HELPING OURSELVES

HELPING OURSELVES

families and the human network

MARY C. HOWELL

BEACON PRESS BOSTON

9 8 7 6 5 4 3 2 1

Excerpts from six poems by Marge Piercy from the book *To Be of Use,*
copyright ©1969, 1971, 1973 by Marge Piercy. Reprinted by permission
of Doubleday & Co., Inc., and Marge Piercy.

"The Universal Explicator" first appeared in *Poetry*. From *Half-Lives* by
Erica Jong. Copyright © 1971, 1972, 1973 by Erica Mann Jong. Reprinted
by permission of Holt, Rinehart and Winston, Publishers.

"The Earth" by Anne Sexton from *The Awful Rowing Toward God.*
Copyright © 1975 by Loring Conant, Jr., Executor of the Estate of Anne
Sexton. Reprinted by permission of Houghton Mifflin Company.

"A Poet Recognizing the Echo of the Voice," Part I, by Diane Wakoski
from the book *The Magellanic Clouds*. Reprinted by permission of Black
Sparrow Press.

Library of Congress Cataloging in Publication Data

Howell, Mary C
   Helping ourselves.
   Includes bibliographical references.
   1. Family.   2. Social policy.   I. Title.
HQ734.H89   301.42   75-5291
ISBN 0-8070-2758-8

*For the students and patients
who have taught me,
whom I have never properly thanked*

CONTENTS

ACKNOWLEDGMENTS

This book has grown like a thing with a life of its own.
I could not have nurtured it without the care and support
generously given, both to the book itself and to me as I
worked. I owe a great deal to: the warm, wise, and strong
man with whom I have shared a household, a family, a life;
our children, who grow with breathtaking abandon and
patiently explain to us the "real world" as they see it; my
friends, who take care of me all ways; my mother and father
and brother, my own first family; the colleagues—Margaret
Adams, Carolyn Attneave, Pauline Bart, Dorothy Burlage,
Roberta Cohen, Arthur Emlen, Ervin Howell, Nicholas
Howell, Denice Johnston, Paul Rosenkrantz, Ruth Sidel,
Victor Sidel, Norma Swenson, Kathy Weingarten, Robert
Weiss, and Richard Wertz—who read my manuscripts and
shared their insights; Barbara DuBois, whose assistance
became a friendship; Joan Coe, whose expert typing was
surpassed only by her sisterly warmth and adaptability;

MaryAnn Lash, editor/midwife, who let the book come in its own due time; and most of all my special friend Kalma Kartell, who fed me cookies, shared both zany delight in good times and gallows humor when things seemed beyond reason and bearing, propped up my failing confidence, coped with my crazy schedules, and added so much of her own wisdom to these pages. You have all nourished me as well as the book, and I thank you.

FOREWORD

We are scared and worried about our families. Our social,
economic, and government agencies, procedures, and policies
often seem to punish families more than they help. All
around us we see some families falling apart, while other
families cling together in a kind of intense and determined
hope. The family unit is rarely credited when individual
family members do well in the world, but if a family "fails"
to have a sufficient income or if an individual family member "fails" in work or school or marriage or parenthood, we
find it quick and convenient to blame the family, to accept
that blame, and to feel guilty.

It is easier to bemoan our troubles than to propose solutions and workable alternatives. This book explores some
means by which family responsibilities can become easier
to fulfill and also more rewarding. Many questions are raised.
If answers were easy and self-evident, our dilemma would
not be so urgent.

Our families seem especially valuable to us when we
are told, more and more often and in increasingly varied
ways, that we have little power to direct or restrain the
changes burgeoning *around* us. At least, it appears, we can
exert some influence on changes *within* our families. Obviously, we need to know more about the forces that initiate
and propel change.

Faced with many uncertain alternatives, it is easy to
postpone difficult decisions and allow inertia to carry us
along. Making decisions about changes in family life can
be worrisome and scary. But our families seem increasingly
in jeopardy; just letting ourselves be pushed around does
not look like a promising strategy.

I am convinced that most people have *good* intentions
with regard to the welfare of their families and real capabilities for competent, sensible, and healthy self-determination. I disagree on this point with some of my colleagues—professionals who, in fact, speak and write as if
families were incompetent. I know from my own experience
that when people have ample information about alternative
choices, and adequate time, support, and reassurance to
reach decisions about family problems, they usually come
to sane and sensible solutions—solutions that respect the
needs of individual members and promote the welfare of
the group as a whole. "How can we help eight-year-old
Johnny, who is doing 'poorly' in school?" "When grandfather has his next stroke, which might kill him, should
he be hospitalized or cared for at home?" "How can I and
the children help our family cope with father's disability
after his heart attack?" In these and similar situations,
families not only make wise decisions but can learn specific
skills that enable them to help and heal. This conviction
of mine must be made very clear from the outset, for it
is the understructure of the change of direction that I ask
you to envision.

The strategies proposed, alternatives to reliance on professionals for direction, are simple in outline, although they

may take years of struggle and effort to work into the reality
of our lives. I believe that our families could thrive by:

1. Working to develop trusting relationships with
a wide human network of kin, friends, neighbors, and
others with whom we feel a sense of community;
2. Insisting that "experts" share with us the knowledge and skills that we need to conduct our own affairs;
3. Utilizing the paid services of professionals at our
own convenience—that is, only when *we* wish to do
so, and on *our* terms.

To turn our backs, even part way, on the widely advertised "benefits" of technology, institutionalized bureaucracies, and professionalism might seem enormously risky.
It is my belief that those risks are, in fact, less than the ones
we face if we continue to expect that purchased services
from impersonal agencies will be beneficial for our own
singular families. The trouble is that *everything* seems risky
to us these days. But the risks associated with learning to
care for ourselves are at least within our own control, as
opposed to the risks associated with putting ourselves still
more beseechingly into the hands of professional caregivers
and authoritarian experts. And the successes we bring for
ourselves are infinitely sweeter than the solutions that come
from the powers of impersonal agencies, which only make
us feel more helpless, dependent, and incompetent.

The arguments of this book also reflect my conviction
that the knowledge and skills that experts and professionals are privileged to acquire—largely at public expense—
are held *in trust*. As a physician and a psychologist, I feel
obliged to share what I know with everyone and anyone
who cares to ask. Exploring ways to share knowledge and
skills *in response to declared demands*, so that families can
become more self-determining, might be seen as *the* major
responsibility of experts and professionals in their work.
But that cannot happen unless we who care about our families demand the knowledge and skills we need and want.

I am simultaneously a professional and a member of a family. Like many women and some men, I cannot separate myself into pieces, a worker some of the time and a daughter/wife/mother at other times. I am always aware of my multiple roles and am most comfortable when what I do "makes sense" simultaneously to all of the persons that make up the whole me. When I was a practicing pediatrician, I always knew, and my patients knew, that I was also a daughter, a wife, and a mother.

For everything I taught patients and their families about health, I learned in return a great deal about how those families lived. I was privileged to know them well over a period of years and to call at their homes when children were ill, when new parents were struggling to cope with wordless and worrisome infants, or when family epidemics struck.

No one had taught me during my professional training how to translate medical terminology into words, phrases, and ideas that could easily be understood by my patients. The children and their parents asked questions, tried to make sense of my answers, and *taught me* in a variety of ways—especially when my answers to them were not sufficiently clear or informative or direct. And much of what I learned from them has helped me in my own family life.

Since then, I have taught in a variety of circumstances, always centering on a core of interest in teaching families about health and teaching professional caregivers about families. I am in some ways a "professional orphan," belonging entirely to no one discipline and in part to many. Like many women I know, I have developed areas of interest that do not correspond to existing and established fields, and have moved work locations in a continuing attempt to assemble experience and understanding about matters that cut across departments and organizational lines. I continue to meet with families—parents often, children on other occasions, and whole family groups whenever I can—to talk about health and about how *they* feel about the experts and professionals whom they consult when they look for help.

I have learned that I am uncomfortable about the authoritarianism that is structured into the professional role. Just as I cannot separate my work identity from my identity as a family member, I continue to be aware, from my own experience, of what it is like to be the *recipient* of care from professionals. I do not believe, for example, that most patients or clients[1] really want a paternalistic style of care that relieves them of the power to make decisions and the consequent responsibility for outcomes. In order to illuminate the problems that beset families, in order to provide care and services, it is *access* to opportunities for learning knowledge and skills that is needed.

I personally am uncomfortable telling anyone what they should or must do except in those relatively rare instances of severe stress and uncertainty when patients or clients wish to be relieved of the burden of responsibility. I would, under usual circumstances, prefer to give as much information as I can in as unbiased a manner as I am able—exposing my personal bias as I recognize it—and to offer space and time to allow them to work through to their own resolutions and decisions.

I am well aware, however, that I sometimes come across as authoritarian, someone whom patients and students might feel compelled to "obey." This happens because patients and students, just like me and my colleagues, tend to confuse "authority" with "authoritarianism." We all need to make better distinctions between the knowledge and skills that make someone an expert or professional— an authority—and the authoritarianism that we can impose for the purpose of exercising power over others.

My own origins are middle class. But many of the students and most of the patients I have known are working class or poor. I am acutely aware of the tremendous differences that arise from class membership (and ethnic group and sex) with regard to family experience and expectations.[2]

While I cannot pretend to speak as other than a white,
female, middle-class family-person/professional, I acknowledge with gratitude the teachings of those students and
patients who have tried to help me to see other perspectives.

My vision of how I like to work and relate to the people
I serve does not correspond to the usual understanding of
the professional role. I have found a different "role model"
altogether—that of the wise old woman of the village, the
witch healer, who has been privileged to learn from her
predecessors and to share with many generations of village
folk their experiences as family members, and who can
convey what she has distilled (what she "knows") to others
so that they too can use that wisdom.

It is my hope that I will become that wise old woman.
This book represents something of a halfway mark in my
quest, and I look to readers to tell me whether what I have
learned fits their own experiences. We teach each other and
we learn from each other.

HELPING OURSELVES

Trust flourishes like a potato plant, mostly underground:
wan flowers, dusty leaves chewed by beetles,
but under the mulch as we dig
at every node of the matted tangle
the tubers, egg-shaped and golden with translucent skin,
tumble from the dirt to feed us
homely and nourishing.

—Marge Piercy

1 BREAKING LOCKS

"Your families are failing," we are told by the experts. The nuclear family, the traditional family style of middle-class aspirations, does indeed seem less plausible and less attractive than it did a few decades ago. But that is not to say that The Family, as a cooperative living arrangement of care and attachment and trust, is either sickly or disappearing.

Many of those who sorrow that their own preferred family style is less popular than it once was would have us believe that no other family styles can sustain healthy collective responsibility and lusty pleasure: their kind of families, or nothing. But most of us have grown up in one kind of family or another, live our adult lives in a close relationship with some kind of family group, and find it difficult to imagine alternative arrangements of personal relationships that might substitute for The Family. Living in families gives intense and long-lasting opportunities to know others very well, to work as part of a collective unit for the good of the group, and to be responsible

1

for the well-being of more than just ourselves. The intensity and duration of family relationships account for their potential both for profound pleasure, gained for oneself and provided to others, and for deep pain.

It is certainly true that families are sometimes pushed into wounding their own members for lack of needed supports. A spate of books has drawn attention to the potential and actual pain and cruelty that family members inflict on one another.[1] But to some extent this is "blaming the victim," in a society in which very little of our economic and social policy has taken the welfare of families into account and in which few of those responsible for that policy have thought the welfare of families of any real importance.[2]

The plan of this book is to look at families as they are now struggling to survive in this society and to propose some changes that might *strengthen people by strengthening families*. To do this, we must first look closely at three systems, three "sets of players," that are involved in the kinds of policies and arrangements that will be altered if family life is to become not just tolerable but really growth supporting. The first system is, of course, made up of the families themselves. The second set of players is that of the experts, managers, and professionals who now affect or even govern some important family functions. The third set of players is the loose system or network of kin, friends, neighbors, and communities of identity—a system that is, I propose, more essential to the healthy survival of family life than is generally acknowledged, a system that is now not very much valued.

Some important institutionalized arrangements that connect these three sets of players are the central theme of the proposals in this book. Some radical shifts in those institutionalized arrangements are suggested. It is relatively easy, and fashionable as well, to criticize and condemn the way things are. It is much more difficult to propose positive alternative arrangements and to ask that they be seriously considered— we are quick to say, "That will never come about," "It won't work," and "This society could never allow those changes to happen."

I ask you to still the ready repertoire of negativism that many of us share. It seems clear that this society, as it is presently arranged, is very hard on families. However, we only make our own family lives worse by shrugging our shoulders and hanging our heads at our individual powerlessness to change society. There is a point where individuals are *not* entirely powerless and where caring *is* enough to make some positive effort toward needed changes; that point is centered in our own families, in our relationships with people we care about and are responsible for, who care about us and take care of us.

The Family itself is an institution and, as such, it both reflects and influences other major institutions with which it interacts. Institutions are simply the familiar arrangements— the relationships and negotiations—of a given culture. In our society, the major institutions that interact with The Family are those of *Work* and *Child Care*, which are arrangements now assigned mainly to small family units, and *Education* and *Health Care*, arrangements now largely given over to experts, managers, and professionals.

To some, the very word *institution* sounds like "glass and steel," a dehumanized structure without life. We could look at institutions through the other end of the telescope, however. If The Family—which we know to be alive, flexibly individualized, and capable of responsive change—is taken as the model of an institution, then we could look at other conventional arrangements (education, for instance, or housing or commerce) and see that they have many of the capabilities and realities of family groups. Institutions are in fact made by *human networks.* Human networks (including institutions) are the work of people.

Examining the three systems or sets of players that take part in these institutionalized arrangements, it seems clear that they are extraordinarily different from each other and that it is not easy to understand how they are interconnected. Even the languages used to talk about families, for instance, and about bureaucracies, are strikingly discordant. Families are highly intuitive, sensuous, intense, elemental; the system of experts, managers, and professionals, on the other hand, is rational, cool, intellectual, and complicated. To comprehend how these systems are related to each other is like trying to puzzle out the rules of an unfamiliar game played by three players who react to those rules very differently—a canny and intuitive child, perhaps, and a computer and a rather shy visitor from another culture. Unless we observe the moves that each player makes, one by one, we will not understand the whole game; if we watch only one player, we will not know how different the other players really are.

But before we look closely at the three sets of players, we need a broad perspective on the game itself. How can we describe contemporary U.S. families? What do we know about family life, and how do we use what we know? How do other institutions shape and influence our families? Perhaps the energy of family life, strengthened and valued, could be turned around to humanize all of the institutionalized arrangements by which we conduct our affairs!

Family Portraits

There is a sense of comfort and familiarity in taking a close and careful look at what family life is like. The pace of change in many aspects of our lives is, at best, merely befuddling—at worst, intolerable. One reaction to that pace is to look to our families for stability, sameness, and warm security. It is as if our ability to make connections with, and investments in, people, agencies, things, and habits is dangerously close to overload. We retreat by narrowing our focus: looking at our own families is a preoccupation of comfortable dimensions.

What happens outside of the family seems almost ephemeral by contrast. People we know move away from us physically or symbolically. Agencies seem impersonal and faceless and beyond reach of easy contact. Things are invented, acquired, or used, and then they are discarded or pronounced

out of fashion, inefficient or hazardous to our health, before
we can make them familiarly ours. Yesterday's face-to-face
encounter with a person has become today's paper form to be
filled out in triplicate and fed into a computer.

But for many of us, the families that we live in are there day
after day. Rituals and repeated encounters are the substance
of family life. We may vacillate in our expectations, worrying
that our families will be either "too much" or "not enough."
Will those others we live with remain available and serve as a
safe haven against the alienating experiences elsewhere in our
lives? Will we feel betrayed because they offer too little shelter, or because they hold us too closely and restrict our adven-
tures? But even when we are ambivalent about the "goodness"
of our own families, The Family appears to be our most
central institution.

While we focus our attention, nervously or hopefully, on
our families, the very fabric of family life in the United States
is changing. Thirty to forty percent of currently contracted
marriages are expected to end in divorce, and that many again
are expected to come to a significant separation. The number
of divorces has increased about ten percent per year for the
last five years. In the most recent statistics the increase in the
marriage rate just exceeds the increase in the divorce rate, but
first marriages have declined and it is the remarriage rate that
has been climbing at a faster pace. One of every six U.S. children lives in a family with only one parent: one and one-half
percent of children live in families with fathers only, and
fourteen and one-half percent live in single-parent families
headed by their mothers. It is expected that between thirty
and forty-five percent of the children growing up in the 1970s
will be involved in a marital disruption for a period averaging
five or six years.[3]

Those of us who are represented in these numbers know
from personal experience about disruption and change in family life. In addition to the statistics of families that shatter and
re-form, there are other changes in family living. More than
half of U.S. mothers of children six to eighteen years old are

now in paid employment, as are nearly half of all wives and more than a third of mothers of children up to six years of age.[4] It costs more and more to rear a child, as goods and services are increasingly purchased rather than provided by household members; a 1969 study estimated the cost of rearing and educating a child through college at nearly $20,000, or nearly $60,000 counting foregone income of a parent who does unpaid work caring for the child.[5] The disjunction between "good" jobs (for which a college or even postgraduate education is one prerequisite) and work for low wages widens social class separations and lengthens the time that some youth are dependent on parents and other agents of society. And paid employment is increasingly a world apart from family life, in distances to travel, in tasks that are specialized and technical, and even in atmosphere and styles of communication.

Reactions to these massive changes in the structure and functions of family life are mixed. Some argue that all change and diversity must be good, while others react with gloom and dread. Almost every change is viewed by some as healthy and progressive, and by others as disastrous if not evil. To the extent that we perceive these changes to be *imposed* on us, we may respond like animals trapped in cages of punishment, alternately snarling at those who are trapped with us and turning away in apathy. But as a counterforce, a positive direction, we could move toward seeking to understand what is known about family life, learning to perform services for family members effectively and competently, demanding time to spend with other family members, and increasing our collective ability to make responsible decisions about the course of our lives as members of families.

Is The Family dead or dying? One might think so, to listen to some who urge or insist upon a return to the family ideal of past decades and who cannot see any possible good in our future. There is so much rhetoric and such powerful emotion attached to concern about families that we often forget that there is not a "best" or even a single family type, but a very

large number of possible combinations and permutations in
family structures and functions. Further, we are often seduced
to overlook the fact that each of us speaks and writes and
thinks about family matters from a position of intense and
blinding bias.

Most of us are heavily invested in affirming that the families of our own lives have been the best, or at least the best
for us. (Some of us reflect the mirror-image and functionally
similar belief that our own families have been the *worst* for
us.) It is increasingly understood that there is little in any
science that is entirely value free.[6] We must then remind ourselves that in social science (the academic bailiwick of family
studies) there are endless opportunities for the interposition
of bias. I am impressed, when I speak about families to academic and professional groups, at the tendency of members
of the audience to talk about their own personal and private
experiences rather than to remain distant and "objective."
In fact, I believe it is healthy and honest for experts and professionals to acknowledge their own membership in families;
it is far more dangerous and misleading when they deny
personal investment and speak as if their recommendations
and pronouncements were absolutely objective and based on
well-established and unambiguous "fact." Heavy-handed
authoritarian pronouncements from experts often signal
opinions with little basis in reliable evidence.

When we consider The Family in the generic sense, it is
important to search for the underlying assumptions of the
experts who describe or define family structures and functions. Much recent discussion has focused on only one family
type—the nuclear family. Sometimes the nuclear family is
condemned as "disintegrating"; sometimes it is scorned as an
institution of coercion, indoctrination, and limitation of personal growth. In its pure (or "ideal") form the nuclear family
is an internally self-supporting, mutually intimate, and exclusive group composed of legally-married husband and wife
living with their biological children in a single dwelling unit,
independent of kin and neighbors for the satisfaction of
"family-related" needs.

But the nuclear pattern is not the only possible family pattern. Probably only a minority of U.S. families conform to the presumed "ideal," although many more aspire, or believe they should aspire, to that family pattern. A significant proportion of families have quite different styles in the numbers and kinds of persons who can belong, in the definition and management of family functions and responsibilities, and in the roles of individual persons living in the group. Some families, for instance, have only one parent; others have grandparents or other nonparental adults living as family members. Some have intentionally acquired children by adoption or by fostering arrangements. In many families both parents earn income; some couples share equally in the responsibilities of earning income and maintaining the household (cooking, cleaning, laundry, repairs, and so on); in a few the wife is the primary income earner and the husband, the homemaker. Many families maintain strong and active arrangements for mutual help with their kin. A few try quite different family forms through marriage contracts, communal households, collective collaboration by several nuclear units, and/or strong neighborhood networks.[7]

In the most general sense we might propose to recognize as a family any group of two or more persons that meets the criteria of living together in a household, exchanging nonmonetized services, and sustaining commitment over time.

Living Together in a Household. Anthropologists sometimes define the family unit in an unfamiliar culture as "persons who use common utensils to prepare food." To occupy the same household with other persons provides opportunities (indeed, requirements) to share, to be intimate, to take care of one another, and to control and be controlled by each others' actions and feelings and thoughts. Families vary a great deal in the manner in which individuals contact each other within the household, but unless there is some common space that belongs to all members for use, some common property, and

common time when they are together, they do not live
together as a family.

Exchanging Nonmonetized Services. In this society in which
so much human exchange is accompanied by money exchange,
the services that we perform for each other in families could,
for the most part, be purchased from others outside the family. For a price, we can buy meals prepared and served, child
care, sexual intercourse, household cleaning and laundry services, and even tolerant, patient, and wise companionship and
counsel. But the family is the only arena in which a great volume and diversity of services are now performed without pay
by individuals for one another.

Although money is not ordinarily exchanged directly for
within-family services, family members do in fact establish an
elaborate system of exchanges or "rules" to determine fairness. Such systems are never static, but change dynamically
over time. In most families, that set of rules is mostly unwritten and unspoken and often agreed to more in practice than
in theory. Exchanges may be immediate and in kind—"If
you'll scratch my back I'll scratch yours," "If you cook dinner tonight I'll cook dinner tomorrow night." Or exchanges
may be metered by an elaborate scheme balanced over long
periods of time.

In its most extreme form the stereotype of the nuclear
family dictates that the husband/father be the sole provider
of family income and financial security. In return, the wife/
mother is delegated to provide the services of day-to-day
household and personal maintenance, child care, and "expres-
sive management" of the family—soothing, listening, comforting, and allowing and responding to displays of sadness,
anger, and worry. In point of fact, this stereotype is gravely
inaccurate for most families, even those that conform super-
ficially to the nuclear pattern. Wives promote the financial
security of their families in a variety of ways, from managing
budgets to earning income. Husbands often take some part in

those aspects of family life that the stereotype assigns to
wives. By the best current estimate, in some ten to fifteen
percent of U.S. families this stereotype is completely erased;
both spouses share almost equally the responsibilities of
income earning, child care, and personal and household
maintenance.[8]

The stereotype is not only inaccurate but also an out-
rageous oversimplification. For most families the system of
exchanges is complex and ambiguous. Individual family members may expect quite different benefits: gifts of property
(household furnishings, jewelry) might be seen as a fair exchange for sexual favors, for instance. Sole responsibility for
child care might be exchanged for public praise—"I have very
little to do with the children; my wife here gets all the credit."
Husbands and wives sometimes make very different contributions to the welfare of their families and to each other; in
other families, husbands and wives both do the same things.
Responsibilities can be shared or alternated. The balance
sheet can be closely watched and openly discussed, or such
attention and such talk can be regarded as taboo, out of fear
that keeping watch on equity would destroy trust or romance.

We all maintain a balance sheet, at least at some internal
level, and have ways of redressing imbalances in the exchange
of services in our families. We can openly ask for more, or use
wiles, or we can withhold favors or perform services rudely
or carelessly. But for the most part, it is agreed that within-
family services should not be paid for directly with money.
The question of housewives' wages has provoked debates
that reveal a great deal about our different views on exchange
equivalences and how balances are calculated over time.[9]
These debates also demonstrate how important it is to many
that within-family services are performed without pay—a
salient part of our collective idea of what a family really is.

Commitment over Time. The experience of family life includes
the expectation that others plan to be part of one's family tomorrow, the tomorrow after tomorrow, and for a long time.

Perhaps few contemporary marriages are based on the assumption that they will endure "till death do us part." But anyone, child or adult, who lives on the premise that "tomorrow I could split" is not, by our usual understanding, living *in* a family. Part of the willingness to be open, vulnerable, trusting, and involved with other family members is based on the belief that those others will be around; we hope and believe that we will have time and space to rectify our mistakes, resolve our misunderstandings, and even out the balances of temporary inequities in our demands on each other.

Commitment over time is not easy to measure. Marriages come to separation or divorce. Adolescent children leave, sometimes unexpectedly or "before their time." Family members are ejected—alcoholic spouses or parents, for instance, or adolescents who are "throwaways" rather than "runaways." Marriages are reported as satisfactory, or even happy, up to the very point of separation;[10] presumably many separated spouses would have said shortly before their separation that they were committed to a continuing marriage.

In our contemporary society, with divorce and separation such ready (and increasingly respectable) solutions to family discord, our firmest model of commitment over time is found in an adult's attachment to a dependent child. We become attached to those we care for. Even this form of commitment is not inviolable, for many children are abandoned psychologically and/or physically by their caretakers. But it is plain that children in this society have few alternatives for care and that children discarded by their own families are likely to fare badly. The attachment that serves as an anchor to commitment is more readily developed toward a dependent child than toward a relatively independent and autonomous adult. Sometimes the adult/child model is recapitulated between adults when one is deeply dependent on the other ("I can't live without you") or when that deep dependency is mutual. Adults who are less intensely and exclusively dependent may be committed to each other on grounds of mutual respect, admiration, or pleasure.

The adult-to-child attachment evolves whenever (1) an
adult takes a major responsibility for the time and energy
requirements of care for a dependent child; (2) when the
child is developmentally so young as to require that care for
physical and social survival; and (3) when the circumstances
of the adult's life provide reasonable support for that role.
Adults who care for children *in the absence of support*—when
a father is challenged or ridiculed on the basis of the social
stereotype that men cannot and should not care for small
children, or when a mother is distracted by poverty and isolation from other adults, for instance—may fail to develop
a firm sense of attachment to the child. Those parents who
abandon their children, physically or psychologically, are
inhibited in their attachment. Perhaps they did not personally invest real time and energy in child care, perhaps they felt
imposed upon and unjustly obligated, or perhaps their own
personal needs did not allow them to engage themselves in
caregiving.

Sustaining a commitment over time requires, for most of
us, some internal or external sanctions (either positive, as a
reward, or negative, as a threat of punishment) to get us
through the bad days when the aggravations of living with
others seem intolerable. The social, religious and legal prohi-
bitions against divorce and separation that formerly provided
some of those sanctions are now loosened. New opportunities
for economic independence of wives have altered the sanctions
of financial need. Similarly, when husbands participate responsibly in daily chores of personal maintenance, such as preparing food, they are released from practical dependence on
their wives. What remains, however, are our attachments to
the members of our families.

In our collective sense about the nature of the family, there
is a fourth characteristic: the belief that *any given family is
more than the sum of its individual members*. A family is a
group with a spirit of its own. Some of that spirit or essence
arises from the family's past history and presumed future.
This notion of a group implies more than a simple pair;

even a family of only two persons (parent and child, or child-less spouses) is peopled with members who are not physically present.

Each adult brings into a new family the tales, traditions, and expectations of his or her family of origin—"ghosts," as it were; their families of origin had their own "ghosts," and on back through family memories. In addition, many families have members who might be imagined to be present, as when one parent does not live in the family or a family member has died or an adolescent child has been launched. "John always joked about arguments like this. He would poke fun at us if he were here." History and future combine with absent members to remind a family that they are more than themselves as individuals, more than the sum of their pairs.

These defining characteristics of families range from a clear and objective criterion of family living (the shared occupation of a household) to a descriptive comment that almost eludes prose, much less measurement (the spirit of tales and traditions that unifies and symbolizes a family). This progression moves from what we can know by the ordinary methods of our science to what we know by an appreciation of the intuitive.[11]

What Do We "Know" About Family Life?

We could begin to gain perspective on our own families, the kinds of events and circumstances that stress families, and our hopes and designs for a society that supports and is supported by them if we had a clearer understanding of what is really known, and likely to be known, about how people live in families. In fact, the study of families has not yet been seriously undertaken by experts and professionals compared, say, to their investment in the study of weapons development, space exploration, or consumerism.

While there has been a great volume of research and writing about and around The Family, much of "family studies" seems strangely divorced from the reality of how we live our lives:

> Families are agencies for caretaking, and caretaking is a little-valued activity in our society. In every service profession, climbing the status ladder has meant becoming free of the responsibilities of face-to-face care of clients or patients: nurses leave their bedpans and become administrators, psychiatrists spend less time as therapists and become consultants, social workers stop doing casework and become supervisors, and "general practitioners"—the least esteemed of physicians within the medical profession—become trained as specialists. Individuals are rewarded with higher salaries when they leave caretaking work; paradoxically, paying the salaries of administrators is said to promote an "efficient utilization of scarce human resources." Housewives and mothers are judged to have "no skills" for the job market, meaning that their experienced understandings of how to feed people and nurse them when they are ill and how to comfort them when they are tired or worried or upset are rated less than the skills of transcribing someone else's words on a typewriter, operating a switchboard, or working a keypunch. When caretaking is so little valued and the family is the last resort of caretaking in this society, it is not difficult to understand why family life has seemed so little worth studying.

> Our most respectable tools for the study of any subject have been those of science; the results of scientific study have been used energetically in the service of *dominion* and *control*. The woman's world of family life has hardly seemed worth investigating since it has not appeared to be a world worth conquering for gain and power. "Family studies" has been a low-status field in the academic world.

> Vision and hearing have been the major sensory tools of scientific study. They are the senses that permit us to

view and analyze at arm's length or more, avoiding personal involvement and subjective sensations. The life of
The Family is deeply rooted in the proximate senses of
touch, taste, and smell. Accustomed *methods* of scientific study have not been appropriate to the study of
families, and The Family as a realm of sensuous involvement has not been easily molded to these methods.

The usual habits of *thought* that underlie scientific
study are not entirely appropriate to the study of families. Families are diverse; they are the impromptu and
perhaps the most fully organic arrangements of our lives,
formed around and between a small group of persons
for whom we care a great deal, bringing constant inven-
tions of intuition, opportunity, and necessity. Western
science, on the other hand, relies heavily on abstraction,
reduction, simplification, categorizing, and the use of
averaging and probability statistics. Scientific study is
designed to reduce variety and diversity and to permit an
understanding of generalized, idealized, and "typical"
phenomena. At the farthest reaches of understanding,
scientists are actually far less linear than this in their
thought, tending more toward the metaphysical and the
intuitive.[12] But in the workaday world of ordinary
research and development, understanding proceeds not
by flashes of intuitive genius but by methodical expli-
cation of processes as straight as enzyme reactions—"a
follows b to produce c" or, perhaps, "a and b interact
to affect c, and d is the resultant product." This blurring
of individual diversity in order to explain generalized
phenomena is exactly the reason that we are uncomfortable as we look at what little work has been done in the
scientific study of the family.

This is not meant to disparage the general usefulness of the
methods of science, for there is a likelihood that these methods can be bent to bring us useful clues to an understanding
of family life. There is, however, another kind of concept-
ualization and problem solving. It highlights differences and

individual variations; comprehends a multiplicity of causes; tolerates high levels of ambiguity, uncertainty, and even error in the probable correctness of explanations; acknowledges the impracticality or impossibility of collecting "enough" information to understand and predict with certainty; and appreciates the intuitive leaps of invention. It is the method of art—the art of poetry, for instance, or the art of healing— a method appropriately applied to the interactive human behavior of family life. If we are to learn what we would like to know about family life, we must learn to use the methods both of art and of science.

The Institutional Network

In a society and a time of such rapid attitudinal and techno- logical change as our own,[13] perplexity about what we "ought" to do, think, and feel manifests itself most acutely in family affairs. Our passion for control, a dominant motive in almost every aspect of our lives, drives us to hope that if everything were "right" for us we would not have to suffer pain, disappointment, or the unexpected. Debates about sexual behavior, use of a variety of mood-altering drugs, the value of paid work for the personal well-being of adults, and the needs of infants and children for exclusive parental care fill us with foreboding. The assumptions that there *are* "right" choices to be made, that experts and professionals hold the keys to these choices, that we ordinary folk cannot hope to understand how choices should be determined, and that all misery and pain could be avoided except for our personal "mistakes" reinforce our feeling that we should be in control and clearly are not. We set upon each other: brothers and sis- ters, men and women, parents and children, appear irresistibly drawn into angry polarization. We believe that we ought to be doing much better than we are, that some expert must know enough to tell us what to do, and that it is all our fault. The belief that we are individually and collectively to blame for the troubles that beset our families is only one example of

the vulnerability of our families to the policies and philosophies of other institutions.[14]

The institution of The Family is not only central to our
personal lives but is also a structural base for many other
institutions. Most of our jobs are designed on the assumption
that the worker has a "wife" to salve the psychic wounds of
the workday and to feed, clothe, and refresh her or him for
another day at the factory or store or office. Schools rely on
families to return their pupils prepared for each day's efforts.
Agencies for medical care expect families to determine when
a patient needs professional services, to transport the patient
to the professional's place of work, and to carry out the professional's instructions for treatment. Most importantly, our
interlocked institutions of commerce, manufacturing, housing,
law, and transportation expect small isolated family units to
purchase, own, use, and hoard.

In the interrelationships of these institutions, families
have been expected to be relatively powerless, and they have
for the most part fulfilled that expectation. One consequence
of the powerlessness of individual families has been the virtual
absorption by families of "convenient" attributes characteristic of those other, more controlling institutions. Thus, our
families sometimes display the following:

   1. Constant, driving rivalry between brothers and
sisters, competing for what they have been led to believe
are scarce resources. ("Don't be too trusting, for there is
only a little attention and affection to share among you,
and you must snatch yours or it will be stolen.");
   2. Demand for absolute fidelity and fealty to control
by "authorities." ("Do what I say because I say so, and
then show that you like what you do");
   3. Internalization of disappointment, error, and "im-
perfection" as justifications for blame and guilt. ("If you
were good, you would deserve more; if you don't get
what you want, you must not be good enough");
   4. Acceptance of the labels of "incapable" and "in-

competent." ("We know best, you don't know, we will
do and decide for you");

5. Expectations of endless gratitude. ("Because you
are helpless we must take care of you, and you owe an
incalculable and therefore unpayable debt for our sacri-
fices");

6. Praise for individual achievement, emphasis on competition between individuals, and disregard for collaborative efforts. ("Your school report just isn't as good as
your sister's was at your age. Can't you at least do
better than she does at taking out the trash?");

7. Jealous acquisitive hoarding of private as opposed
to commonly-owned property. ("Now you each have
your own alarm clocks, so none of you has to depend on
anyone else to get up in the morning").

If we hear any justification for these kinds of attributes in
our family relations, it is that families "must prepare children
for the society in which they will take their places as adults."
But why? Why not live within families in a manner that
supports growth and mutual respect, *even if* (or, perhaps,
because?) our children, grown, might then want to change
the very institutions that now oppress, disregard, and devalue
family life?

It is fashionable to brood over our families' troubles, to
believe that if we have been deprived of happiness in family
life it is our own fault, and, at the same time, to wonder
sullenly if our families have *imposed* our misery upon us. For
most of us, however, the largest part of the happy, warm, and
funny scraps of our lives, when we have felt most needed and
wanted and accepted and useful, have come in the context of
living in a family. We can believe that the one arena in which
we as individuals have some real effect is within our families, and that particular effectiveness is integral to our personal wholeness. Those happy scraps are worth savoring, even
worth fighting for.

There is no doubt that the close association of family
living brings the risk and terror of hurting others, and of

being hurt. We are deeply dependent on other humans, even
though our public admiration of "independence" forces us to
conceal dependency and to act as if depending on others and
being depended upon were somewhat shameful rather than
mature and healthy. The need to be held and fed and comforted—and the ability to hold and feed and comfort—underlies social behavior of the highest order. No public policy has
a potential for cruelty to compare with being abandoned by
a spouse or parent or child, being told that one is worthless
or hateful, being starved or beaten or brutalized by someone
to whom one has exposed one's whole self and with whom
one's contract seemed to be for care, affection, tenderness,
and acceptance. Some are crippled for life by such experiences. Others learn, lick their wounds, repair their souls, and
try again with the faith that living in a family, for all its
hazards and terrors, is a hopeful arrangement for good.

The neglect and disinterest that has allowed public policy
to overlook the welfare of families has until now kept us
relatively free of direct interference by government agencies
and professionally-directed efforts at social engineering. As
we begin to look more closely at the nature of family
life and at our personal preferences, hopes, and dreams,
we should be aware of and should question the self-interest
of those social engineers who are now directing their attention to our families.

For currents are stirring. Planning groups, both in government agencies and in the "helping professions," are designing
a variety of intrusions (called "interventions") intended to
change the lives of families and their individual members. In
the past several decades, families were largely private groups
and there was little official (professional, academic, or gov-
ernmental) interest in breaching that privacy. At a recent
meeting, however, a group of child psychiatrists agreed almost
unanimously that their professional organizations should seek
to implement a nationwide system of family-home visitors
(called "child advocates") whose charge would be to investi-
gate every household for possible child-abusing tendencies.

And a group of physicians recently proposed that it should be
made a criminal offense for a family to refuse to obey the
medical profession by failing to obtain certain recommended
preventive medical services.[15] Increasingly we hear talk about
family assistance programs in which functions formerly performed by family members would be taken over by professionals (or "paraprofessionals" directed by professionals)
working out of bureaucratic agencies.

We may soon be at a kind of watershed. If we hope that
experts, managers, and professionals will devise public policies
that are more supportive of "healthy" family life, are we then
also asking for investigation into our private lives, the recording of information about our intimate affairs, and the
official promulgation of standards for family relationships?
We may have to choose.

Demystification and Remystification

There is in contemporary thinking a two-dimensional reach
for "what we want to know." On the one hand is the demand
for dissemination of the knowledge and skills now jealously
guarded by experts and professionals—a dissemination that
would "demystify" by providing access to specialized knowledge and skills for all. But there is also the reach for appreciation (rather than fear) of ambiguity, savoring (rather than
distaste) of surprise, and wonder (rather than distress) at the
wild and magical in natural events of which human events are
a part. This latter reach draws us toward relearning our place
in the real and universal, "beyond" twentieth-century technology into a domain we cannot control or predict. We long
here for a "remystification."

It is becoming increasingly clear to many that to continue
to strive for absolute mastery and control of everything in
the natural world, and to expect "perfect" and "unflawed"
lives, is to risk the further disintegration of our affinity with
the world of nature. The balance between controllable or
predictable events and those that happen in our lives at

random, or as if by other forces, has shifted over the past few centuries through the fantastic growth and exercise of science and technology. The direction in which that balance might change in future years is unclear, as we argue about the priorities of ecological prudence against progress and growth, and economic restraints against technological and industrial development. What does seem increasingly clear is that a dilemma lurks in the balance between the controlled and the uncontrolled. We have allowed ourselves to be pushed one way and then the other, and we have pushed others (and our natural habitat) without giving due concern to the complex moral issues inherent in seeking always to "be in control."

The Family, our closest and most intimate connection with other persons, may serve as a fulcrum for that *balance*: on one side lie the demystified knowledge and skills through which we, collectively, could exercise real and immediate responsibility for family well-being. And on the other side lies the remystified sense of awe and wonder about the unpredictable turbulence of life's events, through which we could experience both our joy and our pain more fully. Men and women alike are increasingly concerned about the quality of life in their own families, and sometimes they are also genuinely concerned about the welfare of families other than their own—especially families that they perceive as being like their own, part of their "communities of identity."

Many of us now have a profound sense of alienation from the progression of much of our lives. It seems that we have little or no control over the organization, policies, and expenditures of governments; the ability to earn, save, and spend money; the ruination of our natural environment and the poisoning of our bodies by the effluents and accessories of industrial-technological "progress." Our national policies seem to be based on an awesome lack of respect for human and nonhuman life.

More and more it appears unlikely that we can redirect national policy toward a more human and more humane society by attempting to force change at the top: bureaucratic

administration is designed to absorb and even convert those
efforts to its own benefit, continuing its preset course with
gyroscopic stability. The changes we seek may only be able to
grow organically from the bottom up, from the inside out—
from within our families and from within bureaucratic institutions at the same time. The first and most immediate arena
in which we can sort out the balance of control through
knowledge and skills, on the one hand, and appreciation of the
uncontrolled magical and mystical, on the other, is in our
families.

It seems to me that if we who live in and care about our
families had free choice, we would take or buy what we could
use from the experts, managers, and professionals. But we
would at the same time fight like fury to retain a power of
autonomy for the individual family and for the alliances that
our families form with others.

The Alternative Network

The hopeless, helpless family is *not* our only alternative to
a dependent reliance on professional services. We are *not*
locked into the choice that experts have presented to us between isolated, secretive, scarce-resource "nuclear" families—
deficient in the ability to care for individual family members
and threatened by guilt-ridden failure at every turn—and an
invasion by paternalistic strangers providing professional
resources and services—dispassionate, objective, impersonal,
uncaring, perhaps even with ulterior motives. There is available to us an alternative system, somewhat atrophied by
disuse and disparagement but still available for our exercise,
exploration, and enjoyment: the social network of kin and
friends and neighbors and communities of identity with whom
we can share energy, knowledge, services, disclosure, and
trust. It is my thesis, and my open bias, that we can nurture
and benefit from our growing interest in and concern for families by joining with others we know well enough to care
about and trust, by giving and receiving the help and support

that our families need, and by insisting that the services we pay for are provided on *our* terms.

My conclusions about the knowledge (now controlled by experts and professionals) that could be useful in the everyday conduct of family affairs are twofold. First, it is improper and deceiving to imply that a body of knowledge now exists that could guarantee our families safe passage through the cycles of life. (One need only look at the family lives of those who should be most knowledgeable about family matters, such as psychologists and psychiatrists, to recognize that expert understanding is insufficient to assure "right" choices.) Secondly, it seems clear that what knowledge is available could, if widely dispersed at the request of anyone who seeks to learn, help us to distinguish between those events about which there is sufficient understanding to make reasonable predictions, and those events that can neither be anticipated nor mastered.

In addition to demanding access to information, it can be demanded that experts and professionals instruct us in skills that are needed to provide reasonable care from within families. Instead of becoming more dependent on professional services, impersonally rendered by paid workers who cannot care deeply about members of families not their own, we can ask for instruction, assistance, and supervision in nursing our own sick kin, educating our own children and ourselves, and coping with our own handicaps and disabilities. Professional services as presently organized tend to replace rather than to supplement family services, to take control rather than to foster self-sufficiency. The issue is again centered on control, mystification, dependency, and trustworthiness.

If we gained a mastery of what can be "known" about families, a respect for the unknowable, and access to the skills by which we can care for and nurture each other, could we heal the world beyond The Family as well? The mire of alienating work, throwaway culture, and the media blasting of overkill consumerism depends upon our separation from each other and on our assumption of personal responsibility for all discomforts and disappointments. Institutionalized professionalism and paternalistic "intervention" into The Family, which rely on our acceptance of guilt and our suspicion and mistrust of each other, drive us further apart.

It is difficult to conceive of our efforts to help our families as a movement *against* anyone; we are all, actually or potentially, members of families that we care for and in which we find care. What is the healing potential of a loving, committed coming together of people within and on behalf of families?

Forgive who insulted you.
Forgive yourself for being wrong.
You will do it again
for nothing living
resembles a straight line,
certainly not this journey
to and fro, zigzagging
you there and me here
making our own road onward
as the snail does.

Yes, for some time we might contemplate
not the tiger, not the eagle or grizzly
but the snail who always remembers
that wherever you find yourself eating
is home, the center
where you must make your love,
and wherever you wake up
is here, the right place to be
where we start again.

—Marge Piercy

2 THE FAMILY WITHIN US

We must first take a close look at families themselves. Each
family is its own center, and the degree of variability between
families is astounding. But suppose we were to approach families as one might wander through a meadow, letting impres-
sions from all the senses swim together. We could then accu-
mulate a feel for the ways in which families—growing organisms
—are similar and the ways in which they can differ. We need
this kind of understanding before we can build a set of proposals about the relationships between our families and
other institutions.

"Unlearning Not to Speak"

To calculate the strengths that lie within families and the
points of stress that need support requires that we learn to

talk about our families and to listen to others talking about
theirs. While the web of family life is intricate, it is with the
family group that we must begin to talk about what we already "know."

This requires a continual effort to envision and talk about
families as groups and not "only" as collections of individuals.
We believe that we can understand much about the springs of
individual behavior and about relationships between two persons. But we are not used to thinking about an aggregate of
people—in this case, people who occupy the same household
and who have a past and a future together—as an organic
whole. When we talk about a family as a collective group, we
seem to overlook its rich inner intricacies and the almost
infinite variety of arrangements for family living. Emphasizing the collectiveness of the family creates a flatness and
monotony that is far from the reality we live.

However, talk about families as collective groups, remembering the complexities that we conceal in our efforts to
focus on the group itself, is far different from the monolithic
notion of The Family that is adopted by the language and
planning of bureaucratic agencies. There, The Family appears
to be a formless lump with each unit indistinguishable from
the next. To combat that family-as-object habit of thought,
we need to recall the infinite detail of life in our own and
other families.

But how can family life be described? We are not accustomed to this kind of talk as respectable, "intellectual" public discourse. When we try now to talk about the happenings
in that private world between our inner selves and our public
beings, our attempt has a luster of newness, as if it had not
been done before. We have been made reticent. As children in
school we learned not to use the homely words, not to give
examples or make analogies from the realness of our everyday lives. With few exceptions, only the private talk of
women with women has, in an unbroken stream from the
past, dwelled on the "dailiness" of ordinary life.

Talk about the everyday events of family life is part of the

tradition of the culture of women, a culture that we have submerged in this society. Because women have traditionally been
assigned and have accepted responsibility for the inner workings of family life (including the rearing of young children)
women have had the opportunity, and men have been relatively deprived, of attending to and caring about the individual events of living collectively. The attending, and the
caring, feed commitment to other persons. Women's talk has
always been full of family matters. But we women have been
persuaded, by those who have invested themselves away from
their families, that what we know and care about and talk
about is unimportant. To discover and celebrate the inner life
of families, one need only look to the talk and writings of
women, and of those men who—in deviance from the "mas-
culine mystique" and in sturdy self-esteem—have not been
afraid to involve themselves in the juicy reality of family
matters.

The language for day-to-day family life is old and simple.
There are striking regional variations: a sick child is "up-
chucking" (vomiting) in Minnesota, "throwing" in Massachusetts. The vocabularies and events of everyday family life
are called "trivial" from the perspectives of technological
development, scientific discovery, and bureaucratic power.
But are they? The struggle between those who squeeze the
toothpaste tube in the middle and those who roll from the
bottom is deadly earnest.

The quality of talk about family events often has a ram-
bling, nonsystematic order from which insights and possible
solutions can be plucked as they lie—a contrast to the apparently unambiguous answers provided by the conclusive
printout of a computer run. Discovering the richness of the
inner workings of family life, we are "unlearning not to
speak."[1]

Family life is compounded of sensuousness and intense
negotiation; freedom from "public" restraint and layers of
private compromise; the demanding insistence of the needs
of others; and the nourishment of our own bodies, minds,

souls. Family life is made up of sharing, intimacy, caretaking, and control.

Sharing

Sharing among family members involves both tangible things, like kitchens and hairbrushes, and the intangibles of time and energy. Space within the common household must of course be shared, but the variations are almost endless. Each family member may have some private space, or an "own" space may be apportioned according to a hierarchy of privilege (a father has a room of his own, but his child does not). Or every person may have free access to every room. Spaces may be used for many purposes, or areas may be set aside to be used only for eating, for sitting quietly, for playing wild and giggly games, or for sleeping. Families negotiate rules about who can depose whom from a space and about what rooms are "really" to be used for. But these rules, like most others, are constantly challenged and change over time.

Many physical objects in the household belong "to the family," but ordinarily each family member has some possessions that are private and more or less valued. Valuing our belongings, within the family, can be a counter to the acquisitive throwaway culture outside. "Taking care of your own things"—protecting them from disintegration and loss—is a constant struggle; so too is proscription against filching, misplacing, and using up what belongs to another. The question of whether the distribution is "fair" according to ages and needs and interests creates tension between sisters and brothers and also between spouses. Clothing is usually individually owned, but may be passed along from one child to the next; outside clothing, such as jackets and scarves and mittens, is often shared or traded. In some families, property used for the common welfare may belong to everyone, but in others—especially in families in which adult roles and responsibilities are sharply segregated—there is "Mother's

washing machine" and "Mother's sofa" and "Dad's car" and
"Dad's hammer."

Patterns of sharing energy and time also vary. We know
families in which the entire group is almost never assembled,
while in others everyone's presence is required at prescribed
times: at breakfast or at dinner or when relatives come to
call on Sunday. Managing private time is complex. Some of
us salve our wounds and celebrate our joys alone, others seek
human contact; and these may be contradictory needs. Transition time, from school to home or from work to family
bustle, is often experienced as a time of need for quiet and
solitude. Some find that block of time traveling to and fro,
while others must ask to be "let alone" when they reenter the
family realm. Still others may seek immediate and intense
contact with household members as a relief from the boredom and isolation of their jobs.

There are more subtle matters that are shared between and
among family members, such as goals. A husband/father
might work long hours and devote the greater part of his
energy to getting ahead in his job, believing that a better
house in a "better" neighborhood was a goal for everyone in
the family, only to discover at the point of moving that his
children never wanted to move and his wife would rather have
had him participating in day-to-day family matters than
spending so much time at his job. Similarly, parents may
manipulate their children into silence about their miseries in
school—this step endured for the sake of the next step, with
a college education as the triumphant end point. The goal
may explode if the children do not enjoy or even want to
complete that college education for which so much has been
sacrificed.

It is always hazardous for a family to try to agree that any
distant goal is worth making today miserable, especially since
the substance of family life is so knotted into the immediate
present. We may bear the costs of distant goals with different
effects—children are especially vulnerable to the ruination of

today for some far-off tomorrow. And there is always the risk
that the distant benefits, once gained, will seem too small to
have justified their cost in the time and energy lost to the
appreciation of "little things."

In every aspect of sharing, families vary in the degree to
which they are open and explicit about rules and expectations. A wife or husband might avoid asking the other about
daily events, believing that privacy was desired, while the
spouse might judge that behavior as evidence of disinterest
and unwillingness to share. It is a struggle for parents to convey to their adolescent children simultaneous interest in their
children's concerns and activities, and respect for their with-
drawn adultlike autonomy. When expectations and rules are
only implicit and not discussed openly, there are unending
opportunities for misunderstanding, resentment, and suspicion. Even with the most explicit marriage contract or system of family conferences, it is almost impossible to expose
all of the rules and expectations that each family member believes is, or should be, in existence. This is partly because
these rules and expectations change over time, often in unexpected directions. It is difficult to learn to ask others both for
privacy and for permission to share, and to learn to hear the
requests that others make of us.

The blend of sharing and privacy, the common and the
personal, is never just the same for any two of us. The family
demands compromise so that we can live together in common
space and time. Willingness to share and willingness to leave
alone are often taken as signals of our good will toward each
other. Redefining what is "mine" and "yours" and "ours"—
things or activities or goals or responsibilities—is a device we
use to position ourselves simultaneously as individuals and as
members of a family group.

Never to learn that there are options about sharing, that
one *can* ask and be heard, that one *must* listen and respond,
is a grave handicap to impose on a child. When the arbitrary
code of rules and expectations within a single family is experienced as inalterable and universal, a family can become

a prison. The struggle to negotiate and then renegotiate sharing is both wrenching and painful, involving a balance between not wanting to hurt and not wanting to be hurt, wanting to please and wanting to be pleased. I think that one of the most challenging aspects of being the parent of an adolescent is to hold on to the thread of intuition that tells us what our nearly grown child wants to share, and what is becoming "private." Children need the chance to learn to participate in the struggle. They can do so by observing older members of their household, and by being told directly that they may ask for what they need of the family's resources and must acknowledge requests made of them.

Intimacy

One consequence of sharing is intimacy—closeness and familiarity. We know the closeness of intimacy by our proximate senses of touch, taste, and smell. In the public world of the media, and in everyday psychology, there has been a tendency to regard these sensations as both "dirty" and "arousing"—they have become especially linked to orgasmic sexuality. Breast-feeding infants, backrubbing and caressing and holding another close, have come to be looked upon as sexual equivalents, generally taken to mean that they are located somewhere along a two-dimensional space leading from arousal to orgasm. One can instead put genital sexuality into a larger context of the intimacy of closeness and thus enlarge the understanding of how familiarity is experienced with other persons.

The touching that happens between family members is both active and quiet. Leaning together, watching TV or the play of one's children, reading the same book or magazine or newspaper, talking softly or confidentially, lying together asleep or resting, lap sitting, and working or eating together closely enough for intermittent contact are all variants of quiet touch. Such "comfort-contact," which confirms for us the warm reality of other persons, is symbolically skin-to-skin

even when there is clothing between us. It is likely that our
need for and our deep pleasure in touching is part of our
mammalian natures. The need and the pleasure are reinforced
by infantile experiences of being cared for, but they are far
more real and important to our adult well-being than we acknowledge if we regard them as "only" immature residuals of
the neediness of infancy.

More active forms of touching in families include caressing,
backscratching and rubbing, hair tousling, and feeling, as in
"feel this giant mosquito bite on my arm." Both active and
passive touching can initiate genital sexual arousal, and generally (in this culture) we do not know what to do with such
arousal except to think of immediate orgasmic satisfaction.
Immediate gratification is out-of-bounds except between
assigned sexual partners and at certain times—that is, sex is
usually forbidden between parent and child, or at mealtime
when little children are eagerly hungry. As a consequence,
we may restrain our initiation and enjoyment of touching.
At one extreme, casual touching does not occur except between wife and husband, and then only as a signal to initiate
sexual intercourse. At the other extreme, touching can be
enjoyed as an undercurrent to a wide variety of family contacts, and concomitant genital arousal can be recognized and
then banked, "saved up" for the times of genital sexual activity. Within this perspective genital sexuality is one facet of
our familiar understanding of other persons.

We taste each other by kissing or licking mouths, ears,
tears, genitals, hair, and any other body part. Tasting is an
important component of the infant's early exploration of the
world, when hand coordination is too limited to control
touch and when information brought in by ears and eyes is
too complex to be readily used. Infants taste breasts and
mouths and fingers and noses and any parts of their own or
others' bodies that are handy; they test resilience (and human
response) by gumming and biting. Infants also taste good, and
many adults who might be reticent about enjoying the taste
of another can allow themselves to play baby games of

tasting, licking, and pretend-biting—baby toes are especially inviting. We also share the tastes of each other in families by more distant contact: sharing toothbrushes, drinking from the same glass, using the same spoon or fork. Like touch, the taste of another's body has a well of rich experience behind it, the kind of experience that is not readily available to us to talk about "logically"; it belongs in large part to our non-verbal selves, and we may have been discouraged from using words to think and talk about these associated meanings.

We smell each other whenever we are close, without any extra effort except recognition and acknowledgement. Perhaps the extra effort comes when we *deny* that we know each other by smell. Different bodies have different odors, and different body parts have distinct odors: mouths, armpits, genitals, feet. Small children have special access to the smells of the bottom halves of adult bodies. Babies themselves have very strong and distinct odors; the strong diffuse memory of caretaking that possesses us (those of us who have taken care of infants) when we smell again a distinctive baby smell—like the acrid stool of a teething baby—illustrates the family-memory potential of odors. We guess about the activities of others by smell: "You've been outside," "Smells like cabbage for dinner," "Did you buy some new soap?" "You've been chewing gum," "I'm glad you started a fire." In this context of rich and intense experience of the closeness of other family members, we are betrayed when we willingly go along with the notion that we are "better" when we are deodorized—the message of so much TV advertising. If we despise or hide our smell we lose an essential part of what we are and what we can know about and share with each other.

We can actively initiate or we can quietly permit or enjoy intimacy. Family rules about who can be close to whom, like all family rules, are learned by nonverbal cues more than they are directed by talk. Talk about closeness is often unclear or, even, double-binding, in which case whatever one does is wrong—"You never act as if you like to be near me" and "Don't muss my hair." Each person entering a family brings preferences for styles and modes of closeness; even newborns can show what they prefer in closeness, by relaxation or tenseness. If we are free to say what we like and don't like, we can negotiate with less misunderstanding.

We also become intimately familiar from watching and listening to each other. When we live together we see each other naked, bathing, disposing of menstrual blood; brushing teeth, cutting nails, and washing and brushing and combing hair; half-clothed, disheveled, and dirty. For most of us there is a minimum standard of neatness, cleanliness, and intactness of dress that we impose on our "public" appearances, and a much wider range of dishevelment, undress, and filth that is permissible with family members.

Similarly, there is "family talk"—softer and more tender, rougher and more angry, sadder and more tearful, and more tremulous and afraid. Obscenities and "swears," bigotry and blasphemy, corny jokes and wildly improbable schemes, tears of grief and bellows of rage and giggles or shrieks of pleasure, are all part of the noises that we make in families, the noises that we hear from each other and by which we know each other.

We often think we know, even without words, when another family member is lying, when something hurts, when something momentous has happened, or when a new "act" is being tried. Our base of intimate knowing is so complex and detailed that we can hardly explain how it is that we recognize changes. Sometimes we block this intuitive awareness about another, keeping distance by personal boundaries that prevent intimate knowing. We are not always close in the same way with each member in the family; we might share close intuitive knowing with a spouse and hold back from a child, or *vice versa*.

The freedom to know or not know rests on the commitment over time that defines a family. The paradox of commitment is that it is good only for this single moment in time. Even the tie of intimacy does not guarantee that another person will remain, either physically or psychologically; but

to doubt or reject the spoken or unspoken promise of intimacy is only a different kind of leaving. We act as if we know
there will be another day, when what has been done and
shown and spoken and cried about today can be repaired or
made up for if it has hurt or bettered if it was not enough
or erased if it offended or repeated if it matters enough to be
reaffirmed. There is always the tantalizing or dreaded possibility that the tomorrow we count on may not be, that
someone in the family (including even ourselves) will shift
or withdraw or go away. And then we must regroup and the
family is changed.

If intimacy brings pleasure—from being known and approved (or even found delightful) and from knowing and
approving (and being delighted)—the pleasure is intense.
But intimacy sometimes brings displeasure, disapproval,
disgust, hatred. The stakes are very high. If something we do
causes distress—going to bed without bathing, making fun of
women, leaving the lights burning, beating the children,
chewing with open mouth—it can be changed, it can be done
away with, or it can be strengthened. Sometimes it is easy
to change our offending ways, but sometimes it is very difficult. Part of the rhythm of living in a family is asking—beg-
ging, demanding, pleading—that others conform to our sense
of what is "right" and "reasonable" and "good." Short of
hurting another, physically or psychologically (and only the
other person can tell us when that happens), our standards
are arbitrary. They may not *feel* arbitrary, but that is only
because they are so deeply rooted.

In my own family, we have sometimes had "other" adults
live with us as temporary family members. One unexpected
benefit for us, noticed at wry moments, is that our stale-
mated struggles about "how we should do things" can sometimes be seen through another's eyes. From the perspective
of the "outsider," our struggle looks like magnificently important trivia with no logical or rational grounds for resolution—and then *how* we negotiate with each other can be
recognized as more important than the outcome.

Intimacy between family members depends on how each of us perceives the risks and rewards of allowing ourselves to be known and of knowing another. The potential for intimacy challenges us to define what of ourselves "belongs to" others and what is inalterably personal and private. These definitions change from day to day or from decade to decade, and vary in relation to different family members. As intimacy deepens and lengthens over time, we intensify our ability to sense moods and associate thought by the tiniest clues. A husband and wife, driving together in silence to work, simultaneously begin to hum the same melody: neither can say what brought it to mind. A mother impulsively decides to bake a pan of brownies, and in the next instant her small son marches in from the next room to demand "brownies for lunch!" The magic of those connections is awesome and spine tingling.

Caretaking

Caretaking is another central concern of family life. Feeding is probably the symbolic peak of our taking care of one another: choosing, preparing, and serving food that is both essential nourishment and comfort. It may be that man's deepest envy of woman is for the ability to suckle, to produce from within a life-sustaining and utterly satisfying nutriment.[2] How fortunate it is, then, that we all need to be fed and that any family member past early childhood can take part in the profoundly gratifying responsibility of preparing and offering food to others.

Grooming each other is also an essential part of caretaking; we recapitulate the rituals of other mammals by cutting, washing, brushing, and braiding hair, trimming nails, and washing, oiling, powdering, and annointing bodies. Grooming is always done for small children, but as children grow older grooming may be done for them as it is done for adults—only as a favor, caretaking-as-an-event.

Sheltering/protecting is a form of caretaking that in some

societies includes constructing shelters as they are needed against sun, wind, and rain. In our society of permanent dwellings, sheltering/protecting has primarily to do with clothing, which has to be selected, cleaned, and put on or taken off in whole (as for small children) or in part—stubborn snaps or buttons, difficult-to-reach zippers, deciding on right versus left or front versus back, and adding or tucking in a scarf or mittens for warmth.

Caretaking in families also involves keeping order so that everyone's belongings can be found when needed—picking up, sorting, putting away. Nursing and "doing for" a family member who is ill are caretaking. So is helping with work— explaining, showing how, commenting on, making suggestions, giving helpful criticism, holding or bracing an object that is being repaired or constructed. Being supportive— listening to, advising, encouraging reachable goals, *not* advising, setting reassuring limits, sympathizing, approving, accepting—is taking care. And so is comforting—holding, forgiving, waiting until a storm of tears or anger has passed.

In most families there is also some impersonal caretaking to be done. Families vary in the extent to which they value these tasks, require that they be done, and share responsibility for them. Property must be maintained—cleaned, dusted, oiled, swept, scrubbed, not allowed to spoil or rust or get lost or fall apart. Like all caretaking tasks, these responsibilities may fall to one member of the family by some implicit or explicit arrangement, or each person may care for her or his own property and the care of common property may be shared.

A perversion of our wish to take care is imposed by the commercial world that tells us to buy insurance, funeral arrangements, loans, and mortgages to provide "what every family needs." The caretaking that we share with each other is somehow demeaned: *"what we buy is 'better' "* is a message that belittles our own abilities to take care with time and energy.

The ebb and flow of caretaking may at one extreme

proceed entirely according to a contractual arrangement, even
by a schedule: meals prepared and baths given and stories
read and backs rubbed by the clock, roles never varying. At
the other extreme there can be a continuous assessment of
who needs to give and who needs to receive: dinner prepared
by the one who feels most energetic and creative for the one
who feels most in need of being fed. The latter arrangement
is extravagant of time and energy, with endless decisions to
be made and reversed and even argued over; the former is
wasteful of spontaneity and flexibility, with needs overruled
by the dictatorial schedule. Caretaking in its essence is responsive to the needs of the recipient—*not* to take care, an act of
restraint rather than neglect, may be most appropriate when
needs for autonomy and competence are preponderant, as
when a child is learning how to get dressed. There is also
reverse caretaking, when the recipient submits to care because
the other needs to give care: a competent child may gracious-
ly allow a parent to button a coat and tie on a scarf, or a
parent may agreeably accept tea and toast brought by a small
child. The balance of caretaking is negotiated constantly.
"Who takes care of whom and how? When can I allow myself
to be taken care of? How do we pay each other back? What
will you do for me? What can I do for you?"

As with intimacy and sharing, the family code about caretaking is at best an effort to respect the abilities and the
needs of each family member. The potential for "intimate
oppression"[3] is at least as great, and perhaps more obvious,
with caretaking as with intimacy. To be forced by tradition
or by an implicit contract or assumptions about "native"
needs and abilities, to be always in the caretaker role—and to
be expected to go about one's duties with a smile— is no
more and no less an oppression than to be forced always to
be the recipient of caretaking, and to be expected to be helpless and grateful. Husbands and wives, parents and children,
all need to be taken care of sometimes and to give care to
others sometimes. As individuals, we relate to other family
members through our own particular expectations and hopes

about our abilities to take care and be taken care of. Some of us know that we are accepted only while we are being cared for. Some cannot measure our own worth except by taking care of others. Some look on every offer of caretaking as an effort to control, a threat to autonomy, an offense against privacy. The rules by which we guide the care that we give and the caretaking that we expect to receive within our families are shaped by the tolerances of other family members.

When caretaking is routinized—children bathed in a herd or in assembly-line succession and rushed into bed, meals no more than nutritious, brusque and painful hair combing and nail clipping (a duty to perform and a duty to submit)— the pleasures of giving and receiving care can be lost in the service of time and "efficiency." We can lose sight of something elemental in ourselves and in our relationships with other family members whom we "care about" when we overlook the delicate reciprocal balance of caretaking.

Control

We control, and submit to control of, each other's actions, thoughts, and even feelings. To occupy the same household, to live in the same space with other people, requires a most delicate balance of give and take in the modulation of individual idiosyncrasies. In ways that are sometimes open, obvious, and unambiguous, and sometimes devious, subtle, and disguised, we damp the extremes of our own and each other's behavior to a level between tolerable diversity and monotonous uniformity.

We have cultural norms for control in families: parents control children, husbands control wives. (One of our daughters, aged five, gave her own opinion on these conventions: my husband said at the dinner table that a male colleague had commented on my work and then had asked, "What I want to know is, who wears the pants in your family?" As we all groaned and laughed, our daughter first looked puz-

zled and then joined the laughter. "That really is silly," she
said. "In this family, *everyone* wears pants!")

Even in a family of rigid patriarchal style, control is more
complex than just direct commands conveyed by word or by
gesture. The interplay of control is layered, like an onion.
The person who is ostensibly controlled may submit, ask for
direction, postpone a response, fail to hear, misunderstand,
or carry out a command reluctantly or inefficiently, and
thereby exercise covert control of the other who is "in control." Among the strongest mechanisms of control of each
other's behavior are responses of attention and positive
emotion: lecturers emphasize points that members of the
audience smile and nod at, parents repeat games that make
their children laugh, and psychotherapists can make their
clients talk about some problems and be silent about others,
by looking attentive and nodding assent or by looking bored.
"Tell me when I bother you by correcting your speech, and
I will stop" has three levels of control: correcting another's
speech is controlling, saying that those corrections are
bothersome—should stop—is a second layer, and directing
the speaker in need of correction to request that the corrections stop is still another layer of control. At the far extreme,
control of the behavior of others (and resisting the incli-
nations of others to control us) can be a game of fierce
competition. I may not care whether the juice bottle top is
replaced nearly so much as I care about my power to tell you
what to do.

Thought control and feeling control are usually more
subtle than direct control of another person's actions. Some
occurs by contagion: if one person cries while listening to a
Mozart aria, another may be swept into the same mood. If
one parent shouts angrily at Billy for his misdeeds, the other
may join with a surge of anger. Parents control the thoughts
of children by the power to label: "Of course you don't hate
your little sister—nice children don't hate anyone—you *love*
your sister." Authority or special knowledge can be invoked:
"Your father and I know much more about the real world

than you do, and we're *telling* you that you will be sorry later if you don't practice the piano now." Sometimes efforts to control thoughts or feelings only succeed in controlling action—we may appear to be compliant but continue to disagree and keep that disagreement to ourselves.

But control is not entirely malevolent, nor is passive acceptance of control always a weakness. Not only can we control each other, in a reciprocal fashion, in order to reduce family life to a tolerable level of chaos and confusion; but we can also take comfort and respite in submitting to another's direction, and we can relieve each other of worry and unhappiness by taking charge on behalf of another.[4]

The balance of controlling and being controlled, submitting and resisting, demanding compliance and allowing protest, is delicate. Family groups can invest a great deal of energy in seeking what they agree is a generally "fair" and evenhanded balance of control. In our society, this ordinarily means that we recognize, and often go against, the accepted order of parents' control over children and husbands' control over wives. Age and male sex are the traditional badges of the right to control others in this society; part of resultant stereotypic female and child behavior is a passive resistance to control, and covert sabotage with wily techniques for getting others to do what is desired. These threads of oppression and retaliation are difficult to unravel unless they are confronted directly and talked about openly.

We have choices about the way we deal with control in our families:

1. *We can be more or less open* about the rules that determine who can control whom, and when and how to resist. "I don't feel like wearing that dress, just because you tell me to. Why can't *I* decide what I wear?"

2. *We can be more or less uniform* in our control relationships with other family members, or we can vary the amount and kind of control with individuals. "We won't choose any vacation plan that one person vetoes."

"Your sister can choose her own schedule at school, but
we think you should let us decide for you." "When your
father speaks, you must obey."

3. *We can be more or less consistent* over time. "We
never allowed you to go downtown alone at this age;
but now we think that was too restricting, so your brother has our permission to go." "I used to want you to
tell me what to cook for dinner, but I don't want you
to do that any more."

There is no single solution, no "right" way. In some families, what would appear to an outsider to be most grievous
inequities of the direction and degree of control are agreed
upon and acceptable. The real balance of control may not
even be discernible to an outsider. However, every family
evolves its own set of rules and expectations, used to resolve
questions about matters of control.

Choice and Necessity

In every episode of family business, sharing and intimacy,
caretaking and control, are intermixed.   If I prepare you a
meal and then eat some of the food from your plate, I am
taking care with a degree of sharing and intimacy that I
control. If you ask for the meal and then ask me to allow
you to eat in peace and privacy, you alter the momentary
balance of control, sharing, and intimacy. Sexual intercourse,
because it so intensely involves our whole and most vulnerable selves, often reflects partners' momentary needs for
sharing or reserve, intimacy or restraint, caretaking and being
taken care of, controlling and being controlled.[5]

In each of these four modes of family interaction, we do
have choices. There is no family pattern that is "best" or
predetermined by our biology. What is distinctively human
is our ability to learn, and by living in families we learn habits
of sharing, of intimate familiarity, of how we want to be
taken care of and to take care of others, and of the balance

of control. We can also unlearn, and relearn. Because family life is so private and intense, because space is limited and time seems endless, because we do the same things over and over and over, we can, in our families, learn to arrange ourselves in relation to the others we live with in accordance with our own individual and collective needs and abilities. We know each other well enough to hurt, and to support and help. If we trust and are trusted, we can spend the time and energy to hurt as little as possible, and to support and help as much as we are able.

How time consuming! How would family members get anything "important" done (work? studies? housecleaning? helping "causes"?) if everything that happens in the family must be examined and negotiated? The alternative question, the core of our new concern for the inner workings of our families, is simply: how worthwhile are those "important" activities if in order to accomplish them we must overlook the changing flow of needs and strengths in the members of our own families? In point of fact many arrangements for sharing, intimacy, caretaking, and control are decided with relative ease in each family and they remain comfortably habitual and unchallenged. It is the certain belief that they *can be* changed—that they are not predetermined and forever—that saves us from perpetrating on other members of our families the worst consequences of greed, selfishness, injustice, and despair. To have "time for family" really means the time (and energy) to spend in talking, enjoying, giving and receiving, and especially in paying attention to how we are doing, how we are hurting, and how we can help each other.

The freedom to arrange ourselves within our families is sharply contrasted with the limited range of relationships between families and the larger institutions of our society. There is before us now a simple choice: we can take care of our business privately within the family, with little or no attachment to agencies outside of the family, or we can apply to those agencies and give over family responsibility and control.

By convention, we have accepted the notion that maintaining family income to meet individual and collective family
needs is a responsibility of family members; families who
must apply for help with regard to income maintenance are
stigmatized as "unsuccessful" or "problem families." Similarly, the care of preschool children has been assigned wholly
to the private family unit, and families that look for assistance
in child care are looked upon as deviant or incompetent. By
contrast, the family function of education has been given
over almost entirely to professional educators; families that
seek to determine the nature of their children's education
violate convention. And caring for the health of family members has also been assigned outside of the family, to professionals; families that do not rely on professional medical
services are gravely criticized.

It is important to remember that these assignments, too,
are arbitrary conventions. In some ways, they are less easily
unraveled than the arbitrary arrangements that we make
within our families and that we can alter by our own efforts
and without public comment. But these connections to the
official agencies of our society—our places of work, of
childcare assistance, of education, and of health care—strongly affect the levels of time and energy that we can invest
within our families, and they even influence our attitudes,
needs, and abilities to hurt or help the people we live with.

Because the convolutions of power in our society are
focused in a relatively few persons, we can easily throw up
our hands and blame "Them." Or, because we have avoided
responsibility through the devices of agencies and committees, we can easily believe that Society, an impersonal faceless machine, rules us implacably. But Society is also us, individually and as members of our families—a network of human
networks. In all of the interactions of families with other
institutions, we can choose between passive acquiescence and
active participation. If we believe that the way we live in this
society abuses families and requires families to absorb more
castoff fatigue and bad feelings of anger and sadness and

self-doubt than most family units can endure, then we must change the relations between families and other institutions through our own efforts. By determining what our families need from other institutions and what those institutions have to offer us, we can help ourselves and strengthen The Family—the institution that is most *ours* to determine.

The Universal Explicator
is tiny & fits
in the palm of your soul
If cornered will explode
inside you

—Erica Jong

3 STRIPPING THE EMPEROR'S OLD CLOTHES

Our families are but one set of players in the arrangements that we use to get money, nurture and watch over our children, educate each other, and find help for our births, sicknesses, and deaths. In our present society, all of these arrangements are strongly affected by the activities of experts, managers, and professionals. Before we consider the details of these functions, we must first look closely at how experts become experts, at the agencies that managers govern, and at the services the professionals provide. The "system" of experts, managers, and professionals is very different from the "system" of families; even our talk about it is different— crisp, spare, and linear.

Some of the knowledge and skills that we need to conduct family affairs wisely and with care are the stock-in-trade of experts and professionals. To learn how best to nurse a parent who is recovering from a heart attack, the expectable consequences of the alternative treatments available for breast cancer, the techniques of teaching a child to speak a second language, or the nutritional effects of vitamins and other food additives, we consult experts and professionals, either in person or through their writings.

But we have become very reticent about asking to be given information that we have been told is complex and requires lengthy explanation. Our reticence is in part because we tend to think that we won't be able to understand the knowledge and skills that are "possessed" by experts and professionals. However, our reticence also comes from knowing that experts and professionals prefer to *distill* what they know into opinions, advice, and recommendations, rather than to *share* the information and the reasoning that led to their conclusions.[1]

We have been urged also to believe that we provide "better" services for our families by purchasing professional services than by trying to fashion those services for ourselves, in and around our own homes, with the help of family members, kin, friends, neighbors, and others whom we know and trust. "Homemade" or "self-help" services are generally regarded by layfolk and professionals alike as evidence that the users of those services are deprived when these are provided in poor families. When self-help or homemade services are used by families that have "enough" money to buy professional services, the families are regarded as suspect, ignorant, eccentric, or negligent. Following this reasoning, we don't "need" to know what experts and professionals know.

The domain of experts and professionals is reinforced by access to, and use of, very complex machinery. Much of what experts and professionals know and do can readily be learned in a useful form by layfolk. But the special status of experts and professionals is confirmed, "proved," by the fact that they learn and work in places that are equipped with very expensive, very complicated products of technology. Devices like computers and equipment for audiovisual recording and display; special lights that improve on the sun's rays for the treatment of skin diseases; equipment of discovery and detection to examine breath, urine, blood, and bones; and artificial brains, kidneys, and hearts—these are *not* readily available to layfolk. Although these marvels are complicated to understand, operate, and maintain, it is their high cost of purchase and the fact that only certified experts and professionals are allowed to arrange to purchase them that most firmly separate experts and professionals from everyone else. Only established organizations like schools, clinics, hospitals, laboratories, and commercial bureaucracies can own and use these mechanical adjuncts to expert and professional status.[2]

I do not mean to argue that the knowledge and skills of experts and professionals are trivial or not to be respected. My colleagues and I have spent months or years in special training, are paid to work at jobs that reinforce this training, and maintain contacts with others in similar and related fields. Experts and professionals know of, understand, and use a depth and breadth of information that is not available to, or reproducible by, anyone else except through the same processes of learning and use. But much of what experts and professionals know *could* be taught to layfolk for their own use as the need arises—for only the specific information related to an immediate problem must be learned by the layperson at any one time.

The experience and complicated trappings of technology are necessary (as opposed to convenient) only for a narrow range of the work done by experts and professionals. For most episodes of everyday illness, for instance, physicians find out enough to diagnose and treat by taking a "history" and doing a physical examination, relying on their own trained and experienced eyes and ears and hands and a few simple instruments; physicians do not make house calls for most common complaints, not because they always need extravagantly complex mechanical or automated equipment to do their work, but because house calls "waste time," decreasing both their efficiency and income. Similarly, teachers need not use computers or audiovisual machinery for most of their teaching. The distinction lies between what many experts and professionals enjoy and prefer to do, and what the recipients of the services need: the two are often quite different.

One consequence of the professionalization of education and health care has been to cause the average layperson to retreat from an ordinarily useful level of competence in these matters. Paradoxically, professionals simultaneously retreat into areas of rarefied and abstruse complexity, leaving a broad area of everyday human needs poorly attended to. Patients wonder, nervously or hopefully, if their colds, backaches, digestive upsets, or headaches might be treated with some wonder cure, or might possibly be a sign of a more rare and dangerous disease. Physicians are taught in elaborate and painstaking detail about the wonder cures and about those rare and dangerous diseases. They are led by their training to believe that their job will be to apply specific treatments that will cure, and they are taught relatively little about the trustworthy, simple remedies and the everyday disabilities that make up the great majority of human ills.

We patients have to a large extent lost our awareness of our own potential to heal our bodies and to heal others because we believe the professional can do it "better." At the same time, many physicians tend to disparage, as beneath them, the health problems that do not fit the neat (and "interesting") categories of named diseases, diagnosed by technologically elegant devices and treatable by specific modern means: drugs, surgery, machines. There is appallingly little "health care" available, either from lay resources or from professional agencies, for many of our ordinary or ambiguous or chronic ills.

In a similar fashion, the knowledge of experts in other specialized fields becomes increasingly unavailable for application to everyday problems and dilemmas as the experts themselves choose to use their time and energy working on matters of greater sophistication and reward—both money reward and power/control reward. It appears that it is almost distasteful for experts to invest time and energy in a practical approach to problems of immediate impact on everyday lives: food, housing, transportation, neighborhood life, and so on. Self-help projects—for legal aid centers, health clinics, parent-cooperative daycare centers—rarely receive agency funding. It is not easy for self-help projects to find experts willing and able to work collaboratively and who do not attempt to "take over" and control policy. The projects that do soak up funding resources are just those that are controlled by experts, which ofteń have the most tangential relevance to the everyday needs of people. But the funds that pay for both research and service projects are public (tax) monies, or monies skimmed off the top of corporate profits from *our* purchase of goods and services: in either case, we are supporting the work of experts and professionals.

To understand the power relationships relevant to helping ourselves, we must look closely at the interlocking network that links experts and professionals to the managers or administrators of the agencies of training, work, and "service delivery."

The Badges: Expert, Manager, and Professional

Experts are simply persons who know a great deal about a particular subject. We have come to assume, however, that "real" experts will have credentials: usually an academic degree, often a certificate or a license as well. It is not the mere possession of knowledge that is so important to the experts' influence and power. More critical is the role that has been assigned to experts in this society, the manner in which experts are expected to relate to layfolk, and the expert's right to *exclusive* possession of knowledge acquired.

Most experts feel comfortable about expecting or demanding respect or even awe as perquisites of their privileged status. As layfolk we demean ourselves by assuming that we know "nothing" and experts know "everything"—usually both are exaggerations. *Our* motives are compounded of anxiety, wishful thinking, passivity, responsibility avoidance, and submission to authoritarianism. Although it may be tempting, we cannot blame experts entirely for our own diminished status, for we clearly find some comfort in "leaving it to the experts." We can, for instance, avoid responsibility for "bad" outcomes by denying our potential competence to solve our own problems. We also, of course, deny ourselves the satisfaction of "good" outcomes that we might have created. A cultural philosophy that insists we could (should) be living "perfect" lives (free of pain, disease, ambiguity and unpredicted or uncontrolled happenings) makes the chance of a "good" outcome seem infinitely smaller than the risk of a "bad" outcome and encourages us in dependency.

Further, the philosophy of *individual* responsibility— the blame/guilt mechanism that makes us all believe that anything short of perfection is shameful and inadequate and evidence of personal failure—frightens us away from wanting to try to do our best and to find contentment in our own best effort. Only the outcomes, the "products" (career, children, even physical appearance) are valued, while the process, the means by which we work toward these ends, is overlooked. The price paid for an almost exclusive investment in products, and the concomitant belittling of process, is great. If only perfect products can be acknowledged and praised, it is better to give over responsibility to professionals and experts than to risk attempting something that might well bring blame. We surrender the possibility of rewards and satisfactions from our own efforts in exchange for avoiding some of the shame or guilt associated with our (inevitably) less than perfect lives.

Much that we need to know to solve problems and be of help to our families, kin, friends, and neighbors could be learned if we only knew which experts to go to to gain that knowledge, and if we could find responsible teaching and supervision. For instance, many children with "learning disabilities" have an unusual neurological function that affects the way they take in and use information. Such children can

learn best when other persons in their world present information to them in the special forms they need; understanding
the relatively simple neurological principles involved permits
anyone who wishes to help such a child to be creative and
perceptive in those efforts. A family with a child who has a
"learning disability" should be able to find experts and/or
professionals who will teach these principles to family members, kin, neighbors, and any other potential caregiver. This
kind of knowledge can be learned through written and spoken
language—face-to-face teaching, books, articles and leaflets,
television and radio programs.

Experts may use what they know in a variety of ways
with layfolk.

1. They may teach what they know formally and
continuously, as in courses. Experts are usually given
wide latitude in determining what they will teach and
how. This is not an unreasonable arrangement, since
only the teacher can determine what she or he likes to
teach and teaches best, and since both satisfaction and
self-determination (control) are likely to have some
positive effect on the quality of teaching. On the other
hand, both student apprentices and learners who are
layfolk can be expected to have thoughtful and reasonable notions of the subject matters and emphases that
are most meaningful for them. In addition, motivation
for learning is increased when learners have some degree
of control over what is taught, both in content and in
process. Ideally, neither teacher nor learner can command what is taught, unresponsive to the other. In
practice, the authority to so command is often arro-
gated by the expert as a prerogative.

2. Experts may be consulted by layfolk with particular problems and may respond by teaching some amalgam
of specialized knowledge as it applies to the particular
situation and need. For example, a couple anticipating
the birth of a child may seek from a biochemist/nutri-

tionist information about the nutritional tolerances of the fetus, with special concern for the effect of chemical food additives on the developing child. They need a distillation of what is known and what is not known about the fate of ingested foodstuffs and chemicals, as well as the needs and susceptibilities of the fetus, presented in language that layfolk can understand—that is, ordinary language free of the mystifying concealment of jargon—in terms that relate to the choice of foods in the market.

3. The knowledge and skills of the expert may be held closely by the expert and shared little or not at all with layfolk. In this way, what experts know is essentially mystified beyond the reach of others, except other experts. Only summary conclusions are presented as advice or as orders—a physician sometimes implies or even says, "If you don't follow my orders I refuse to act as your doctor." When only advisory conclusions are presented their bases cannot be examined, nor can we understand the expert's own personal bias of interpretation; further, we feel incompetent to make decisions of personal and private importance. A school principal may decide that a "special class" will be a "better learning environment" for a child. Unless the child and her parents know all of the information the school has about the child, all of the possible options, and can compare the options with each other (characteristics of teachers? division of space and time? classmates? outcomes for similar students in the past?), they cannot participate in making the decision. As a consequence we must either remain in the consultative relationship, continuously dependent on the expert, or do without the benefit of the expert's special knowledge.

Consultation is bidirectional—that is, the person who needs information is said *to consult* by seeking to learn, and the expert is said *to consult* by applying special knowledge. That

bidirectionality implies an interaction of teaching and learning. Experts in this society, however, rarely assume any responsibility for sharing what they know, except in the most
tangential and mystified manner.

Techniques for sharing one's special knowledge are not
usually taught in, or approved by, the agencies that provide
experts with credentials. Students, while learning to become
experts, sometimes look for opportunities to share what they
are learning with layfolk—in free health clinics, for instance,
by working with parent's groups in schools, or in "science
for the people" meetings about ecology or nutrition held in
churches or at gatherings of community groups. But students
are not rewarded for these activities by their teachers and are
sometimes actually punished. Those who make such efforts
usually are only part way toward defining themselves as
experts and still believe themselves to be somewhat like
their communities of origin—they may identify with adolescents or with young parents or with "under-served" groups
with whom they feel a kinship: ethnic minorities, women,
poor people.

Since their own teachers are heavily invested in teaching
students to identify *with experts*, and it is greatly to the
advantage of experts to define their status as "special," such
efforts by students are "reasonably" punished: by classroom
humiliation for their presumed lack of intellectual interests,
maturity, and competence; by receiving bad marks in arbitrary grading situations; by being unable to find a faculty
sponsor for a research project; or by not being recommended
for needed scholarships and loans. Most university faculties,
for instance, would refuse to allow a student to use a
knowledge-sharing project as the basis for a doctoral dissertation; most medical schools and hospitals would refuse to
give a student or a resident credit for working in a cooperative
("consumer controlled") clinic. The pressures for conformity
are severe, and accreditation may be withheld from students
who do not appear to be willing to accept the prevailing

attitudes of the expert role toward which they are being
socialized.

Nor do employers usually pay experts to teach layfolk
enough to enable them to become independently knowledgeable in their own lives. It is as if the expert's knowledge were
a personal possession to be jealously guarded; it becomes a
commodity, to be bargained with and for, to be bought and
sold to consumers. There is an implied dread that if experts
shared what they know, they themselves would be "out of a
job," as if teaching others were not an activity to be rewarded. Layfolk often collude in this arrangement by believing that the teaching-consultation meetings sometimes arranged
with experts should properly be done by the expert only as
a volunteer, after-hours activity.

Experts have a further handicap: they are usually not
trained to teach succinctly, in lay-comprehensible language,
and directly to the point of a particular problem or need. Nor
are they instructed in the procedural arrangements to make
themselves and what they know available for repeated and
continuous access by persons who have need of their special
knowledge. When I talk with other experts about using our
knowledge in this way they often blink in surprise—"How
could I do that?" "Where would we meet?" "How could we
decide what to talk about?" "Those people don't really want
to learn." (I have come to believe that the phrase "those
people" is often an alarm signal: it means that the expert
believes him- or herself to have little or nothing in common
with the persons who are the *objects* of the discussion or
activity. Experts who include persons other than experts in
their use of the term "we" are rare and to be cultivated.)

Implicitly by the models of the established and "successful" experts who teach, and explicitly by the rules of conduct that students are taught and required to work under,
experts are permitted and encouraged to mystify their special
knowledge. Jargon plays an important part in this.[3] The
convenience of jargon between experts is not an adequate

explanation and excuse for their failure to learn to explain to
layfolk what they know in everyday language, and this must
be seen as a device to keep their special knowledge as an exclusive possession. In fact, the ideas of *any* field of expert
knowledge can be taught in an intellectually respectable and
useful way to all who have need of that knowledge.[4] That we
do not in this society now use and expect such teaching
reflects both the experts' jealous guarding of the prerogative
of access to knowledge and the nonexperts' lack of confidence
in their own ability to understand what the experts know.
Both assumptions are reinforced by the experts' use of
jargon.

Much of the unnecessary use of drugs in the United States,
for instance, is fostered by the accustomed unwillingness of
physicians to explain to their patients the pharmacologic
action of drugs and the probabilities that available drugs will
affect a patient's illness or complaint. For instance, many
patients hope that their colds will go away when they use an
antibiotic drug—such as a penicillin or a tetracycline— or a
"cold pill." If it seems fairly certain that the illness is viral,
none of the commonly used antibiotics will have any beneficial effects—and the use of most drugs entails some risk.
"Cold pills" have as their most prominent ingredients anti-
histamine drugs, which may cause secretions to dry and
symptoms to decrease, but some symptoms, like a tight cough
or a wheeze, worsen when secretions are dried. These medications in *no* way speed the body's work of combatting the
underlying infection. Of course, patients often prefer to take
drugs—and almost any substance will do—when they feel ill,
because they can then believe that "something is being
done"; that preference would not be unreasonable if the
drugs were known to be harmless. But no drugs are guaranteed to be entirely harmless, and most are reasonably expensive. Sales of the drugs used for colds, like sales of many other
kinds of drugs, would decrease precipitously if physicians
explained *in lay terms* the nature of illnesses and the probable
safety and efficacy of the kinds of medications available.

Patients could then make reasonable and informed decisions
by balancing the possible benefits (including the psychological "placebo" benefits) against the known and suspected
costs and side effects of drug use.

Experts are one kind of elite in this society. If the knowledge possessed by experts were more readily shared with
others who had specific needs for information, their elite
status might well diminish. But there would surely be no
lack of "work" for experts to be occupied with: it is part of
the human condition to be in trouble, to have problems that
need to be worked out, and to need to be taught new ways
of coping with new problems.

The elite status of experts is guaranteed by the nature of
the educational process leading to certification as an expert:
schools of certification, graduate education, or professional
training. To enter such advanced training one must usually
be able and willing to spend the time and money needed for
undergraduate education. One must be sufficiently competitive, compulsive, and "achievement oriented" to forego
both broad areas of personal development and the immediate
needs of one's family, kin, and friends, in order to meet the
requirements of getting "good grades." And one must be
willing to conform in dress, demeanor, and attitude to the
image of senior experts in the field that is being entered—in
fact to "identify" with them so that conformity becomes
thoughtless and automatic.

One reason that women and minority students are not very
much wanted in the elite fields is that those students cannot
really identify with their white, male teachers ("wrong" sex,
"wrong" skin color), nor can their teachers identify with
them by remembering their own student days. An occasional
token black or woman is tolerable as an oddity as long as the
token person tries very hard to act like an "honorary" white
male.

The established power structure in any field of expert
knowledge has an awesome authority to discipline junior
members of the field. Even for high-status, well-paid experts,

job security is a mechanism of threat. Relatively few elite
jobs have secured tenure, and the possibility of becoming
unemployable in the institutions of business, government,
or education that use experts is a very effective mechanism
to enforce conformity. For those very few jobs with the
security of tenure (for which most experts strive) the selection mechanism requires that senior experts be pleased—
almost never are students or layfolk or "low-level" co-work-
ers asked to give their views about the decency, honesty,
morality, or public responsibility of a candidate. Employment opportunities in our society *seem* sufficiently scarce,
even to high-status experts, to serve as a firm barrier to the
exploration of useful ways to share knowledge with others
who need information. This reasoning is, however, usually
well concealed: for instance, there is at present a comfortable
agreement among many high-level physicians and public
health administrators that "health education of the public
has been tried, and it just doesn't work." The rationale given
is the unwillingness of the public to want to learn.

Our experts are almost always specialists. We give more reward to an expert who knows "more and more about less
and less" than to one who knows something about many areas
and can make connections between those areas. Some areas
of highly technical knowledge, and areas in which there is
very rapid "breakthrough" development, provide useful
work for narrow specialists. But it is striking that specialism
is currently in such high favor and that generalists are
despised as "shallow." Even in the narrowest realms of the
work of experts, it would appear that their work would
profit from some contact with generalists who understand
the wider applicability of that work to other related fields.

Scandals of dishonesty in abstruse research work involving,
for instance, the falsification of research data and the alter-
ation of experimental results occasionally come to public
notice. Such deceptions can most easily occur in a field in
which the subject of study has only the most distant application to everyday events. In two recent cases the investi-

gators were working toward the treatment or cure of rare diseases; despite promises that their work *might* lead to information useful in everyday medical care, the validity of those promises could not be checked until after many years of expert energy, and many millions of dollars, had been expended.[5]

It is precisely the avoidance of "everyday" applications that makes dishonesty and dishonor so possible. If every expert were required to spend some time each week talking to layfolk, sharing what is known and teaching those who have immediate need of research information, extravagant uses of research time and money would be balanced by the immediate practical utility of the shared information. Should experts be allowed to talk *only* to other experts and to work *only* on problems that have no demonstrable relevance to the everyday lives of ordinary people?

The right to determine where and how work will be done is a jealously guarded prerogative of experts, subject only to approval by others like themselves, seniors in their fields. Consider the health needs of children in the United States. The most important and least studied causes of childhood death and sickness are poor nutrition, accidents, and environmental poisoning. To solve each of these problems would require a collaborative effort of experts from several fields—medicine, sociology, law, economics, education, engineering, and others—and some one or more persons would need to understand enough about all of these fields, as "generalists," to direct and tie together the efforts. In fact we have made very few coordinated and serious efforts even to approach the solutions to these problems. Problems such as these are usually cut into bits that correspond to what each expert is interested in and to what each knows how to do; "symptoms" are attacked, but the whole, the underlying disease that ties all of the symptoms together, goes on unabated, neither recognized nor defined. Experts do not like to work on interdisciplinary projects because they have been trained only to talk to others like themselves and to be competitively jealous of other experts. Further, the problems of "ordinary" people (and especially the problems that beset poor people) are not often considered sufficiently "elegant" or "interesting" to experts when they choose the areas in which they like to work. Of nearly $180 million spent through the National Institutes of Health in 1974 on research related to the health needs of children, less than ten percent went to studies related to the problems of nutrition, accidents and environmental poisoning *combined*.[6] Who is accountable for this diversion of our scarce resources of expert talent and money?

Managers are essential to our present bureaucratic structures. The most common form of bureaucracy in our society is a *large* organization that requires managers or administrators to maintain hierarchy, coordinate several areas of specialization, and regulate adherence to the rules. There are a few persons at the top who set policy and many persons at the bottom who carry out those policies—make the product or deliver the service that the bureaucracy sells. Sandwiched in between are the managers, who tend to the internal affairs of the organization. Managers are concerned with such matters as personnel and employment negotiations, the purchase, storage, and dispersal of supplies, the maintenance of the building and the grounds, and the control of the budget for operation.

Managers are supposed to:

1. *Perpetuate the existence of the bureaucracy and, if possible, keep it growing.* Managers thus have a conservative effect; they work to guarantee the continuation of organizations, even when the organizations have outlived their usefulness. The managers' responsibility is essentially amoral, for they are not concerned with questions of the good or evil effects of the organizations that they oversee.

2. *Protect the interests of the organization.* Managers are concerned both with the competitive strength of

their bureaucracies vis-à-vis other similar organizations and with the "protection" of their bureaucracies against the complaints, or even the helpful suggestions, of consumers or clients. Although managers of similar organizations often band together to protect the interests of their common "industry," they ultimately see those others as competitors for scarce resources: universities, for instance, are in competition with each other for "good" faculty, "good" students, public and private funds, and the prestige of published books and research reports. The "interference" of consumers or clients is handled by managers in some form of a complaints department or public relations department, which, when it functions smoothly, receives information and reassures informants that they have been heard. The organization then changes not a bit; in extreme instances, it may change just enough to appear to be responsive and to pacify consumers, whose interests are, by definition, "foreign" to those of the organization itself.

3. *Smooth the efficient operation of the organization.* In the service of efficiency, the manager is usually required to reduce the extravagance of diversity in a variety of ways. For instance, individual preferences of workers for hours of work and styles of effort are not observed. Changes in work procedures, determined by worker preference, are correctly seen as dependent on the nature of the work force at any moment in time and, therefore, likely to change or even be reversed as worker composition changes over time, with a consequent reduction in "efficiency." Alterations of the "product" (things manufactured or services provided) according to the needs of consumers or clients are similarly regarded as "impractical." If such changes are "only" in the direction of greater adaptability to the individual needs of those who pay for what the organization sells, they are outlawed as inefficient; if they are in the direction of providing a product or service that has

permanence so that the purchaser need not continue
to buy, they are regarded as economically imprudent.

While managers serve the interests of experts in the top
or policymaking roles, most experts are actually only high-
level workers and are themselves subject to the controls
established and enforced by managers. In some bureaucracies,
especially those that are nonprofit, the most critical policies
to be set are those that assure the perpetuation, protection,
and efficient operation of the organization, which then exists
because it exists—its function and purpose are not even
defined by the self-interests of owners. Experts in such organizations are allowed to choose their own fields of work and
their own styles of work, but only insofar as these do not
threaten the efficient operation of the bureaucracy.[7]
Because our bureaucracies are increasingly large, employing
many people and handling large sums of money, we are all
pushed from outrage into fright at the thought of the effects
on our economy of "a collapse of our major institutions."
The perpetuation of inflexible and sometimes outmoded
institutions thus has wide support. Witness our continued
dependence on automobiles when we need not and should
not expend the fuel that automobiles consume.

Professionals are perhaps the most highly valued of all in
our society. There is a not so subtle insult in the terms
"nonprofessional" and "paraprofessional." House painters
and house-cleaning services, for instance, advertise that they
provide "professional quality" work.

Almost everyone, it seems, would like to be considered a
professional. We vary our definition of the term according
to different contexts. Professionals, for the purposes of this
discussion, are experts who have special skills and can provide
specific services. These skills are (like the knowledge of
experts) useful to layfolk who wish to take care of family
members, kin, or others who have need of a particular
service. The three categories of services that are of special
concern to families are those of child care, education, and

health care. The special skills that professionals can teach
are usually best conveyed by some form of demonstration
(in person, or by film or videotape) in contrast to the teaching of knowledge by language alone.

The title of professional promises work that is potentially
worth a high salary—although not the highest in our present
society, for that is usually reserved for a few entertainers and
corporation executives. Professionals also enjoy relative freedom from day-to-day supervision and review of their actions.
While not all professionals actually earn high salaries, the
esteem in which they are generally held by the public implies
that they deserve earnings as high as any. And while in
actual practice professionals are not entirely free of super-
visory control (from their peers, from those who receive
services, and especially from managers), their work is more
self-determined than most jobs in this society; again, traditional public esteem judges this freedom to be warranted because of the notion that professionals are "more ethical"
than most people.

All that has been said about experts applies to professionals
as well, for professionals are experts—experts with special
skills. The services they provide are based on these skills.
Professional training is designed to induce trainees to adopt
the ideas and attitudes of their teachers. Usually more time
in medical school, for instance, is devoted to teaching students to doubt the veracity and accuracy of patients' accounts
of their illnesses than is devoted to discussing ethical questions of patients' rights or the potential for victimization
of patients or research subjects.

It is not difficult to devise changes in professional training
that would redirect them to learn a role of "service to the
people." Many such changes have been proposed, but their
adoption is firmly resisted by those who now hold professional status. This is not surprising. The professional role
is one of great power—the power to control not only one's
own actions but also the actions (and thoughts and feelings)

of those who come to request services. And power that professionals now hold will not be given over lightly. Professionals are in the business of "the delivery of human services."
(The expression itself has a mechanistic flavor: I envision
a giant forklift thrusting huge crates labeled SERVICE into
the faces of recipients.) At a rapid pace, most purchased
services are now being organized into bureaucratic "delivery
mechanisms"; the solo service practitioner, like the ma-and-
pa grocery store, is being forced out of operation on the
grounds of "inefficiency" and avoidance of bureaucratic
regulation. As this society becomes more and more entrapped
in a network of gargantuan bureaucracies, both inefficiency
and the absence of bureaucratic regulation are widely believed
to be "dangerous."

The Flaws in the Ointment

We should consider why human services provided through
large bureaucratic agencies governed by managers *must be
flawed*:

> 1. The managerial function *damps feedback*, both
> from the recipients of services and from the workers
> who actually provide the services. A patient who says,
> "I came to the hospital clinic because I wanted some
> exercises for my weak ankles, and I got a series of
> health-screening tests but I never got my exercises,"
> is accused of being ungrateful and not knowing what he
> really needed. A student who says, "I wrote in my ad-
> missions application that I intended to become a teacher
> of family planning and sex education in junior high
> schools, but when I got here no one would advise me
> about training for that role, and I couldn't take any
> classes to prepare me for what I wanted to do," is
> blamed for having "unrealistic" career aspirations.
> Several years ago, a group of medical students docu-
> mented the poor treatment received by women patients
> at a municipal teaching hospital; a recent union health-
> insurance study similarly documented the recommenda-

tion of "unnecessary" surgery in more than one in four instances of recommended surgery. In both cases the reports were dismissed by senior physicians as "immature." This expression is frequently used by professionals against their critics; it generally is meant to imply that the persons offering criticism have not yet learned to behave, or to express themselves, in the proper manner as certified members of their field. There is a corollary in the arrogant proposal that no one but a certified professional could comprehend the complexities of the work being examined.[8]

Those workers in a large organization who actually provide purchased services are low paid and low status, doing what has been described as the "dirty work of seeing and taking care of people." Because they do the actual work, they usually have the clearest and most practical ideas about how the services they perform might be improved, becoming better suited to the needs of recipients and better fitted to their own capabilities as workers.

House calls, so that clients receive services on their own home grounds rather than in the forbidding and unfamiliar offices of the agency? After-work agency hours, so that employed persons can receive services without losing time and money from their jobs? Follow-up contacts by telephone to assess the effect of services provided? The scheduling of appointments in a manner that does not imply that clients' time is worthless? Scheduling of caregiver work hours so that no one is required to work at an unrelieved full-time job of responding to the needs of strangers? (Taking care of strangers, or even friends, in a responsible and responsive manner is exhausting work that should probably be limited to four or six hours a day and interspersed with other kinds of work.) Worker time set aside for thoughtful supervision by peers doing the same jobs? Time for meetings among workers to enhance teamwork and reduce competitiveness between them?

These and similar recommendations are not novel. They are generally rebuffed by managers on grounds of "economy" and "efficiency," meaning both that the bureaucracy will not pay the costs of changing policies in response to the requests of particular groups of consumers or workers, and that administrative policy must not be controlled or even significantly influenced by those who do not carry "managerial responsibility."

2. The managerial function *demands a reduction of variety* in the interests of economy. The conditions of work in large institutions are stringently regimented, and recognition of, and response to, the personal styles and needs of recipients and caregivers are discouraged or forbidden. Most of the workers who provide "bad" service—thoughtless, careless, disinterested or controlling—are not themselves malevolent. Many agency workers despise the scheduling practices that keep clients waiting long hours for a brief visit with a professional, but they are powerless (or feel powerless) to change the system. The only possible alternatives to their own feelings of discomfort are to quit their jobs, or to detach and harden themselves to ignore or even disparage the discomforts of their clients. The powerlessness of the immediate caregiver is reinforced when the responsibility for client contact is put into "paraprofessional" work roles, low paid and clearly of low status: "It does not require a highly trained and highly paid professional to do the actual work of giving service."

In some instances, the persons who provide service—physicians, teachers, nurses, attorneys, and "paraprofessionals"—have been trained in the very agencies in which they ultimately work or in agencies that are functionally similar. They may not then experience their conditions of work as limiting the range and variety of services they could provide, for the only work they have witnessed or done themselves has been restricted by the managerial functions of a bureaucracy—"That is how things are done."

3. The managerial function *resists change*. Devoted to protecting the organizations from "wasteful" swings— "from one fad to another"—managers tend to regard all proposed change with suspicion. If the population living in the community that surrounds a medical clinic changes, as when a formerly all-black neighborhood becomes mixed with Hispanic newcomers, certain changes in the provision of service might be well recommended: the hiring of more Spanish-speaking doctors and nurses and clerks, the addition of several "floating" translators to the staff, and the printing of information materials in Spanish as well as English, at the very least. Managers are likely to resist such recommended changes, out of habit and out of their need/desire to maintain control for control's sake. Similarly, as old habits of provision of service become displaced with new ideas, some of which might even be better for recipients—the establishment of a day ward for out-patient surgery, for instance, or the allowance of around-the-clock parental visiting for child patients in a hospital—it is usually very difficult to convince managers of the wisdom of instituting change except by demonstrations of increased income or decreased operating costs. It is not difficult to devise schemes that would make the services provided by agencies more responsive to the needs of individuals receiving those services, but it is extraordinarily difficult to alter set practices in a large bureaucracy.

4. The managerial function *increases the disaffection of workers* with the consequences of their work. Because a major responsibility for managers is to protect the policymakers at the top of the organization from harassment by low-level workers, the sandwiching of managers between those who actually carry out policies and those who set policies acts to guarantee that workers

will feel powerless to improve the quality of their work.
Complaints or suggestions from workers are accepted,
reassurances are given that their comments will "receive
every consideration," and then no change ensues, or
change is so minimal as to be cosmetic. Those who do
provide services according to organizational policies
and don't try to "make waves" are often rewarded by
being offered jobs as managers themselves—jobs that the
bureaucracy defines as of higher status than actually providing service.

The disaffection of providers from the needs and
satisfactions of recipients assures that services will be
provided on the terms of the agency and not on the
terms of the recipients. There are some obvious benefits to providers of service in this assurance, not the
least of which is the face-to-face control that they are
permitted —encouraged—to exert over those who come
to the agency for help. But the benefits to providers of
service offered by bureaucratic rules particularly numb
the service providers who have the highest status, the
professionals.

Despite the unfavorable conditions of training for experts
and professionals, and despite the unfavorable conditions of
work (in a bureaucracy-smitten society), some experts and
professionals retain a strong desire and the energy to share
their knowledge and skills. Such persons will only rarely be
found in high positions in the most wealthy and powerful
organizations of their particular areas of work: "making it"
in these organizations almost always requires conformity to
the bureaucratic philosophy and a skillful development of
jealous and competitive individualism. More often, experts
and professionals who are willing to *collaborate* with layfolk
and clients can be found working in small organizations—
especially organizations so small that they do not "need"
managers, or in new or relatively poor organizations.[9]

The sharing of knowledge and skills that they can provide

is contrary to their training and to the accepted policies of the work of their colleagues. Is is not easy to collaborate to renounce the power of control and there are few credible models to follow. We shall consider later how we can encourage and support experts and professionals who are willing to teach us some of their knowledge or skills so that we can help ourselves by helping our families.

Weave real connections, create real nodes, build
  real houses.
Live a life you can endure: make love that is loving.
Keep tangling and interweaving and taking more in,
a thicket and bramble wilderness to the outside but
  to us
interconnected with rabbit runs and burrows and lairs.

Live as if you liked yourself, and it may happen:
reach out, keep reaching out, keep bringing in.
This is how we are going to live for a long time:
  not always,
for every gardener knows that after the digging,
  after the planting,
after the long season of tending and growth, the
  harvest comes.

—Marge Piercy

4 WEAVING THE NETWORK

Between our families and the knobby necklace of professional
services that encircles each of them lies a wide swath. Beyond
family, but not so distant and different as experts and professionals and bureaucracies, are our interlaced networks of
kin, friends, neighbors, and communities of identity. These
networks have much the same flavor as families themselves,
and they call forth the same kind of discussion. I am conscious of a similar sensuous complexity, very different from
the machinerylike complications of the system of institutionalized professionalism. This kind of human network,
then, is the third "set of players" in the functional arrangements for work, child care, education, and health care, which
we shall look at later.

Again, my plan is to sketch what we really *do* in relation
to our social networks, which can be different from what we
are told to do or what we sometimes think we "ought" to do.
For while we are told that professional services are always

"better," in fact we sometimes do use and exchange and enjoy the services of our networks. The seeds are there. But "community" has come to mean different things to different people—it can mean a neighborhood or an ethnic group or the working class. It is feared as much as it is sought. The concept of "community" is readily tarred with our mistrust of irrationality, conservatism ("against progress, against our own best interests"), and destructive negativism. For many of us the idea of "community" is tied to a fear of losing what little control we seem to have over the business of our own lives, fear of becoming part of what we see as a potential mob.

Thus, family has become the agency of our *in*dependence, a group of a few with whom we have private dealings (not to be spoken about publicly); these private dealings are supposed to nourish us so that we can face "the real world" as energetic, enterprising loners, dependent on no one. While we might yearn, on the one hand, for some kind of permission to be *inter*dependent, to be supportive of others and to receive support in return, yet we fear that these yearnings are signs of weakness and lack of resolve and anxiety—personal, private, and individual inadequacies. When one fails in independence one "should," therefore, repair to paid professionals. Payments to experts are made in dollars, but more agonizingly, perhaps, in self-esteem.

Increasingly we grumble: a nation of discontent, worried and apprehensive *individuals*. Our depression and apathy seem to be more acceptably explained as personal—the shameful evidence of our inability to "make it." We worry about our children and their future lives, hoping that they will not be lonely and sad. We feel as powerless to arrange their lives hopefully as we are to overcome our own circumstances.

No matter how strongly we value and how well we understand our immediate families, they seem insufficient as our only resource for sustaining nurturance. If The Family is to be pushed to "failure," it will likely be the result of our having asked and expected too much of it. The intensity of giving and taking and support requires masses of energy and time we don't have and good will we cannot sustain.

Open and Closed Families

Closed families represent the mythical standard of the "ideal" for contemporary U.S. life. These families provide for their needs either by drawing on their own insular resources or by applying to agencies outside themselves. They are inward-looking units with tight boundaries. A husband and wife live in their own home with their own children. For a large proportion of their needs as a group and as individuals, they are expected to be quietly self-sufficient and entirely competent. Parents are expected to assure that the family has sufficient income, and the family is expected to be content and to make do with whatever income they have. Mother and father are expected to smooth over emotional upset and see to it that individual family members "behave" in a manner that is not upsetting to people outside the family. And parents are expected to watch over children, ascertaining that they are given both the best possible care and the best possible early education.

When families fail in these or similar responsibilities, "society" provides resources in the form of professional services: public welfare or sliding-scale negotiations for families with "inadequate" incomes; social, psychological, and psychiatric services to repair "unsatisfactory" feelings, attitudes, or performances; daycare services for small children to compensate for the "deprivations" or "deviancy" of their own family life. While services are most readily available to families with ample means, they are made available also to those who have "failed" in securing income and have become selected as recipients of public aid. But families in the broad middle-income range are often "deprived" of these kinds of assistance.

Frequently the announced goal of professional services is to "strengthen" the family according to the mythical standard of the nuclear "ideal." This is the family pattern most

familiar to the great majority of professionals, either because
it was the stated philosophy of their own middle-class up-
bringing or because it was emphasized in the training they
received in their professional schools. It is natural for professionals to assume that reinforcing the ideal of the closed
nuclear family is a goal of unquestionable validity; the very
human desire (or need) to defend the choices made by one's
own family can interfere with the ability to see others' families on *their* terms.

Formal teaching in professional training programs rarely
includes an effective program to blow away the biases of
trainees with regard to "desirable" and "healthy" family
relations. Should a couple get a divorce? Should a mother
be partly or wholly responsible for earning family income?
Should a father "sacrifice" his success in his work by spending some of his time caring for his small children? Should
parents remain unmarried and maintain two households?
Should an elderly relative come to live in the household of
a nuclear family? Professionals all too often attempt "yes"
or "no" answers to such questions, assuming this to be
their proper role. Only rarely do professionals know the solid
information that inquiring families need in order to reach
their own decisions. There is, after all, an alternative to the
authoritarian pronouncements of the professional who
"takes over" or manipulates the control of *our* decisions, for
our own families: it is the sharing of relevant information,
based on the tenet that family members can and will take
care of each other and make responsible decisions.

Professionals—educators, physicians, psychologists, social
workers—can even contribute to the weakening of existing
family bonds: by encouraging family members to put a
senile grandmother into a nursing home when they are prepared to include her in their household; by urging institutional placement for someone who is ill or unhappy or de-
mented when the family is willing to provide care at home;
by advising that a dying family member be hospitalized when
the family is prepared for that death and can cope in a

positive fashion; by dire warnings about the consequences for
children when a mother enters paid employment and her children attend a daycare center;[1] by advising that mothers are
always the best custodians of children after a divorce.[2] In
many of these instances, professionals disparage reliance on
the family's social network and even encourage the "independence" of separation from that network.

I believe that our families need a different kind of support,
that some kinds of "support" now available—controlling and
interfering services that we purchase from professionals who
work in bureaucratic institutions—are more debilitating than
strengthening. Even if the outcome is good—the child learning competence and "good work habits," the patient cured,
the anxiety dispelled—credit is given only to the professional
or to the faceless agency, and we are diminished by the
demonstration of our helplessness.

We can retrench. We can find links to others that simultaneously net us into a web of trust and build a substantial
structure of competent caring to reinforce our families. That
retrenchment will only come about if we dare to rely on the
imperfections of other persons. No electronic automation
will replace the richness of continuity and caring that can be
gained from equitable and mutual human contact.

But we *do* have a wealth of those human resources, other
people whom we see often, whom we know well and trust,
and who care. We are close to losing sight of a broad band of
resources—the social network that lies between the tight,
tiny nuclear family and the cool, distant system of paid
professional services. Our kin, friends, neighbors, and communities of identity are real resources of time, energy, talent,
and caring. Within that network, we have a choice between
exchanging services in kind or by monetary payment.

We also have a potential safeguard in the quality of services
provided: unlike professionals I may consult, the members of
my family's network have reason to care about our welfare
and have a responsibility reinforced by history and promise

of continuing contact. If I help my neighbor by nursing her ill child when she is away from home, I already know something of what the child is like; my sense of responsibility is increased by the understanding that the neighbor and I will have to face each other in the future, and by the assumption that I will undoubtedly have some favor to entrust to her when my own family needs help.

Families that cannot call on members of their network of kin, friends, neighbors, and communities of identity for help and support are *closed* families. They are attempting to follow the recommended pattern of the "ideal" nuclear family. Sometimes families find it difficult to maintain or build a strong network because of geographic mobility, as when a family moves many times in rapid succession to follow the father/husband in his work. More often, the firm boundaries of the closed nuclear family are constructed from a psychological aversion to asking for help. That aversion is strongly encouraged by social scientists who praise the nuclear family. It is further "substantiated" by psychoanalytic theory, a theory preoccupied with the *conflicts* arising in families. These conflicts, in the views of psychoanalytic theorists, inevitably send parents, children, and siblings flying apart in all directions as soon as they are able to get away from each other.

Open families, on the other hand, can define their boundaries more loosely, according to their own needs and the needs of other persons whom they trust and care about. In our contemporary society three groups of families most often defy the prescription of the closed nuclear family. The very rich, who have much to share with each other and the resources to maintain several homes and travel long distances, can easily maintain a strong extended-family network. The very poor, who must share what they have for survival and are relatively immobile, can value the exchange of services and goods that they would otherwise have to do without. And some ethnic minority groups, who may rightfully feel abused or misunderstood or neglected by the majority, find solace and joy in networks of others like themselves.

In fact, however, only a minority of U.S. families really "measure up" to the recommended pattern of independent self-sufficiency within the walls of their own households. Despite strong pronouncements about independence as evidence of maturity and good health, despite hammering prescriptions about the necessity of traditional sex-role stereotypes in family relations, and despite dire judgments on families that accept help from nonprofessional sources beyond their four walls, many families deviate from this "ideal." They not only visit kin but rely on them for help. They turn to friends and neighbors for information and advice.

Families that use kin, friends, and neighbors as sources of information, advice, and help often feel guilty or apologetic. They fear that they are violating the guidelines for proper family behavior—guidelines that they subscribe to, or believe they *should* subscribe to. (The usual professional view of these sources of help, information, and advice is reflected in a scathing drug advertisement that shows four women playing cards and has the caption, "because her 'medical society' alarms her about 'the pill' . . . ."[3]) They also risk being scolded by the professionals they may eventually turn to, and sometimes as punishment they get more careless service than usual. The standard view among most professionals is that the closed family pattern is most acceptable; families with open boundaries are made to feel uncomfortable if not inadequate.

Kinfolk

Our usual sense of obligation toward our kinfolk (relatives by blood or marriage) includes the exchange of unpaid services.[4] At the same time, the "ideal" of the closed nuclear family urges us to call upon kin only in the most unusual emergencies and to use purchased professional resources in preferences. Kinfolk are persons with whom we feel a bond of long-term commitment; they do not occupy the same household as the family.

Our definition of kinship is to some extent ambiguous and arbitrary. Sometimes a friendship is so stable over time that it seems like a kin bond; friends sometimes act as if their commitment to each other to exchange services were as firm an obligation as it would be for a brother or sister. Sometimes we use "honorary" family titles for such friends: brother, sister, aunt, uncle. Adolescent children, moving away from the parental household, may teeter for a while on the brink between family membership and the kin relationship. When parents are divorced and their children live sometimes with one parent and sometimes with another, parent and child are alternately members of one family (when they live together) and kin (when they are living apart).

Most of us do, or could, call on kin in times of great need. But we do not know who belongs to the "extended family" of kin as precisely as we know about the membership of the nuclear family cluster. One reason that it is easier to know the limits of the nuclear family is because it is *exclusive*. Our extended families, on the other hand, have loose and shifting boundaries, and they can vary in composition from one decade to the next. An open nuclear family is like an extended family when it has acknowledged bonds of privilege and obligation to near kin, including especially parents and siblings and other kinfolk one has lived with. But at any point in time only some of those kin bonds might be actively in use. More distant kin may be included in the active extended family net for a time and then move out of contact. Since we have no prescribed norms for extended family relations, we usually think of our kinfolk as only those relatives with whom we have frequent contact.

With kinfolk we are close to, we most often exchange such services as child care, loans or gifts of money, nursing care for those who are ill at home, visiting and cheering for those who are ill in a hospital, sharing sorrow and giving comfort

at times of death, preparing food for special occasions or as
a gesture of help. We also exchange special knowledge and
skills—plumbing or carpentry, know-how about medical,
legal, or educational problems, access to work opportunities,
and experienced savvy about the manipulation of bureaucratic agencies like the telephone company, the school
system, the outpatient clinic of the local hospital, or the welfare office.

Kinfolk who make active use of their exchange-of-service
network often keep close contact with each other—and provide opportunities to let each other know when they need
help—by ritual gatherings. Ceremonial occasions for gathering
(birthdays, weddings, funerals, anniversaries, holidays, and
celebrations) usually include sharing a collectively prepared
meal, bringing everyone up to date on recent news and happenings and plans, repeating familiar stories of shared history,
commenting on which members of the collected clan our
children are growing to look like, and making music or playing traditional games together.

Gatherings of kinfolk, families related to families, are
usually part pleasure and part prickles, for we sometimes
misunderstand each other, make jokes about the wrong
things, or fail to keep up with each others' small changes.
Recent and wide- ranging experiments in family styles confuse our expectations of each other. We react—with wonder
or disapproval or shocked disbelief—at the ways our brothers
and sisters and aunts and uncles and nieces and nephews
choose to live. Old expectations are no longer fulfilled, and
we bristle at each other as if we were looking for disapproval.

Situation comedies on TV, and ubiquitous ads, play on
those discomforts of ours. We are told that we *should* dislike
our kin at these gatherings—we are instructed that mothers-
in-law will nag, small nephews and nieces will be offensive
and bratty, grandparents will be agitated or forgetful, brothers
and sisters will be competitive. One memorable TV ad shows
a veritable crowd of kinfolk seen through a fisheye lens so

that their unpleasant faces look enormous, chattering and scolding about spots on the glassware.

Those who want to sell us goods and services have much to gain by convincing us that our ties to our kinfolk are distasteful and should be limited or forsaken altogether, and much to gain by urging us to overlook the pleasures of renewing contacts with that circle of flawed but very real people to whom we have ties. We are more likely to buy their goods and services if we do not trust our kin. So we are subtly programmed to suspect those ties of obligation, responsibility, and affection that are born of a common history and a promise of continuing commitment; we are urged to focus on their *inadequacies*. Anyone who intends to maintain a kin network must challenge the message that it is foolish to trust and rely upon such flawed and "ordinary" relations.

When the kin network is used only rarely or made to seem distasteful and tarnished, we can feel uncomfortable about calling on kinfolk for needed help. If we do not have an actively functioning and defined system of exchanges we are not certain that we can or will want to "pay back" any favors, nor are we clear about what might be adequate or appropriate repayment. Human relationships are like muscle tissue, or a complex skill like piano playing. Used frequently, they grow in strength, stamina, intricacy, and the potential for enjoyment. Unused, they remain small or seem unfamiliar and foreign. Used to excess, they become fatigued, dull, or painful. But even a kin relationship that has withered from disuse still remains as potential—my parents, my brother and his family, my cousins, are still connected to me, and I to them, by obligation and responsibility, no matter how distant we grow in time and space and understanding of each other.

The demands of employment (arising both from need for income and from desire for work that brings satisfaction) may lure us to move far away from our kin: extended families are sometimes scattered to the corners of the world. Some young adults move away from their kin because that seems

the only way that they can create or enforce their transition
from being members of a family to being kinfolk. But separated kinfolk also move back together after an interval,
create contacts by mail and travel and telephone, or even
find adoptive kin by creating new kin relationships with
people who "might have been" mothers, uncles, sons,
cousins, or granddaughters.

Friends

Friends also participate in the exchange of unpaid services, but they do not live in our households and we do not
ordinarily expect to share a commitment over time. We value
our friends while they are close and are sorry, but not sur-
prised, when we grow away from each other.

We have family friends and individual friends. Our individual friendships grow in our contacts with the world outside of family life, at work, school, in the neighborhood.
Those who are tightly bound to the family—toddlers, the ill,
the handicapped, and some housewives—are dependent on
other family members to bring them friends, or they must
hope to remain close to friends from the past.

Exchanges of service between friends are more variable
than those between kin. Obligation and responsibility are
much less, and much less clearly defined, so that the relationships seem more voluntary and arbitrary. Friends allow
us to diffuse our energies, our worries and fears and celebrations, outside of the immediate family and allow us to
dilute our investment in family members. Among my friends
are some I call upon to talk about troubles, to share good
news and commiserate over bad. Some I see relatively infre-
quently, but often talk to on the phone. Some have taken
care of our children when all our family adults had to be
away. Certain of our friends are especially close to one of
our children, and they sometimes can help us resolve perplex-
ing worries about a child's temporary difficulties. Others do
shopping errands, read and criticize manuscripts, or nurse my

sick plants back to health. We do not always do the same
things for each other—I have a spare bed to offer and a place
at our table, hours to listen and talk, and hands to launder
clothes and shampoo hair.

Relationships with friends may compete with family ties.
When the competition becomes chronic, so that we have to
choose between family and friends, we can lose in one realm
what we gain in the other. We are limited in time and energy
and the ability to make connections with other people. But
short of the point where the fullness of relating overflows,
we can find a vivid extension of ourselves from the family
center into friendships. That reflection of energy can make
living in a family richer and less solitary—our friendships
increase our sensitivities to others. Because friendships are
voluntary and arbitrary, far more so than family relationships usually seem, we can use them to explore our capacities to share, to be intimate, to take care, to control.

Friendships, unlike kinships, require accessibility and
availability to survive. Friends widely separated by space
may "keep in touch" (symbolic of intimacy) by letters,
phone calls and visits, but there is no guarantee of commitment over time. The waxing and waning of friendships reflect our individual growth and change—in interests, abilities,
philosophies, needs, and daily activities. Most friendships
end by attrition, withering by happenstance rather than
intent. We suddenly realize that we do not see each other
very much any more, and while we may regret the loss (and
hope that the regret is mutual), the separation does not seem
like the violation of an assurance. Sometimes friendships,
like kin and family relationships, come to a violent break
by a misunderstanding or quarrel, and the loss seems bitter
and wrong.

Because some friends "belong" to one member of a family
and others "belong" to the family as a whole, and because
all our friends bring us into potential contact with their own
networks of kin and beyond, our access to an informal system
of exchange of unpaid services is greatly increased through

our friendships. The arbitrary and variable nature of our friendship bonds permits a vast resource of help, if only we can discover our assumptions about the fairness of exchanges. "Would you trade a tub of homemade ice cream for information and help in preparing my income tax form?" "If you come with me to an appointment with my doctor, may I take your children to the zoo?" "Will you type my papers, and let me iron your shirts?" "Will you tell me if you think the proposed exchange is not fair?" "What can I do for you, and what can you do for me?"

Neighbors

Neighbors are simply all those persons and families who live near us, often neither kin nor friend. Their proximity allows an enormous potential for exchange, and opportunities for repeated contact make it possible to develop trust. The varieties of service that can be exchanged between neighbors are almost endless.

In the past, some believe, neighborhoods were always networks of trust and helping, families who were friends of families. Whatever the reality of the history of neighborhoods, we generally assume that they have in the last few decades become less than they might be. As neighbors we are often wary of each other. The habits of mistrust, suspicion, and a search for *the* scapegoat, someone to blame for whatever hurts us, dilute our sense of affinity with neighbors.

Our wistful wishes for a network-neighborhood have been violated by the myth of the desirability of family "independence", by pressures to anticipate that we or our neighbors will move away, by urban renewal projects that tear apart the most stable neighborhoods, and by the striking contemporary phenomenon of our great divergences in personal philosophy. Vertical city housing, in apartments and projects, and horizontal "developments" of identical units so dilute opportunities to establish the individuality of families that it becomes necessary to retreat and separate in order to preserve the haven and identity of personal living space. Sometimes it is difficult to think of calling on neighbors for help, or offering services to help them, because of fears that the relationship might be short lived, suspect in validity and trustworthiness, and flawed by differences. One of the most striking characteristics of our society is the enormity of our differences in religious affiliation, preference for political party, beliefs about childrearing, ethnic background, or identification with conservative, liberal, or radical definitions of "what this country needs." Sometimes these differences between neighbors are irreconcilable. More often they are *irrelevant* to the exchange of a lawnmower or the running of errands at the corner store.

Neighborhoods of trust and trustworthiness are often found in those ethnic pockets of city or town life where families live, intentionally or by the unwritten rules of housing codes, with others "of their own kind." In neighborhoods that are mixed and unsegregated, our differences with our neighbors may loom larger than the convenience of nearness.

Sometimes "neighborhoods of intention," taking advantage of all of the easy means of connection and communication, are newly created as alternatives to the loneliness of living amidst strangers. Neighborhoods of intention usually arise from some experience of frequent contact with people who work together at the same place, who work at similar jobs and meet in larger organizations, whose children attend the same daycare center or school, or who participate in the same church or political organization. By using telephones, bicycles, and automobiles, by reserving time and energy to make contact with each other, a network of families who are "near" is created to substitute for a network based on literal nearness in space. Children visit one another and share toys and excursions. Adults call on one another for help, the exchange of services and the celebration of happy personal events and formal holidays. And the space of houses and yards and the use of property (especially the expensive equipment that no single family needs to use continuously) can be shared. Buying food cooperatively in large discounted quantities is sometimes the nucleus of a neighborhood of intention, sometimes a consequence of such a neighborhood that has been created out of other connections. Although such "neighborhoods" are intentionally invented, they are modeled on memories or tales of neighborhoods of the past.

Maintaining a sense of neighborliness, like maintaining a kin network that functions actively and agreeably, is often "easier" for persons and families who define themselves as different from the portrait of the white, middle-class, "average" family pushed upon us by advertisers and social scientists. The differences may be chosen by preference—"We are not like that"—or may come out of forced alienation, of being outsiders from the approved "mainstream." The steady message that tells us that we ought to be in those "average" families, from those who want us to buy what they sell, is very loud and persistent, but more and more people seem less and less inclined to listen. We are learning that to be homogenized into a mass of interchangeable units carries a high price, and some of us are turning away by valuing and celebrating our differences. Just when computers and statisticians are becoming proficient in analyzing and describing those average tastes and preferences and reactions, many of us have begun to react by proclaiming that we *are* different and that our differences are important.

For those who find strength and self-esteem in valuing their peculiar differentness from the generally accepted portrait of "most Americans"—whether the sense of that difference arises by their own intent or by the rebuff of others—an active social network serves both to define and to affirm their differences. The exercise and enjoyment of strong networks of kin, friends, and neighborhood serve in defense against the pain of alienation, turning a discomfort into a joy and a strength. As individuals and as families we are reminded by the people in our networks that we are not alone in our differences and that our *own* culture is a valued source of pride and of resources for help.

This recent phenomenon of celebration of our different cultures began, as far as public (media) recognition goes, among blacks. But the germ seemed to sprout instantly and everywhere; its roots were already deep and strong. Even the culture of women—a culture of difference at once more profound and more disparaged than that of any ethnic minority group—is beginning to flower into pride and forthright joy.[5]

The force of authority carried by the media, the bureaucrats, and the experts and professionals whose convenience and profit is served by the myth of our sameness, is difficult to resist when we are isolated as competitive individuals and nuclear families. The stain of self-doubt and apology weakens us. But surrounded and nurtured by others who hold and live by the same values and beliefs, who perceive a similar reality born of similar experiences, and who honor similar ritual celebrations, we find strength in helping ourselves by our own best efforts.

Should we then live only amidst others "like ourselves"? To some, the clustering of people who are highly alike in values and customs is antidemocratic because it thwarts the "melting-pot" goal of assimilation of diversity.[6] It seems to me that neither pluralistic voluntary segregation nor individualistic voluntary mixing can be said to be better, in and of themselves. What is important *for the good of us all* (over and above the importance of choice in how and with whom one will live and associate) is the promotion of tolerance. The "melting-pot" ideal, which has in our past tended to overrun ethnic pride in association, has also promoted competitive individualism. Individualism in a "scarce-resource" society, in which we are driven to compete with each other, works predictably as a counter to tolerance. If the strong currents we now feel toward ethnic pride and voluntary separatism could also promote secure personal self-esteem, then we might move again in the direction of a tolerance for personal differences.

Communities of Identity

Communities of identity are broad groups with which one feels the bond of similarity in values, interests, and style. While neighbors are named and known, members of a community of identity are largely unnamed and unknown, to be discovered and joined as occasion arises. My communities of identity are not identical with those of others in my family, nor with those of my family as a whole: women, certain small networks of activist physicians and educators, feminists, mothers, and women health workers are communities attached to my family only through me. Some of my kin belong to my communities of identity, some of my friends are in those groups, as are a few of the neighbors who live near me and almost all of my neighbors-by-intent. But I am very certain that I do not now know personally all of those persons who would join with me if need arose.

Communities of identity are greatly promoted by and often flower into being through "political" organization. The central value of such a community may be one's occupation, ethnic or racial origin, sex, or strong belief in an idea or cause. At a time when astonishingly wide philosophic differences divide us from each other, and when many of those philosophic differences concern who shall have power over whom, communities of identity almost always have a political base, in the broadest sense. Communities of identity also have the power of political action, whether through a buyers' strike, worker organization, refusal of participation as research subjects in a study, or a voting bloc. Many such common efforts are considered to be negative, simply because resistance against power is *always* defined—by those "on the other side"—as being negative.

Other kinds of community action can gain substantive benefits. The network of a joined community of identity can rally to raise money, as when a "block party" raises money to buy trees in a new, or newly renovated, neighborhood; to feed, clothe, and shelter the displaced and homeless, such as political refugees or neighbors burned out in a fire; or to resolve the dilemmas of a distraught family by a coordination of help, as in "network therapy."[7] Neighborhoods have organized to demand that traffic lights be installed at dangerous corners or that construction trucks be rerouted away from streets where children play. A coalition of U.S. health workers worked to raise money and to press for government action on behalf of imprisoned health workers in Chile. Incipient efforts at union organizing at a work place have been supported with massive volunteer contributions of time by persons who are knowledgeable about the strategies and tactics, the successes and the discouragements, of the efforts of worker organizers. Feminist authors gathered to sit long days in a courtroom in support of a woman suing her publisher.

The persons with whom we regularly exchange services on a daily basis are relatively few, and must be so for reasons of energy conservation. Equitable and efficient exchange of services requires that the network be used frequently and with intent and good will, and for most of us there is a limit to the number of people with whom we can relate with caring, trust, and concern. We know that our wider communities of identity exist and that they are potential sources of help. Our own helping acts are at least as valued as the insurance we can buy from a corporation, for they help build the communities that we can draw on.

Affirming the Strengths of Networks

We have grown far from a *formally* approved system of barter for unpaid services. We wonder if it is not more civilized, more sophisticated (and therefore "better") to *pay* for what we need. A barter system of exchange of unpaid services must rely on human frailty and human good will, both notoriously variable and unpredictable. If my sister takes care of my children for an afternoon, she may feed them only tuna sandwiches, which they hate. If I defend a fellow worker

against our mutual employer, will she remember when I need
to ask for help? Every instance of unpaid service carries the
risk of disappointment, anger, hurt feelings, and resentment.
Could we not bypass all of this aggravation by arranging to
pay for services with money?

The most energetic efforts to increase our personal network of service exchange will not greatly alter the system
we now have of paid professional services. Most of these
services are directed to narrow, exotic needs and use the
complicated trappings of technology. We are not thinking
about performing brain surgery at home on the kitchen
table, but we do need occasional or part-time childcare assistance, help in deciding whether a sore throat will be cured
by drugs, and news about job openings. Although we might
offer competition to some existing professional services,
most of what we could exchange with kin, friends, neighbors,
and community is not now well provided in the system of
services for pay. Child care, consolation, food preparation,
home nursing care, and the maintenance of personal property
are for the most part considered to be the responsibility of
individual families and are difficult to obtain from the paid-
services system.

There is no guarantee that the services we now purchase
are performed with any greater reliability and satisfaction,
or with any less misunderstanding and grief, than we risk
when we try to develop private networks for helping. Healthcare providers, for instance, often are strangers; we meet them
in the clinic or hospital, and more often than not we are
treated as a disease or a complaint, not as a person with a
full life, nested in a family with multiple ties to a social network. Those who teach us and our children in the formal
institutions of education often seem to want to relate to us
only through a specific instance of teaching/learning and
apparently want to avoid an integration into *our* context
of student, family, network.

These are services that must in the most usual instance
be performed by human heads and hands. Even when they

are purchased directly, these services may be performed badly. When they are arranged through "third-party" intermediaries— referrals to educational specialists from a school, or to medical or surgical specialists from a general-care clinic, for example—the caregivers' responsibility to recipients is still more diluted. If the person who performs the service that we purchase is a stranger to us, and is governed more by organizational policies than by concern for our ultimate welfare, it may be even less likely that we will be served well than if that person is someone we will see again and will someday repay by our own efforts.

We act as if we were trapped in a rut. The inadequacies and errors, both of omission and of commission, of purchased professional services are well publicized.[8] The discrepancies between what families say they want and need from professionals and what professionals say they want to provide in services are painfully documented.[9] Patients, for instance, say that they want to be listened to, to be known as persons and not as "objects"; physicians say they want patients to consult with them only for illnesses for which there are "treatments" and not to keep returning only for solace and "hand holding." Yet we continue to act as though we had no resource for needed services *except* the professional establishment. We act as if we forget that we have kin, friends, and neighbors whom we know and trust.

In the area of child care, for instance, where professional services are not yet institutionalized, we seem perilously close to opening yet another area of family life to professional intervention by the legislation of *professionally run* daycare centers. Although the degree of risk to our children in this new instance of bureaucratized professionalism is not yet clear, we have little assurance that a daycare system controlled by professionals will not also become inflexible, unresponsive, uncaring, careless. And yet there are few serious proposals for alternative arrangements for child care.[10]

Neighborhoods that do not have any, or enough, expert

and professional resources are deprived in one sense. Neighborhoods that have professional services unsuitable for their
needs may also be considered to be deprived. Most of us are
deprived of those services that appear to fall "beneath" the
interest of the professional caregiver and "beyond" the
competence of layfolk.

Are the outcomes of professionally arranged maternity
and childbirth services, for example, really more beneficial
than they are harmful for the infant, the parents, and the
family unit? Do we *know* the benefits and harms of deliveries by drugged mothers separated from other family members and attached to electronic monitoring equipment—with
the newborn whisked away into a nursery distant from his
or her parents? Have we had the wit to challenge the pronouncements of the professionals and really measure the
costs and benefits of well-equipped and competently served
home deliveries, compared to those in assembly-line hospitals?[11] Similarly, are parents who feel incompetent (or intimidated) about their understanding of their children's readiness to read really providing the best education for their
children by surrendering them to the schools? What about
children whose reading readiness is "too young" according
to established school procedures or "retarded" beyond the
prescribed age of six or seven? Are we well served by a medical service system that requires us to visit a physician for
symptoms of the flu (lest we be scolded for neglect), when
we are then told—the joke is sadly more than a jest—"I
can't do a thing for you. Come back when you get pneu-
monia and I can cure you"? Surely some other combination
of scientific and technical knowledge and service delivery
would be less predictably depriving.

We do not use our networks of kin, friends, neighbors,
and communities as much as we might, as consultants and
"experts" in their own right on the basis of their experience,
skills, and knowledge. We are reluctant, fearful, and apprehensive about choosing not to use professional services.

We have been well trained; these fears and discomforts are

directly related to some notions that are very predominant
in our society:

*Never are we systematically taught that good can come of
cooperative effort.* "It's a competitive world" is the principal
reason given for the necessity of rank ordering children, from
the beginning of their school experience, in an officially
recorded array from the "best" to the "worst." We are taught
in our histories and novels, in our civics courses, and in our
observations of the world of work and commerce that there
is never "enough" to go around and that our individual
worth will be measured by the amount of money and power
we can grab and hold by competitive individualism.

This competitive individualism that we are so carefully
taught defeats both trust and trustworthiness. If we are each
striving for something that will identify us as worthy, something of which there is not "enough" for each of us to attain,
then we are all always in competition with each other—family
members, kin, friends, neighbors, and those who make up
our communities of identity. We jockey for money only in
certain areas of our lives, but we are taught to jockey for
power (control over ourselves and, whenever possible, over
the lives of others) continually.

We have little patience with patience. In the context of
competitive individualism, if an opportunity is not seized
(or wrested from someone else) it will be lost. If we are rebuffed the first time we reach out to a neighbor, we are
likely to assume that he or she is worthless, antagonistic,
and certainly untrustworthy. By contrast, those of us who
care for small children on a day-to-day basis learn perforce
that tomorrow can be better, that rough spots can be
smoothed over, that storms of tears and anger pass, that
aggravating baby habits are "grown out of." Taking care
of patients, we learn similar lessons: I learned, for instance,
that I grow to like, with genuine affection, almost everyone
I have an opportunity to know. But that process requires
repeated face-to-face contact, for there are many people that

I do not like very much when we first meet. Child care and
long-term contact with the same patients are low-status jobs
in this society, and the lessons one learns in this kind of work
are not recognized as very important. But lessons about
patience are of enormous importance if we are to learn to
trust those outside of our immediate family with whom we
could develop a system of exchange of unpaid services.

*Our individualism is constantly nourished by shame and
guilt.* This shame and guilt are part of our Western religions,
nourished by the American pioneer dream-culture, dramatically reinforced by Freud's poetic creation of "the true story
of family life," and hammered home by advertising. We are
taught that a "perfect" life should be ours, were we but
worthy enough: anything less than perfection—any pain, any
inadequacy, any less than alluring appearance, any grimy
shirt collar—means that we are guilty and will be shamed
(for what?). In that enormously risky dilemma, we often
lack the confidence to turn our backs on what the experts
and professionals advise. If grandfather says he is ready to
die, and we are ready to attend him at his death, and he
wants to die at home—we are still likely to put him in the
hospital: "What would the neighbors say? What would our
doctor say? Suppose he might live another week, or three,
in the hospital?" In fact, we have been robbed of participation in the deaths of those we love, just as we have been
robbed of participation in their births; the risk of feeling
shamed and guilty is a powerful mechanism that causes
us to hesitate before seizing experiences that might enrich
ourselves and others.

We are taught to feel incompetent in every area of expert
and professional endeavor. If experts and professionals have
a "right" to keep and control their knowledge and skills, we
must play the counter role of incompetence. Many of our
ordinary problems of living, for which we are directed to
seek professional services, require an integration of knowledge and skills from several expert areas. Although our
problems are often best dealt with by a "generalist" or

coordinator, we are continually led to believe (1) that no one but a professional can solve our problems for us; and (2) that the higher the status of the professional, which usually means the more specialized, the "better" will the service be. Management experts regulate the conditions under which we work; our daily pains and ills are put in the care of medical specialists who hope to discover that we are suffering from exotic illnesses; and our children are educated in schools whose excellence is judged by the elaborateness of the audiovisual teaching machines and not by the quality and content of the teachers' interaction with individual students.

Our training in mistrust, impatience, guilt, and incompetence keeps us from trying in a serious, sustained, and hopeful manner to act on our care and concern for our families by expanding beyond the closed boundaries of our nuclear enclaves. We are taught *not* to exercise and enjoy our networks of kin, friends, neighbors, and communities of identity.

With mutual cooperation we could not only provide services that cannot be purchased and that we are hard pressed to provide within our small units of immediate family; we also could work to rearrange those central functions of family life that are now dominated by experts and professionals:

1. *The conditions of work.* Families are not now able to decide freely who of their members should work, for what hours, and where. The issue is critical both for parents and for their children.

2. *Child care.* The "rules" (actually better described as fads) of child care are set by experts and professionals, most of whom have had little direct personal experience in the day-to-day care of children. The requests of contemporary families for assistance and advice in childrearing may in the near future become the rationale for a professionalized bureaucracy of agencies for early childhood education.

3. *Education.* Family members have been encouraged to believe that they are not competent to educate their

children, nor should they seek to influence or advise
professional educators.

4. *Health care.* Families have not had access to the
kind of basic knowledge and teaching/consultation/
advice that would permit them to make reasoned and
informed decisions for their individual and collective
good health, and that would encourage competent
home-based care for a broad spectrum of injuries,
illnesses, and disabilities.

The work of the world is common as mud.
Botched, it smears the hands, crumbles to dust.
But the thing worth doing well done
has a shape that satisfies, clean and evident.
Greek amphoras for wine or oil,
Hopi vases that held corn, are put in museums
but you know they were made to be used.
The pitcher cries for water to carry
and a person for work that is real.

—Marge Piercy

5 WORK VERSUS JOBS

We value work and despise our jobs. Few of us have jobs so
comfortable and so substantially rewarding that we find them
to be sources of recognizable pleasure. We are accustomed to
believe that jobs must be draining, aggravating, taking (of our
heart's blood) in return for needed income. Even those relatively fortunate few in jobs with high status, high pay, and
some autonomy complain about *their* jobs: too demanding
of time, too tension filled, and too pressing.

We believe that work, on the other hand, is inherently
good; we celebrate honest toil and labor in our arts and
literature. The "work ethic" prescribes a positive attitude
toward work, a belief that work should be both necessary
and deeply satisfying. We are taught in a thousand ways that
the rewards of work are worth the sacrifice of other, perhaps
more immediate, gratifications. Freud proposed that a
primary index of maturity was the ability "to love and to
work."

We embrace the values of effort, mastery, and competence; these values combine with whatever drives are inherent in human beings toward creative completion of tasks—we *are* strongly impelled to believe that we want to work and to do our work well. It seems impossible to discover exactly to what degree those values and drives are "wired in," as constitutional predispositions of our human existence, and to what degree they are learned from our culture.

What we extol is work that is done competently and with an investment of creativity, involvement, pride—even passion. Since few existing jobs permit that investment, an institution has evolved that justifies, indeed demands, that it is "enough" to work for income alone. We are carefully instructed, from our early years on, that most people *would not work* at necessary jobs unless it were arranged that their very livelihood (the ability to feed, clothe, and shelter themselves and their families) were at stake. The dreariness and the impossibility of creative investment in most jobs-for-pay is thereby accepted, for we have been taught that we are basically lazy and will only do what "needs" to be done with that stick of financial fear at our backs.

This schism between valued work and the jobs we are allowed/required to do forces a condition of profound emotional conflict into our everyday lives. Often we turn away from that conflict (as too painful to confront) and argue that the conditions of our jobs *have* to be unfulfilling: it would be futile or foolish to expect more. Yet we cannot consistently deny the undercurrent of our needs for creativity, mastery, and competence in work, and that undercurrent feeds our resentment about jobs. Jobs do not *have to be* bad, we then think, they just *are* bad.

Our jobs are key factors in our relationships at home, for they are both the means by which we provide money for our families and the major reason, if not excuse, when we fail to provide other kinds of support to family members. Our jobs dramatically affect the lives of our families.

Because the institution that ties together work, jobs, and

the earning of family income has such a central and pervasive relationship to the quality of life in families, it is the first extra-family institution that we must examine. Perhaps no other institution in our present society has the fate of families so firmly in its grip. No other institution seems so impersonal, so driven by its own *animus*. If our investments in our jobs were fully rewarding—permitting energetic and creative work in the most positive sense—and if we could moderate our job responsibilities in accord with family needs, we would discover a key element in our design for a family-supportive society. We exist now amidst conventions that are the polar opposites of family supportive: most of us labor at jobs that discourage the investment of our individual talents, that are arranged for the profit of others, that are personally demeaning and inadequately paid, and that require schedules that disregard our membership in families.

Work That Is Productive

Although most of us are not permitted to have creative work to do, we are allowed to be *productive*. At best, our opportunities for work permit us to know that we have accomplished something worthwhile through a measure of productivity. An exertion of energy and effort that has no recognizable productive outcome does not seem to be really worth the label, "work."

The product that can result from work may take one or more forms:

1. The product may be a tangible thing, a whole. Craftswork results in objects of decorative or useful purpose. Farmers and gardeners grow food, authors write plays or novels or poems, cobblers make shoes. Relatively few paid jobs now permit a single worker to create a whole product. Some workers—artists, crafts-workers, and many farmers—are "self-employed" and create products that they may then sell. But this is

not often a source of sufficient income for a family's
needs.

2. The product may be part of a whole. Most factory
jobs limit the individual worker's contribution to a relatively small part of the whole item produced—the principle of assembly-line work. Workers have described how
they sometimes mark the bits that they produce so that
they can later be recognized or identified, even by a
mark that is defacing.[1] Construction workers also contribute to the making of a whole, and—perhaps because
their projects take a long time to complete and are one
of a kind—these workers may point out, years afterward,
their contributions to "that building" or "that road."

3. The product may be measured in the aggregate, as
tasks completed. Those who do repair work, or piece-
work, and most service workers (barbers, nurses, clerks
in stores) can identify a product in the number of
pieces of work done in a day or a week: TV sets repaired,
patients cared for, items sold or customers served. The
more discrete the tasks, the easier it is to count the
aggregate as a product.

4. The product may be measured by a demarcation
of time. Toiling "a full day," with or without punching
a time clock, may identify the productivity of one's
work as time set off from other time. Work begins and
work ends, and the time spent in between is a product
that can be identified by its duration.

5. The product may be a paycheck or money earned
as fees. Work for pay is the most usual definition of
"productive" work in our society, but it seems re-
strictive to exclude work that is productive by other
criteria.[2] Still, we do tend to rate effort according to
the salary that is paid for it. Salary scales are critical
determiners of the flow of money, goods, and services
between us, even though many of us would also agree
that the income of some workers does not correspond
to the "true" value of their work. United States census

reports list the earnings of adults employed full time,
and that list gives a kind of ranking of the "worth" of
various jobs in our society. Workers who provide services to people (caregivers) are among those who earn
least; caring for children—when it earns any salary at
all—is so disgracefully ill paid that it is hard to believe
that children have any value, even as objects, in the
institution of work and jobs. Taking care of garbage
(that is, collecting garbage) is a more valued occupation
than taking care of children or other dependent folk.[3]

Adults Without Productive Work

About one-third of adults in our society spend most of
their time in another kind of effort—the maintenance of
their households and the personal sustenance of members of
their families. "Are you a housewife, or do you work?"
accurately reflects the irony of the arrangement.[4] Taking
care of family members and their property does not, according to our present definitions, meet the criteria of productive
work. No products, either in whole or in part, need be made
by the homemaker, nor is her work defined by a limited
schedule of hours, nor is she paid directly for her efforts.[5]
There are few products that a contemporary homemaker
needs to make with her own hands; almost every conceivable
kind of household good can be purchased at a price less than
the cost of "homemade." Store-bought socks and bread, in
their inexpensive varieties, may not be as well made nor as
suited to family tastes as the products that most homemakers could create, but by their very existence they negate the
necessity of the homemaker's efforts to make socks and
bread. It is usually an *extravagance* of time and money to
create a product for family use.
Can the child one cares for, or one's husband, be counted
as a "product"? Certainly in many societies children have
been looked upon as their parents' property, to do with as
parents will without outside interference. And wives may

take surrogate pride in their husbands' appearance, behavior,
and career success. But to count another human being (no
matter how much one has worried and fussed and invested
in the other's welfare) as a "product," a thing, is really
deeply demeaning of that other person. "Behind every good
man there is a good woman": if she has "produced" him,
what credit goes to his own efforts? If my children are my
products, they are only objects kept in good repair, without
the inner stuff of humanity. Further, both husband and children are then obligated to act "for Mother's sake" in order
to validate her sense of productivity. Husbands of traditional
homemakers find ways to defend against their wives' needs
to regard them as "products." Children have fewer defenses,
and the children of traditional homemakers can be made to
feel that they are required to confirm "Mother's work" by
their very existence.

Most of the tasks the homemaker accomplishes are continuous and have no end point. In any family with several
members, neither the kitchen counters nor the floors stay
"clean" for any perceptible length of time: as soon as the
cleaning task is finished (and sometimes before it is done)
crumbs and dirty dishes and toys and coats are strewn
about. One of the sad/funny games of family life is the
"stay out of the kitchen for an hour; Mother has just cleaned
it up" game—an artificiality of pretense to counter the fact
that her efforts are unending. Many of the "traditionally
male" chores of household maintenance are discontinuous
and can more easily be counted as tasks completed: building
shelves, repairing electrical appliances and laying carpets are
once-only events, or at least chores to be done on separate
and discrete occasions. Unlike the "traditionally female"
chores, the jobs customarily assigned to men and boys can
also be postponed to a moment of convenience, while feeding hungry people, keeping clothing in wearable condition,
and washing dishes cannot wait.

Homemakers do not, of course, punch a time clock. "Woman's work is never done" is an apt description of the

responsibility of housekeeping. It is also an acknowledg-
ment that the never-ending chores of homemaking have
readily been assigned to, and (perhaps not so readily) accepted by, women. The responsibility of sustaining the members of a family runs for twenty-four hours of the day and
seven days of the week; there is no sick leave, often no vacation, and almost certainly no sabbatical. Time passes without
the humanly satisfying landmarks of productive work.

Finally, the homemaker is not paid a salary. "Housewives' wages" have been proposed: the discussion has arisen
more and more frequently in recent years and warrants careful consideration.[6] Will the wage be at a very low level, thus
further reinforcing our regard for the responsible care of
other people as "of little value"? (Does "priceless" sometimes mean "of no value"?) Is the rationale that assigns
this work primarily to women, or to any one person in a
family, so clear and so desirable that it should be reinforced?
What will happen to our already fragile family solidarity if
we exchange money for the services that we have been doing
for each other in unpaid exchange? If the exchange is now
uneven in traditional families (as many believe it is), will the
translation of personal caregiving into wagework resolve
irksome inequities? Could that monetary adjustment really
enable men and women, husbands and wives, fathers and
mothers, to participate in adult life more evenhandedly?

I believe that the creation of a system of wages for personal
housekeeping could threaten family life as no other recent
change has done. To discredit our private systems of exchange
of unpaid services, and to bring government regulation into
our most personal relationships, will change families profoundly. To seal any adult, male or female, into full-time
involvement in a single one-sided role—either in a role that
severely restricts the satisfactions of productive work or in
a role that precludes the satisfactions of contributing to the
personal maintenance of one's family—could shatter the very
bonds that now seem most likely to hold us together as
families.

Despite these forebodings about the effects of instituting housewives' wages as a long-term strategy for "strengthening" our families, such a scheme may be useful or even necessary as a tactic *in the short run.* There is no question that segregation of the bulk of the responsibility for family and household maintenance into the hands of only one family member now stands as a major impediment to family solidarity and collaboration. The arrangement is justified mainly because it allows the adults who are "taken care of" to invest the greatest part of *their* time and energy in paid jobs. This arrangement suits the needs of employers; it is a lynchpin of our commercial economy. If all family members shared their mutual responsibility to maintain themselves, their dependents, and their property, jobholders could no longer make the same degree of personal investment in the commercial interests of others. Every worker would have to create a balance between work investment and family investment.

It may be that the most direct redress of an *economic* ill is to be found in an *economic* solution: a temporary institution of housewives' wages. The effects of paying family members for their family-maintenance efforts would include a near overthrow of our usual and customary conventions of Gross National Product, unemployment calculations, employment benefits (including vacations and retirement income), and taxation. If we go through and *beyond* this upheaval, we might then be able to revise policy to promote a livable range of options, permitting each family member to work productively *and* to take care of family responsibilities, with the latter again secured in the realm of private and unpaid exchange of services.

It is important to reflect on the distinctions between paid work and productive work. While paid work is always productive in the sense that the paycheck or salary is one kind of product, productive work need not be paid work. Many who are not employed for a salary (and many who are) find or take the time to work productively at home or at volunteer jobs, making wholes (paintings, furniture) or parts (collective quilting, fund raising) or aggregates (house-to-house canvassing, neighborhood service projects).

Do adults *need* to do productive work? Like most questions about human needs and motives, that question is very difficult to answer as an absolute. What do people tell us about their lives when they don't do productive work? It is evident from personal testimony that:

Productive work is, in our society, so highly valued that it serves as a measure of self-esteem. This self-esteem is in part internally imposed: men and women who have engaged in productive work and then have lost their jobs give eloquent testimony to their ensuing self-disparagement, depression, self-blame, and guilt. The reaction is similar whether the employee is male or female, and whether the job was lost because of a layoff or because family needs were incompatible with job requirements.[7] In addition, there is self-esteem externally derived from the opinions of respected others: anyone who is not a productive worker is disparaged, sometimes subtly and sometimes openly, and is assumed to be less than adult in an essential dimension—whether one is an unemployed male, a retired worker, a homemaker, or a mother on welfare.

Productive work, if it accrues any income at all, offers a degree of economic independence. The converse, economic dependence, is for an adult a condition that is both demeaned and insecure. Young adults who are still students, not welcome in the job market and therefore engaged in prolonged education/training programs preparing them to find "good" jobs, are belittled for their dependence on parents or on scholarship funds. Their behavior is often closely monitored and strongly censured *because* they are not economically independent. Homemakers with no personal income are equally subject to stringent control of their behavior, both by their husbands and by others who believe

that economic dependence justifies or requires sub-
jection to supervision. (The fact that some homemakers do not perceive themselves to be closely supervised
is not contradictory to this statement. For many of
them, a serious "error of judgment"—in management
of the family budget, care of household property, or
childrearing—would bring criticism from their husbands,
as arbiters of "errors of judgment," in a manner more
appropriate to a disparaged employee or an immature
child than an equal partner.) Single parents using Aid
to Families with Dependent Children funds are similarly
subject to regulation in return for the receipt of public
funds.

Effective protest against such conditions is difficult
if there is no foreseeable means of becoming economically independent. If protest involves risk of losing one's
means of financial support, there is reason for fear; the
precipitous drop in the living standard of most women
who are divorced is well documented.[8]

In our society, a large proportion of the goods and
services needed by families must be purchased. As a
consequence, economically dependent adults who are
nominally and psychologically responsible for the
welfare of other family members find their own sub-
servience reinforced by the real needs of others. Being
autonomous, apportioning one's use of time independently, and acting on principle to do what seems right
may jeopardize the well-being of those others—children
and dependent adults who are unable by age or infirmity
to earn incomes for themselves. To defy a husband, to
regulate one's expenditure of time, energy, money, and
emotional resources according to an independent per-
ception of priorities, to risk "only" one's own means
of financial support, is one thing; it is quite another to
risk the welfare of one's children by toying with *their*
financial support. When economic dependence is inter-
woven with the unpaid responsibility of overseeing the

well-being of other family members, the bind to do
"what is expected" is tight indeed.

Further, when family responsibilities are entirely
segregated—one adult produces income, the other main-
tains the household—both parties may feel aggrieved,
may argue that their burden is the more onerous, and
no reasonable comparison can be made between them.
(Apples and oranges cannot be precisely valued against
each other.) We can assume, however, that the marriage
partner who is unwilling to share his or her responsibilities—and to undertake a share of the other's burdens—probably believes, despite any verbal arguments
to the contrary, that his or her present status is the
more privileged.

*Productive work gives a variety of personal benefits
over and above self-esteem and the capability for economic independence.* Unless the job is done alone, there
are opportunities to talk with others about a variety of
things, to have conversations that might never occur
with members of one's own family. There are opportunities also to develop strong and sustaining personal
friendships. We know, understand, and develop affection
for those whom we see repeatedly on a face-to-face
basis and with whom we share space and time. If the
work is away from home, there is refreshment in the
daily cycle of leaving home and returning; some adults
virtually imprison themselves at home when they have
no reason or obligation to separate from home base.[9]
There may also be opportunities in work to learn new
skills, which can be valued as opportunities for personal growth and change; some workers change jobs as
soon as they feel that they have learned all they can in
their present situations.

Any given work opportunity offers a mix of these dividends; sometimes the dividends of social contact, friendships, bits of gossip and news, a change of scene, and the

development of a sense of competence in the minutiae of
one's work are the predominant benefits of our jobs. Something like three quarters of adults holding paid jobs say that
they *would* continue at their work even if they did not
"need the money," which attests to the varied benefits we
perceive to come from our jobs over and above the incomes
we earn.[10]

Some adults are denied productive work: no jobs are available to them; they do not have access to education and training
in skills that enable them to find work, paid or unpaid; they
are victimized by discriminatory employment practices; members of their families forbid them to take employment; or they,
themselves, are caught in a net of self-definition that damns
them if they do not hold jobs and damns them in a different
way if they do—the conventional obligations of full-time
housewifery make many employed mothers feel guilty.[11]
All who are excluded from opportunities for work are deprived of formal and informal benefits. As individuals, we
"need" these benefits in different proportions and give them
different priorities, but it seems likely that most adults
would profit from the experience of doing productive work.

Jobs and Families

At present, most jobs in this society are unsuitable for any
adult who is deeply engaged in the life of his or her family,
especially when the family includes small children or any
member with special needs.

Most jobs require a time and energy commitment that
leaves the worker little to invest in family affairs. When a
parent substitute is hired to fill in at home while parents
work at their "forty-hour" jobs, wages must be paid not
only for work time but also for travel time, often an additional ten or more hours a week. Many workers hold more
than one job to try to meet their families' financial needs.
Others, especially in "career" jobs, find themselves obligated
to work many more than forty hours a week. In one specialty

department of a hospital, the chief of service boasts that his
physician staff works on the average, from sixty-five to
seventy hours a week. In fact, most of these staff members
have preschool or school-aged children. Responding to an
article about flexible training hours for young physicians who
were also parents, one young man wrote about the "system
that trains us to help others solve marital and personal problems . . . [and is] designed to weaken or destroy our personal
and marital lives."[12]

Over and above the formal requirements of time spent at
the job or in job-related activities, there is an assumption,
sometimes implicit and sometimes made forthrightly to job
applicants, that the affairs of one's work will be a consuming
interest and will take priority over "merely" personal matters.
In fact, many employers expect workers to be cheerfully
willing and able to work overtime on short notice, no matter
what the family's needs or the expectations for one's presence
at home. Few employees would feel comfortable taking time
off from work to nurse a sick child or spouse, to shop for
family needs, or to attend a child's school play or a spouse's
seminar. The activities of caring for one's family are somehow
counted as "frivolous." By the time employees rise to executive positions they are often so well trained in this attitude
that they regard a game of golf or a long lunch with business
contacts as permissible, but equal amounts of time on behalf
of family needs as totally out of the question.

The psychic devotion to job, employer, and corporation
that is expected of the worker is, in the long run, probably
more destructive to family life than the flat fact of hours at
work. Up to a point, energy, time, and interest invested in
our jobs can refuel or refresh our availability to family members. Beyond that point we are drained, preoccupied, and
irritable; we may even resent expectations that our relationships within our families involve personal giving as well
as taking. The irritability arises not just from fatigue, but
also from our own repressed desires to give, and from

internalized guilt about our impotence in becoming more
available to family.

Many jobs are so physically distant from our homes that
the world of work is an entirely separate realm from the
world of family life. If our places of work are near our homes
we can, when we wish, go home for lunch; drop by during
the day to help resolve a quarrel or comfort a hurt child or
just chat; tend to shopping chores, let in an electrician or
carpenter, or measure a window for new shades. Children and
other family members can stop by at the job with messages
or to do errands for us.

The great physical separations of most workers from their
homes and neighborhoods reinforce the principle that *our
greatest devotion is owed to those who pay our salaries.*
Workers are "saved" from the distractions of family matters
during work hours. I know of no study that has measured
time lost from work, or incompetent or careless work done,
because workers were preoccupied with worrying about a
sick child left at home, or about the cat who could not be
found to be let in before everyone left the house, or about
unresolved differences with family members. The unremitting
sameness of staying for the entire day in one building—even
a new and modern building designed for the worker's comfort—and the sense of having one's life broken into pieces
that do not connect with each other may cause a falloff
in worker performance significantly greater than any that
might come from flexible options of trading work time and
family time.

The effect of this separation, this distance between home
and job, is unquestionably one of great hardship for families.
A family member who is also a worker is sometimes virtually
out of communication with other family members during
work hours: these workers cannot know what happens to
their families during those hours, nor can spouses and children know about the worker. Several years ago, I practiced
pediatrics in a middle-sized town where job–home distances
were not nearly as great as those for many suburban and city

families. I learned that, even in such a setting, not only
were children generally ignorant about the work that their
employed parents did, but spouses as well often had no
clear, concrete understanding of the nature of the jobs held
by their husbands and wives.

It has suited our economic system to strengthen big, corporate, commercial organizations and to punish or fail to
support small collaborative or family-owned businesses. The
vast majority of our jobs now are components of large bureaucracies in which the workers who make products or
perform services have little control over the policies that
determine what those products or services will be. Most jobs
also forbid the worker any real control over the *process* of
the work. Workers and their families are affected by such
matters as hours worked in relation to family needs, flexibility of time commitment over the family life cycle,
opportunities to include one's older children in parts of
one's work, on-worksite daycare facilities for preschool
children, and limitations of the hours spent in personal
service to consumers; these could well be subject to collective control by workers. However, the managerial function in
large bureaucracies of employment effectively prohibits any
significant degree of worker input or control.

Finally, many of our jobs do not pay enough to permit us
to meet family monetary needs. In many families, two adults
working full time (with little time or energy to give to family
affairs) still cannot earn enough to purchase the goods and
services that, we are trained to believe, all well-cared-for
families *must* have. For some, two full-time salaries are insufficient even to buy food and shelter; some couples who
are poor must divorce in order to feed their children. The
great majority of "middle-class" families attain their class
status because of the salaries of both parents, thus violating
the definition of the mythical "ideal" middle-class family in
which only the husband/father earns income. Having attained
middle-class status, a family must purchase still more goods

and services; there is never "enough" money to buy the
myth, and the circle entraps.

Change Agents

Can the conditions of work be changed so that workers
who are also members of families will not be so torn away
from their families by the institutionalized arrangements
that govern employment? It seems unlikely that government
and corporate policymakers will, of their own accord, alter
the responsibilities and obligations between employers and
employees in order to strengthen families. As individuals, we
are for the most part helpless in the face of an arranged
scarcity of jobs and inadequate salaries. Joined together, we
have an impact. We have yet to explore our collective power
in this domain, on behalf of our families:

1. There is a small group of workers, sought after by
employers, who can demand that the conditions of
their own work reflect the needs of their families.
Included in this group are some professionals, some
persons with advanced academic degrees, and some
fledgling managers "tapped" by their employers to
prepare them for high-level administrative work. Only
a few of them will be entirely successful in naming
their own terms of work, and some will risk loss of
employment or a fall from the "career ladder."

Those who are not in the position of demanding
improved conditions of work for themselves will be
tempted to be angry and resentful that others can do so.
But, as in every self-help movement, a coalition of those
on the "inside" with those on the "outside" has a significant increase in effect. If a physician employed by
a teaching hospital, or an attorney employed by a large
firm, is willing to make such demands, she or he will
need massive support from others to sustain that plan
against an onslaught of accusations—accusations against

the employee's maturity, suitability for work, professional commitment, and even reason and sanity. If, in
fact, some gains are made in high-status jobs for the
feasibility of part-time work for parents, then there is
greater likelihood that similar working schedules will be
considered for other employees.[13]

2. For most workers, organization and collective
support for the priority of contract demands related to
family needs are the only routes to change at the policy
level. Unions have not, in the past, been much concerned
with conditions of work as they affect workers' families—both because of early priorities of wage rates, benefits, and hours, and because policymakers in unions have
not themselves counted family welfare as a high priority.
Only recently have contract negotiations acknowledged
workers' dissatisfaction with the inflexibility of exceptionally heavy demands, such as obligatory overtime.[14]

With so much threatening change "just happening"
to us, it is especially difficult to negotiate *planned*
change. Unprecedented, never-before-tried contract
demands are likely to be resisted with arguments predicting the economic downfall of corporations and individuals. If we can at least expose the argument that our
present system *prohibits* the support of family welfare,
we will have gained control of what issues are going to
be dealt with. The focus can then shift from individual
blame and guilt to a recognition of the constraints imposed by our present policies in support of commerce.
As with arguments about priorities regarding the preservation of our natural environment, arguments about support of families will go on for a long time. Corporate
interests are now very powerful, and they will surely
never bend unless workers' demands are strongly voiced,
again and again. Only by organizing in broad coalitions
based on mutual self-interest in the well-being of our
families will we make those demands heard.

3. There are many workers who do not now have a

collective organization to work through, and whose
conditions of work are such that organizing to affect
the relationship between their jobs and their families
will be a slow and halting process. For them, as for all
of us, public policy responsive to public pressure is a
possible avenue of change. Recently expressed concern
at levels of local, state, and federal government about
"the quality of family life" in our small and large communities gives voter groups an opportunity to begin
public dialogue about the needs of families with regard
to the conditions of employment.[15] Public policy,
effected through legislation, regulatory agencies, and
tax surcharges and credits has power to change employer-
employee relationships in support of families.

These three mechanisms, then—individual case-demonstra-
tion, worker demands expressed directly through unions and
other collective organizations, and public policy decisions by
elected representatives—are our avenues of change. The specific changes we require are most likely to happen as the
result of steady efforts over a long period of time, with all
three mechanisms being exercised relentlessly toward the
same ends.

Nailing Down the Priorities

What changes in the conditions of employment would most
benefit our families? The following goals have the highest
priority:

A job for everyone who desires paid employment.
Our present arranged scarcity of jobs serves to keep
workers "in line." Only arbitrary conventions determine
what kinds of work are worth a salary and what salaries
they are worth. We might, for instance, overturn
present conventions and decide that taking care of
people and of our natural environment were jobs worth
very good pay.[16]

A guaranteed minimum income for all workers, which is reflective of the cost of living and assures that all can earn enough to "make a living" for their families. The experience in other countries is useful to examine, but our situation is not identical and our solutions need not be the same.

One debate should be attended to carefully: should benefits be provided to families "in cash" or "in kind"? Benefits in cash allow families to decide how they will spend their funds, and involve "waste" when some families spend their monies in ways disapproved by others. Benefits in kind, on the other hand, are for the most part service benefits—education, health care, child care, and other "social" services—and maintain control of the use of all the monies involved in the hands of policymakers and professionals. Considering the quality of, and even "waste" in, our present professionally run services (education and health care, for instance), and the inherent difficulties in providing human services through bureaucratic organizations of professionals, we should argue against providing nothing but benefits in kind. In point of fact, most nations more advanced than we in social policy have as base policy a provision for a minimum income.[17]

Worker-controlled balance of distribution of job time and family time, with wide options for flexibility. As an overall master proposal, our goal should be flexibility throughout the life cycles of families: options for parents to work as little as half-time when their children are young (a period of about seven years for the average two-child family); three-quarter to full-time work for the parents of school-aged and adolescent children (another thirteen years); full-time work, or more if the worker desires, during the years before children are born and the years after they are grown and launched (some twenty-five years of the worker's span); and decreasing job time when workers age to a point where they wish to diminish their job involvement because of a fall in energy. For some workers and some families, this loose schedule will not always fit: family illness, for instance, might require a drop in work participation, as might some special neediness of a child—a learning disability or an emotional upset. In terms of the numbers of workers available to the work force, however, this scheme will provide more workers rather than less, as both parents will have the option of working in paid employment throughout their adult lives. In terms of productivity, it is likely that part-time workers are relatively more productive, hour for hour, than full-time workers. In terms of family supports, such a scheme will encourage workers to consider family needs as their highest priority, without threat of punishment by job loss. In terms of family autonomy and self-determination, the option of setting work obligations in accordance with family needs will strengthen families. A first step is the recognition, in employment policies, that the needs of families are accorded high priority.[18]

The support of small businesses and solo entrepreneurs. This policy will represent a thorough change from our recent preference for massive support of large bureaucracies and punishment of small units. Small units allow greater flexibility and the opportunity to know *all* fellow workers, at every level, on a face-to-face basis; workers can in these circumstances more readily determine the policies that affect both the product and the process of their work. It is fair to assume that we have abandoned policies that protect small business concerns precisely because of the "threat" that smallness entails. A concentration of money and power promotes the establishment of policies that preserve and augment that very concentration.

Policies that encourage the employment of workers close to their own homes. By so doing, we can overturn our present difficulty in integrating our jobs and

our families, an unavoidable by-product of extreme
geographic separation of home and work. Because per-
son-to-person solidarity requires a quantum of face-to-
face contact, neighborhoods will also be strengthened
when most workers have jobs close to their homes, and
when most businesses employ nearby residents.

The inclusion of children into the world of work.
Tax-credit incentives and supplemental funding for daycare centers at our places of work are clearly needed.
Opportunities for older children to visit their parents at
work will promote an integration of family and work
for children and parents alike. In many kinds of employment, children can provide occasional assistance to their
parents, just as parents can assist children in their school-
related work. Many of the tasks of adult jobs are quite
suited to the capabilities of children—photocopying,
stuffing and addressing envelopes, running errands,
sweeping, sorting—with the understanding that the
attention span for children is relatively short and that
they have other activities to attend to. An hour or two
of effort by a school-aged child can be engrossing for
the child and helpful to the adult.

Perhaps our most serious present deficit with regard
to the inclusion of children into the world of work involves our adolescent children: if we argue that opportunities for productive work are beneficial (perhaps
necessary) for mature self-esteem, then we greatly de-
prive and handicap our older children by excluding them
almost without exception from the "real" world of
work.

Child-labor laws, probably passed primarily to secure
the jobs of adult men, had the consequence also of protecting children against the horrendous and harmful
imposition of "sweat shop" labor.[19] But these laws have
not been entirely beneficial for our children, for they
now have almost no opportunities to participate in paid
work. We have gone from one indecent extreme to

another. What we seek are moderate and humane solutions: in this case, the guarantee that adolescents who *choose* to hold paid jobs will have that option.

To design and promote policies that will allow adolescent children to work on a restricted time basis, when and if they wish, doing work that provides them with learning experiences, will require the most careful and alert caution. Some economists have wryly observed that the recent influx of women into the labor market can be explained in part as a consequence of the needs of our economic system for a constant supply of "disposable" workers who can be overworked, underpaid, and fired with little difficulty.[20] If there is truth in this observation, then we must be concerned about the possibility that our hopes for allowing opportunities to older children for productive work will coincide with bureaucratic interests in pulling in the next cohort of "disposable" workers, to be hired and fired in concert with the goals of efficiency and profits.

A system of adolescent apprenticeships, with pay at least at minimum wage for their work, will enhance the self-esteem and potential for self-determination of our children. As a side effect, it must also alter our educational system: if *all* adolescents have work opportunities as alternative options to schooling, we will progress more quickly toward the establishment of "open" education in which we all can participate intermittently throughout our entire lives.

Policies that allow experimentation with options of sharing jobs between two or more individuals. Many of our jobs, especially but not exclusively those at high levels of responsibility, are clearly too much for any one individual who also participates fully in her or his family. Positions of president, director, or dean are increasingly hard to fill, at least in part because the amount of time and effort required seems out of proportion to the returns experienced by the worker who holds such a job.[21] A more reasonable approach is to split jobs so that two persons, working as collaborating equals, can meet the requirements of a single job and still live as integral members of their own families.[22] When collaboration is a more adaptive characteristic than competition for "success" at work, then we no longer need to train our children to be competitive at home and at school.

When our responsibilities to our jobs become a subset of our responsibilities to our families, kin, friends, neighbors, and communities of identity, we will have tamed the inhumanity of one of our major institutions. The process of *demand* and *response* is essential to these changes. Small offerings, made by bureaucratic managers to anticipate demands and to forestall worker and family organization for collective effort, only enhance the underlying bureaucratic stability and managerial control. Only *we* know what our families need. The process by which we determine those needs and secure the conditions that will meet them (conditions that usually include the availability of our personal time, energy, knowledge, and skills) is the same process that shifts the balance of values from machines, money, and things to life itself. As we relearn to value life, we will have exchanged corporate efficiency for collective self-sufficiency.

To Sustain Our Souls

Collective effort toward long-term solutions provides us with a promise and a goal. But we also need some immediate respite from our pain and guilt, which are reflections of our absolute inability now to be both the kind of workers that our employment policies demand and the kind of participating family members that our families require if they are to survive in good health.

We *can* turn toward the creation of work situations in our own homes, reinventing the kinds of productive work that

families once were required to do on their own behalf and
learning to invest ourselves in mastery, passion, and collaboration. We have already begun to resist the temptation to buy
more and more goods and services by "making do" with
what we can create for ourselves: pottery, weaving, gardens,
bookshelves and tables, bread, shirts and wall hangings, and
refurbished broken furniture and worn clothing. We have
created these alternative options for unpaid work, although
with some hesitancy and apology for turning our backs on
the "better" goods and services we could buy, and with
defiance against the disparaging judgment that what we do is
"cute" or "defective." Predictably, industry is trying to turn
these efforts into yet more "consumer items": mixes to
make bread, kits for making furniture, assembly-line craftswork as a "curriculum offering" in public education. Will we
permit this rediscovery of work that we can do creatively, in
any way that we wish, to be taken from us, prepackaged, and
co-opted by the technology of consumerism?

What we want is a reordering of priorities. What we must
demand is that we, as individuals and families and neighborhoods, determine that reordering. If we cannot fit ourselves
into a model of humanity that holds efficiency, profit, and
progress above all other values, is it really we who are deficient, at fault, to be blamed, and encouraged to feel guilty?
Or is it possible that enslavement to those values requires us
to pay a price that is too high for benefits to ourselves and
our families that are too low? Could we not help ourselves
to help our families by tolerating, even enjoying, some comfortable level of *inefficiency*, and some comfortable option
of refusing to work for "progress" unless it clearly benefits
us in the day-to-day lives of our families?

Androgynous child whose hair curls into flowers,
naked you ride a horse without saddle or bridle
easy between your thighs from the walled garden outward.
Coarse sunflowers of desire whose seed birds crack open
nod upon your journey, child of the morning whose sun
can only be born from us who strain bleeding to give birth.
Go into your horse, let there be
no more riders or ridden.

—Marge Piercy

6 CHILD CARE

A child and a caretaking parent are a prototype family. In our
society the very presence of a young child in the household
gives family members reason to remain committed to each
other on the child's behalf. The strongest social sanctions
against family dissolution arise from the predicament of the
abandoned child. And the neediness of dependent children
invites us to become attached to them.

Who Will Mind the Children?

Because of the critical role that children hold in families,
our institutionalized arrangements for child care take a
central place in any discussion about families. Who *will*
mind the children? The way we see that responsibility, as a
mix of punishment and pleasure, is an important ingredient
in any proposal for family well-being.

The traditional prescription is that the woman/mother/wife

has almost total responsibility for child care. In the "ideal" nuclear family, it is assumed not only that the mother is the child's constant caretaker, but also that she is consistently better able than anyone else to give the child good care. Most of us who are mothers know better: we tire, become bored and irritable, and sometimes fervently wish that we were a thousand miles away. Some mothers, with little else to shore their self-esteem, make central to their lives those wonderful moments when child care really is fun, play down the bad times, and hope for the best.

A man/father/husband may "help," according to the traditional prescription: he might take his children on exceptional outings—the zoo or a fishing trip—put them to bed, or even occasionally "take over" for his wife so she can get away (and presumably, thus refreshed, return to take care of him). But in that "ideal" nuclear family, he never becomes the *responsible* parent, nor can his attachments to his children be relied upon. Mothers always provide the child care of last resort. When the chips are down—parents have a dinner engagement and their child suddenly is sick, or both parents are preoccupied with their own work and the child needs help—everyone in the family knows that Mother will (should) come through.

We only shake our heads at the report of a father deserting his children, but we are deeply shocked, even outraged, at a mother who leaves. When increasing numbers of mothers leave their children, as is now happening, we must wonder if their responsibility was not beyond enduring. Many of the young women who now keep their children who were conceived out of wedlock, and plan to rear them alone, do so with the cynical realization that as a matter of practical fact fathers cannot be counted upon to care for their own children, while mothers are *always* presumed to be reliably (if not always willingly) there.

Child care is, for the traditional nuclear family, an internal responsibility. It has been assumed that "normal" families will manage to oversee their children without recourse to

support from any formal or informal outside agency during
infancy and early childhood, and during the hours when
school children are not in school. Extended-family and other
social network connections have been discredited. A TV ad,
for instance, promotes the value of professionalism in family
service agencies this way: "To whom would you turn if you
had a deep personal problem? To someone you have known
for a long time? That may not be the kind of help you need.
Turn to us . . . ."

From whom "ought" we to seek advice about, and help
with, childrearing? Surely not grandparents, aunts, uncles,
friends, neighbors—the help they can give is looked upon as
inappropriate, uninformed, and even of questionable motivation! Grandparents especially are readily labeled as "invad-
ing," "controlling," "taking advantage because they have
nothing better to do with their lives." Grandparents, themselves, may prefer to keep at a distance; given the limiting
and constricting aspects of traditional nuclear family life
they may want to avoid replaying that experience, even at
some remove. Feeling that they have already met those responsibilities (provided time and energy, cared for and made
hard decisions about their children) they may wish only to
be entitled to "their own lives."

Experts and professionals, on the other hand, extract
their own price: "human service" agencies deal in pathology,
and the family seeking information, advice, or services must
first allow itself to be categorized as "deviant," "sick," "inadequate," or (the indescribable horror) "multiproblem."
With such a label, we may find that when we walk away from
our expert with a prescription for "better" behavior we
really have no clearer understanding or perspective to allow
us to resolve the next question or problem that occurs.

There seems to be an ever-growing number of men and
women both who wish to reexamine their assumptions
about families. They are discovering ways in which life outside the family might be used to enrich, rather than to
deplete, the family ecology. Many husbands and wives are

struggling to work out family arrangements through which they can share the warm and warming delights of being responsible and trustworthy to children, and share as well the messes and inconveniences and irritations of caring for small creatures so willful, helpless, and without common sense.

As families protest that the traditional prescription for child care (mothers only, fathers excluded) fails all concerned—mothers *and* fathers *and* children—bureaucratized agencies seem ready to move in. Is supplementary daytime care for children, both preschool and after school, a new "consumer need"? Should we then be wary of efforts to institutionalize the control of supplementary child care by professionals?

The professionals' most ready point of entry is in the setting of standards that limit access to federal monies; these standards can restrict and regiment day care and prohibit local community options according to parental preference or need. Perhaps if we note carefully the professional/commercial response to the recently developed "consumer need" for supplementary care for old people (profit-making nursing homes and isolated, mass-produced ghettos of old people) we can avoid repeating similar mistakes on behalf of our children.[1] The lure of turning to the experts tempts weary and worried parents, and prospective parents as well. Professionals with special training, experts in child development and in childrearing techniques, are eager to step in and take charge, with our permission, of course. We may hope that they can protect our children from our own mistakes. But can we and our children find protection from their mistakes?

The institutionalization of childcare services into bureaucratized agencies will most likely involve *large* centers with *many* children. The risks of establishing large units of child care include those associated with "economies of scale," which produce almost identical equipment, food, and routines for everyone; these and other inflexibilities, necessarily devised and enforced by managers, limit our children's individual growth and can subtly discourage their proud sense of themselves as unique.[2]

Certainly we must have supplementary childcare arrangements that honor children and the families they live in, and we must find them soon.[3] Experts and professionals may be less helpful in this than we would hope. We know, for instance, that child-development specialists have over the last several decades recommended one contradictory "fad" of childrearing style after another. Each pronouncement is given as an absolute, as if it were firmly based on evidence. But each conceals biases of personal belief and prejudice on the part of its exponents.[4]

Before we rush to hand over any major part of the controlling responsibility for our small children to experts and professionals, we should look closely at the position of our children in our families and our social networks. For our children's sake it is important that we examine the ways in which we value children, our hopes and dreams for their future, and the arrangements we might invent for providing them with growth-promoting and healthful environments, while ensuring parallel opportunities for health and growth for their adult caretakers.

For the Love of Children

Young children cannot know, unless they are told or shown, that family arrangements are arbitrary: for the young child not yet "out in the world," one's own family style seems inevitable. One hazard for parents is that of allowing, or even encouraging, children to believe that family arrangements, family rules, and family codes are fixed and forever, as if according to some hidden decree. In our own family it took years of "trivial" irritability to discover that in my universe it was the husband's responsibility to carve the Sunday roast, while in my husband's universe (derived, like my own, from childhood experience) that job was for wives to do. Until we realized why we were snapping at each other and how arbitrary the resolution was, we could not see that each believed the other to be willfully violating an unquestioned and seemingly absolute "rule."

On the other side, because a true choice always means some sense of loss at the turn not taken, parents wish to protect children against the impression that choices have been entirely casual, thoughtless, or without plan. The degree of *sharing* that is urged upon children, for instance, depends on the amount and kind of space available, on a family's financial means, and on its preference for individual as opposed to family ownership.

Style and degree of *intimacy* are imposed on infants and young children, who have little opportunity to ask for more or less than they are offered. When children learn to move around on their own power and to let others know what they want, they can ask for or refuse intimacy, and show preferences among different family members. But to recognize, respect, and respond to a baby's expressions of preference with regard to intimacy is not always easy for others in the family.

Similarly, individual children vary in their needs for privacy; most children seem to want and use increasing amounts of privacy as they grow through middle childhood. Adolescents, halfway in and halfway out of their families, may wish to have little or no intimacy with family members, while, at the same time, they explore their options for intimate relations with persons outside of the family. It is difficult and painful for parent and adolescent child alike to "lose touch" (literally and figuratively) with each other, but it is also exactly as it should be that the child we fondled and who clung to us, now nearly an adult, is ready to find gratifying relationships with new friends and ultimately, perhaps, with a newly created family.

Like styles of intimacy, *caretaking* is also imposed on infants; even the tiniest infant, however, has some ability to make demands for caretaking. The most critical of all the early learning experiences that seem to have long-lasting effects are probably those related to the likelihood that cries of need will be met with appropriate offerings. To learn that usually someone will come and do for us what we need to have done provides a very different world outlook than to learn that often no one comes, or that what is done is not at all what was needed. In reality no parent, not even a devoted and intuitive *group* of family caretakers, can ever hope always to hit upon the "right" response to an infant's every cry—infants also learn the realities of having sometimes to wait and of not getting the caretaking they desire.

As children grow, they clearly want to reciprocate in caretaking, and they will learn to do so as they are given opportunities and encouraged, praised, or otherwise rewarded. Nuclear families, both because of their size and because of their isolation from other families, often fail to provide children with opportunities to learn how to care for those smaller than themselves.

There is evidence from research to support the common observation that children learn to take care of others when they have models (others whom they can observe in care-taking acts), when they are themselves taken care of, and when they have opportunities to give care to others.[5] (It is especially noteworthy that boys are most likely to learn care-taking if they have either a father who is comfortable in the caretaker role or no father at all; apparently the "average" adult male in this society discourages his sons from learning and expressing caretaker behavior.)[6] In the many U.S. families where the caretaker role is the nearly exclusive respon-sibility and prerogative of mothers, both boys and girls are deprived of opportunities to learn to take care of others; they are led to believe that caretaking is an appropriate activ-ity for adult females only. This vitally important deprivation can be overcome when families become open to their net-works of kin, friends, neighbors, and community, so that all family members can participate in the exchange of a variety of caretaking services.

When children have opportunities and rewards for taking

care of others, they progress steadily as they mature in their
capabilities: preschool children take care of others only
when they feel like doing so, while school-aged children may
give about as much care to other family members as they
receive themselves. Ordinarily, by early adolescence children
are able to put aside their own needs for a while and perform
caretaking that is attuned to the needs of the recipient. Thus,
the essence of caretaking (recognition and respect for the
momentary and future needs of the person cared for) is
learned in stages and only with a great deal of practice. The
caretaker gains in return a respect for his or her ability to
predict, to know intuitively, the needs and responses of the
other. The pleasures of providing help at the right time—like
turning a tantrum into a smile—are also gained. Much self-
knowledge comes from the experience of caring for others;
encouraging and applauding another's milestones of mastery
and learning, for instance, give a sense of one's own balance
between capability and effort.

Small children teach their caretakers well. Their smiles of
pleasure are enormously rewarding, their cries of protest very
painful to hear. In many societies, preadolescent and adolescent children are major sources of the care, socialization, and
teaching of younger children. In this society, we have, for the
most part, excluded children from similar supervised opportunities to learn about caring for small and dependent children. Then we decry their young adult "selfishness," their
inexperience in caring for others in need, and their blocked
intuition.

The interplay of *control* in families can easily victimize
children. Socializing (or "civilizing") children is a major responsibility for older family members, and this can lend
justification to a tendency to be unduly controlling of the
actions, thoughts, and feelings of small children. When we as
adults feel powerless in so many aspects of our lives, it is
very tempting to "keep our children in line" by giving vent
to all of our frustrated wishes for self-determination and our
resentful desires to control others (as we have been con-

trolled). "This soup is too salty"—"It cannot be, I added just the right amount of salt" might be a joke, or just a miscommunication, between adults. But children have little recourse when adults undertake to control and dominate their perceptions or even the naming of their sensory experience.

"Not to hurt others" is a simple rule to understand, even if it is complicated to work out. The smallest child with the simplest level of language comprehension will understand that prohibition in a useful way: "Don't step on the puppy's tail"; "It hurts me when you hit me with your book." Learning *how* not to hurt others is a lifelong quest; helping a child to modify her or his behavior in accord with the needs and vulnerabilities of others is the beginning. There is a vast difference between controlling household behavior toward the goal of minimizing purposeless, uncaring hurtfulness and controlling behavior on impersonal or authoritarian principles, or on no principles at all. To teach children that they must work toward the ability to monitor and control their own behavior in a manner that respects the others with whom they share a household, and whose preferences are to a degree arbitrary, allows them not only to learn these rules but also to see beyond the immediate family circle.

Parental control of children's actions, thoughts, and feelings is sometimes furthered by a general "disparagement" of others who are not members of the immediate nuclear family.[7] Parents may do this, implicitly or openly, on the basis that those others are less valued, less moral, less wise *only* because they are not part of one's own exclusive nuclear group. As a result, a child is severely restrained in learning from any persons other than family members and the "official" teachers in schools. They are thus denied opportunities to gain perspective on (and the needed support to deal with) the arbitrariness of family rules.

Usually adolescent children have the ability to imagine themselves no longer members of their own households; they can wonder what it might be like to be a member of

another family. They can thus gain perspective in understanding the intricate balance of personal control between
spouses, between parents and children, and between brothers
and sisters. This may be one of the last and most important
lessons that the child learns on the threshold of leaving his
or her family of origin. Observation, comments on family
"politics," and an appreciation of the essential funni-
ness of much that happens in the complicated dance of family life all contribute. Our own grown son's sardonic/affec-
tionate observations on the dynamics of power in our family have helped me to understand their ramifications in ways
that I never before could have seen or comprehended. It was
he who cheerfully pointed out our family habit (which we
adults had never noticed) of excessive, joking ridicule for any
of us, child or adult, who says an inappropriate word or even
uses incorrect pronunciation. "In this family," he said, "if
you make that kind of mistake, you pay and pay and
pay . . . ."

Because children are so vulnerable to accept and believe
that the ways of their own families have some basis in *absolute* good, it is both necessary and difficult for parents to
understand and respect that we each have our idiosyncratic
needs to do things "our way." At worst, when parental needs
determine a family style that ill suits the needs of a child, we
may demand that a child acquiesce and participate in the
destruction of her or his self-esteem.[8] If we teach children to
question, protest, resist, and fight the arbitrary rules that suit
the comfort of powerful parents but betray their own integrity, we at least equip them to hope for something better in
their own lives and to believe that what they say and do
counts. At the same time, we can respect them when they
recognize and honor the needs of others or when they modu-
late their own demands in response to "the neediest among
us"—who may be the littlest brother or the weariest parent
or the most discouraged baseball player. I have been impressed
and touched when one of our children takes an incredibly
courageous stand on behalf of a brother or sister, arguing

with an irritable parent that what we have "ruled" is arbitrary and unjust.

More Care, More Caring

In terms of the entire life cycle of a family, the years when children are small, vulnerable, and in need of great amounts of care are relatively few. For a family with two children, born two years apart, there are at most seven or eight years of full-time parental responsibility and an additional twelve or thirteen years of part-time parental responsibility for children in school. Put another way, children in our society need "full" supervision and care until the age of six or seven, "partial" care until adolescence, and "intermittent" care until the adolescent becomes a responsible adult. In an era when our expectable lifespan is more than seventy years, the period when any of us is tied to intensive childcare responsibilities is brief indeed.

Furthermore, the bulk of the time we spend in child care is occupied with other activities as well. Research on how people spend their time ("time-budget" studies) is amusingly unmindful of this reality, for subjects are asked to report how many minutes they spend each day in separate, distinct activities—meal preparation, travel, reading, child care, and so on.[9] But anyone who has been responsible for the care of young children knows that in actual practice one rarely "babysits" in the sense of "sitting and watching the baby." At the same time that we care for children, we cook, iron, garden, walk the dog, shop, and fix broken toasters. Relatively few childcare activities require one's entire attention or the simultaneous use of hands and head—like bathing and diapering a squirming infant, for instance, or checking the calculations of arithmetic homework.

On the other hand, child care done in long stretches of time often brings fatigue out of proportion to the physical energy consumed. There are many subtle reasons for this:

1. When we take care of children we are restricted in our mobility. It is difficult to go visiting or shopping for any length of time with one or more small children who need to be carried or pushed in carriages, fed on demand, or settled for naps.

2. There are many places in this society where young children are not at all welcome—some libraries and restaurants, shops, even museums and grassy yards.

3. The needs of a young infant are urgent and demand an immediate response; a caretaker's schedule is controlled by the demands of the hungry or wet or bored baby. Many children are, in addition, quite naturally resistant to any sort of regular schedule, and their caretakers can hardly plan when they will be interrupted to supply milk, sing a lullaby, read a story, or go for a walk outside to bring new sights and sounds to refresh a toddler.[10]

4. Once a small child learns to creep and then to walk and run, one's freedom to move or even to engage in any engrossing activity is severely restricted by the imperative and frequent need to "go see what the baby is doing." Taking care of young children requires constant alert attention, a readiness to act, and endless decisions about whether to put down what we are doing and act for the child.

5. Most telling in relation to fatigue, child care does not allow "mind-spinning," the awake daydreaming, planning, problem solving, and fantasizing that absorb us and draw us away from the events of the immediate present. Just as sleepers wake unrefreshed if sleep is interrupted every time they begin to dream, so we feel drained at the end of a day in which we could not spin our minds away from the here and now into that private realm of connected or disconnected thought.

For all of these reasons, subtle perhaps to the unpracticed observer but very apparent to anyone who has spent long stretches of time taking care of small children, the responsibility of child care is draining well out of proportion to any literal measurement of energy expenditure.

People who take care of children in well-staffed, well-appointed, and conveniently equipped daycare centers (and who are paid a reasonable salary for their work, have compatible adults to talk to, and are able to share the burdens of an irritable and not-to-be-pleased child or an energetic runabout) report that there is a limit to the number of hours that they can respond with affectionate attention to the needs of little children. That daily span of hours varies for different individuals, but is usually in the range of six; when the limit has been reached, they "tune out" in effect, safeguarding their charges from harm and responding to requests for help or food but failing to observe and care as intensely as they do when they are fresh. This phenomenon too is familiar to anyone who has taken care of one or more small children for a whole long day.

On the child's side, there is ample evidence that children profitably absorb all of the appropriate and affectionate attention they can get. "Attention" is not doing for, playing with, or even always answering requests or complying with demands for help, but being aware of what the child is doing and learning, of where today's pleasures and frustrations lie, and of what new task might be mastered if the child had enough space and encouragement to try and try again. The essence of human child care is to know and respect the inherent properties of the small person who is taking shape before one's eyes, and to clear a way for that growth by removing the obstacles that exceed the child's capacity to cope. There is no such thing as "too much" of that kind of attention for a child.

Given these conflicting needs and capabilities of children and their caretakers, it is a wonder that our children turn out as well as they do: ours is a most peculiar system of regimenting child care, relegating the responsibility almost exclusively to isolated mothers. Only in highly technological and urbanized Western societies has this arrangement for child care been

imagined as practical, beneficent for children, or pleasant to
carry out. In most other societies, child care has been and is
a shared responsibility: mothers, fathers, grandparents, uncles,
aunts, kin, friends, neighbors, adolescent and preadolescent
children, take regular *and willing* part in the responsibility of
caring for young children. The advantages to parents are
obvious when child care is a shared responsibility, with other
people around to talk to and work with; when an irritable or
crying child who wears one's patience thin can be helped by
others; and when there are opportunities to move around
physically, to plan and schedule time, and to "mind-spin"
while others care for the child.

The advantages for children of having multiple, trustworthy, and affectionate caretakers are at least as great, if
not more so:

1. Children with only one caretaker have "all of their
eggs in one basket." If the child knows only one person
to be trustworthy, and if that one person is tired, worried, angry, or irritable, the child has no other recourse
and must suffer the consequences of the adult's temporary and quite normal inability to provide appropriate
care.

2. Children with several trusted caretakers have a
range of adult styles and skills to observe, enjoy, and
learn.

3. Care by only one caretaker promotes the sense that
resources are scarce, a chronic feeling that we are probably going to be deprived of getting what we need.
Since no one adult caretaker can provide as much care
as several "fresh troops," a child with a single caretaker
is much more likely to learn to feel guilty (in reaction
to caretaker failure) than is a child with several caretakers. Given our widespread tendency to blame "bad
events" on individual inadequacy, the child with limited
resources for care often believes that being cared for
depends on being "good." With more than one trusted

caretaker, a child can discover that when one adult is worn out (tired, distracted, bored, needing to do something else) someone can be found who is fresh and delighted to be with the child.

It is probable that very young infants, in the first few weeks of life, are able to tolerate only a limited number of caretakers—one or two or three, perhaps: mother, father and baby nurse is a typical arrangement. The infant's ability to cope with and assimilate variations in caretaker style grows in parallel to her or his ability to deal with other kinds of stimulus complexity.[11] All other things being equal, we would not plan to ask a child to accommodate to the style of a new caretaker at times when the child's adjustment capacities are already stretched—for example, when the child is first learning attachments to familiar persons (roughly in the third quarter of the first year) or just on the brink of learning to talk, starting a new school or moving to a new neighborhood, or experiencing the arrival of a new family member or the departure of a familiar and trusted friend. When children's lives are otherwise serene and usual, they are much more adept at accepting and enjoying the attentions of new caretaker arrangements than professional child-development specialists have led us to believe.

Why Have Children at All?

In point of fact, we live in a society in which the only fully accepted institutionalized arrangement for the care of young children is solitary care by one home-based adult. As it becomes increasingly apparent that this is a difficult and hazardous role for adults to fulfill, more and more young women and men are "postponing" parenthood, or opting for a small number of children to care for, than ever before in our history.

There are other reasons why young adults are deciding not to become parents:

1. Children are expensive. The investment of something like $60,000 in the rearing of a child is an impressive burden when all of that money must be individually earned at jobs that are often less than fully satisfying.[12]

2. Children are draining of their parents' energy and time. As it becomes increasingly acceptable for young adults to decide whether or not to become parents, it is easier to see clearly the personal investment that parenthood involves and to assess one's own willingness and ability to make that investment. Not long ago a decision not to have children was so unacceptable to peers and to kin that it was almost unthinkable, and young adults were therefore prevented from making a reasoned assessment of their ability to invest themselves in child care. The consequence, predictably, was a high rate of children who were conceived and born primarily because their parents believed they had no real alternative. Some of these children never become wanted or valued by their parents.[13]

3. Childrearing is a risky venture, with an infinite number of things that can go "wrong." We have managed to transform parenting into yet another competitive activity, with the challenge to display the "best" entry in the race—tallest, earliest talker, highest marks in school, most home runs. Parents are readily blamed, and readily accept blame, for children's "failures," but are rarely credited for whatever their children do successfully. Given that risk of a "bad" or unhappy outcome, especially by competitive standards, it is no wonder that more and more young adults are questioning whether the venture is worth undertaking.

4. Many of today's young adults are the products of families that made a real effort to follow the prescription of nuclear-family responsibility for child care.[14] They know at first hand how much their parents have sacrificed "for the children": their mothers by isolating

themselves in their homes and cutting off opportunities to engage in productive work, and their fathers by
locking themselves into jobs that they sometimes hated
and rarely really enjoyed. They know how easy it is for
their parents to look upon them as "products" of
those efforts, and the burden of the expectation that
they will fulfill their parents' wishes, justifying by their
own lives so much parental sacrifice. They understand
how difficult it is for parents to be happy when children
choose their *own* family styles, interests in work and
play, attitudes about social activism or retreat from political interests, and concerns about "getting ahead" in
one's work or escaping from established work patterns.
In a time and place when social styles change from one
decade to the next with almost incomprehensible rapidity and scope, it is extraordinarily difficult, often even
undesirable or impossible, for children to fulfill the
expectations and hopes of their parents. As young adults
perceive and agonize over the worry, disappointment,
and distress of their own parents, they are increasingly
unwilling to take on the parental role themselves.

5. When a high proportion of marriages are falling
apart before children have grown to adulthood, it seems
especially risky to bring children into the world only to
subject them to the miseries of parental separation or
divorce. Despite a great deal of good will and firm intention to work out "amicable" arrangements so that children can continue to have two parents, separation and
divorce are usually so wrenching for adults that amica-
bility is difficult to sustain. When separating parents are
angry at each other, children can become pawns, used
by each parent as a means of hurting the other. The consequences for a child almost always involve sadness,
often anger, and sometimes guilt—as if the shattering of
the family group came about because the child was "not
good enough." Single-parent childrearing is a very difficult task in a society that has few institutionalized

arrangements for out-of-family shared child care.

6. For some there is a growing cynicism, despair, and fear about bringing children "into this world." In our lowest moments—when we consider our feelings about our jobs, the possibility of nuclear holocausts, our dying earth, the pressures of "looking for things to want"[15] and buy, and all the hungry children of this nation and world that we have not been willing to feed—the "creation" of yet another child can seem foolish, if not downright reprehensible.

7. Finally, becoming a parent at best invokes ambivalent values. While we pay much lip service to the joys of parenthood and the dearness of small children, in point of fact we do not, as a society, like children very much. Often we openly pity parents. On occasions when I have made this statement to professional groups, I am invariably contradicted by an authority, usually male, who avers, "But I like my children very much indeed." And therein lies a paradox, for we cannot voice or even acknowledge the feelings of sometimes actively disliking our own children as we might dislike any other persons with whom we have close, intimate, and demanding contact. But we are free to show our feelings about other people's children, and, in fact, it is not only socially acceptable but even expected that we regard children categorically as messy, noisy, uncivilized brats. Perhaps we project our quite normal intermittent irritation and anger at our own children, which we cannot freely admit, onto other children, adding strength to our feelings along the way.

We are, for instance, encouraged to agree that children should not be found in "adult" restaurants or at our places of work or in the stores where we shop. When there are children present who are not our own or the children of friends, we turn away or frown disapprovingly or ignore them altogether. World travelers sometimes comment that nowhere are children so publicly ignored as in the United States. (This is a paradoxical twist, for some defend the hardships and difficulties of our institutionalized arrangements for the nurturance and protection of the young—which are sometimes excessively stressful for their parents and then necessarily less than optimal for children—on the grounds that children are so precious that adult discomfort, even sacrifice, is justified.)

In a current lawsuit that seeks to return children to their parents after the children were summarily taken away on the order of a home-visiting social worker, one of the original charges against the parents was that their children "sometimes insulted and pestered adults." [16] On daytime radio, disc jockeys offer jocular comment about "poor Mother" on days when schools are closed because of bad weather—it is assumed that to spend time with children is always annoying if not maddening. This attitude is different from the public enjoyment of children in a society like, for example, the People's Republic of China, where adults on the street stop to admire or give a hand of help to children who are strangers. Slides of the street songs and games of the Loma people, in West Africa, show children and adults clapping, shouting, and dancing together with a joy of single purpose. By contrast, there are public places where my family and I have gone in which the obvious disapproval of other adults has made me uncomfortable to the point of wishing that my ebullient, lusty children were not there with me.

When a child is born, parents are often both congratulated and consoled: *"Now* you're in for it!" On learning that we have a houseful of small children, many people offer both me and my husband murmurings of condolence and head shakings that convey their attitude that we deserve every bit of work and worry we have created for ourselves.

We know from recent research on U.S. families that

the years when families have preschool, and especially
school-age, children (and are, by present conventions,
entirely responsible for providing care for those children from their own limited resources of time, energy,
and money) are years when marital unhappiness or
disappointment are likely to be experienced.[17]

The U.S. birthrate is now below the level of zero population growth, below replacement level. But we have not
entirely stopped bearing and adopting children.
  *What are the current predominant reasons for undertaking
the parental responsibility?*

  1. The choice *not* to become a parent is still not entirely free of social pressures. In spite of all of the
  reasons cited above for remaining childless, most young
  people report that they feel themselves to be pushed
  into parenthood by both peers and parents.[18] Pressure
  from peers is most likely to come from those who are
  already parents; since child care is such a consuming and
  unremitting responsibility for the parents of preschool
  children, their family lives are greatly altered and they
  "fit" less well socially with childless friends. Both
  parents and peers may argue on behalf of parenthood
  from the position that "we did it, and so you should
  too"; the speaker may be reflecting both pleasure and
  pain in that attidude.
  2. Some couples are tempted to hope that the birth
  of a child will cement a shaky marriage, even when that
  hope flies in the face of the experience of others. (There
  are, in fact, only a few instances when pregnancy, childbirth, and early childrearing have a temporarily positive
  and reinforcing effect on a tired marriage, perhaps because of the novelty of the experience.)
  3. The ability to conceive and bear a child, in the
  elemental physiologic sense, is a unique adult experience that we are all probably tempted to try "just to be
  sure that the machinery works as it should." I know of

several women who have had babies (not otherwise particularly wanted at that time in their lives) after they had
been told by a thoughtless physician that they "might
very well be sterile or infertile"—judgments arising from
physicians' views about tipped wombs, prolonged use of
birth control pills, or even premarital sexual activity.
Men, too, sometimes regard the conception of a child
as an ultimate badge, of masculinity. (In some societies
adolescents have a first child, a "grandmother's child,"
to assure themselves and others that their physiologic
machinery is in working order; the infant is given over to
the grandmother to rear, and the adolescent can then
proceed with the business of growing up and becoming
a responsible adult.)

4. There is almost certainly a universal adult mammalian attraction toward young creatures: we find babies
endearing, cute, appealing, lovable. Recently our family
was returning from a visit with an extended family in
another state, and we stopped at a lunch counter in a
train station. A young couple sitting across from us, on
their way to a football game, began to talk about how
appealing they thought children were, but only in very
small and controllable doses. The young woman, around
eighteen, said, "Wouldn't it be neat if we could rent
children, like for the Christmas season, and then return
them to the agency after two weeks?"

I think this symbolizes well the root of the attraction
of small children as cute and cuddly *objects*, who are
looked upon as creatures to "do for" at our pleasure,
satisfying our own needs to be nurturant. I am reminded
of the runaway "street kids" I have known, who found
themselves kittens or puppies to love; when we next
met, the baby pets had "run away," the kids told me
with shrugs of boredom. There is trouble afoot when a
parent foresees that a child will be an object to be played
with and displayed: children often are not cute but
furiously angry or irritable or overwhelmed with sadness,

and often not at all cuddly but screaming, angular, high-energy runabouts playing their side of the game of "control" for all it is worth. While the appeal of the cute and cuddly cannot be denied (and is often to be enjoyed) it is not by itself enough to build a sense of respect for a child as a whole and autonomous person, nor will it carry us through the moments when child care feels like the hardest thing we ever have to do.

5. Finally, in a more positive light, *rearing* a child (rather than simply conceiving and bearing) can be regarded as an elegant adult responsibility of the most rewarding sort. In my own adult life, no work-related accomplishment has seemed so much a source of self-respect as my less than perfect ability to be available to my children when they need me and to behave responsibly as a parent; no discouragement or depression has outweighed my gratitude that I am needed in a way that I can meet. I am not sure that I would feel comfortably competent as a parent if that responsibility were mine alone and unshared; but I have not been a solitary parent—in our family, child care is shared not only between mother and father but also with older brothers and sisters, our friends, and a variety of out-of-family resources, paid and unpaid.

Making It Better

If we have fewer and fewer children, if adults who do not really want to become parents have free options to refuse to take on that responsibility, will we then *as a society* value our children all the more, because they are wanted? Or will we value them even less than we do now, because only some of us will be parents while many of us will not? I fear that we may slide still further in the direction of despising (and harming) our children unless we find ways, very soon, to transform the responsibilities of parenthood into a different sort of undertaking—one that can be accomplished with a degree of pleasure and self-respect by most of those who will choose to become parents.

What could we do to help ourselves and each other and our children and our children's children?

We can demand that experts and professionals give us information and teach us skills that we can use to be joyous and competent parents, to the extent that their understanding is of practical use and not simply "academic." Competence in parenting is not instinctive but learned; most of us, I am convinced, are potentially more competent as parents than we believe. Probably the attitude most antithetical to good parenting is one that is often rewarded in school and at work: it is the attitude of the arrogant individualists who have never learned to work collectively toward common goals, and who build their self-esteem by disparaging others who are less "valuable" or "accomplished" or "learned" than they.

We need a wide range of opportunities to learn to be parents. Children need opportunities to learn caretaking from an early age and to gain a sense that to be a responsive caretaker is a highly valued and creative accomplishment. Adolescents need to learn what little children are like, both as abstract knowledge (for we appreciate best what we understand) and as practical, skilled experience; such learning might happen, for instance, in daycare centers affiliated with parents' places of work, or at neighborhood centers. Young adults anticipating parenthood can learn about children in quite different ways, for they can then imagine the immediate and necessary application of what they are learning. And, for all the learning absorbed *before* we become parents, there is much that cannot be comprehended, integrated, and retained until we actually *are* parents. We need readily accessible opportunities to become students of children and of parenting just before our children are born and while they are growing.

When the knowledge and skills of parenting are learned, in part, by observing warm and enthusiastic people who serve as models of competent child care, much more is learned than facts and techniques. The ability to give care to children also contains components of enrichment for all of our intimate and important relationships. Gentleness, sensuality, gratification, sensitivity, "tuning in," give rise to the impetus (sometimes blocked in adults, especially men) to have more vital, less alienated, less constricted contact with people we love.

In addition to these formal and informal "courses" in child care, we urgently need convenient arrangements through which we can request teaching with reference to our own *particular* and *immediate* needs. If a child becomes anemic, for instance, from having too little iron in the body, parents might want to ask what foods contain more and less iron, what conditions help the body absorb iron, whether there can be too much iron in the body, whether drugs can be used to treat the anemia, and how to keep the anemia from recurring. Any similar episode could become a learning opportunity, with the option of seeking knowledge and skills resting *in the hands of the learner*—which means, among other things, that no one is disparaged for choosing *not* to become expert about anemia. Similarly, a family planning to change the partitions in their living space might want to consult an architect to ask what is known about the effects on children of living in space divided into many small rooms versus a few large rooms, what kinds of connections best promote communication, and how to arrange furniture within rooms to minimize clutter and traffic collisions. If experts and professionals are to be obligated to teach in response to specific questions in these and similar situations, then there must be workable conventions through which those who teach and those who want to learn can come together.

We can institute regular and equitable arrangements to share child care within our social networks. In some cases the most workable arrangement will be an exchange of child care for child care: if you take care of our children on Monday, Wednesday, and Friday mornings, we will take care of your children on Tuesday, Thursday, and Saturday afternoons. Or a group of parents in a neighborhood may pool resources so that a dozen children may spend time together in the care of three adults, the adults rotating their time commitment according to the options allowed by their own job schedules. In other cases, child care may be exchanged for entirely different services: an adult may provide childcare services for other families' children and, in return, receive meals prepared, lawns mowed, or housecleaning services.

The sharing out of childcare responsibilities builds strong bridges between adults and children alike. When out-of-family adults know children well as a consequence of caring for them, their parents have resources to turn to when a special problem arises with regard, for instance, to the child's schooling, or her or his reaction to illness in the family. An amusing story about a child, or a special accomplishment, will be shared and savored by all who are attached to the child by virtue of their investment in his or her care. And children gain an array of adults whom they know well, trust, and can call upon for help, or to whom they can supply help.

At present, a family daycare arrangement (when a child stays in the home of another family) is the most common solution to a need for out-of-family child care. The possibility of expanding family daycare relationships represents a largely unrecognized, and little-valued, potential system of exchange of service in a local network context. The usual low to moderate fees involved can often be supplemented by repayments in service. The sharing of love and concern for a small child, jointly cared for, can create firm links between families. When a child stays in the home of another family, and when the arrangement proves to be a compatible contact of family and childcare styles, the two families involved can grow to be very close.[19] The family daycare arrangements of my own family have created relationships very like kinship.

We can insist that there is no more appropriate investment of monies collected through taxation and commercial profit than in the children of our society. We need a *variety* of daycare centers, enabling different families to supplement their own care of their children in ways that suit their own

different styles. We should remember the advantages—to
children and parents and paid staff—of small centers that
avoid the inflexibilities that usually come with having a manager or administrator who does not also actually take care of
children. We should demand that there be an adequate ratio
of adults to children (one adult for every three or four
infants, for every four or five toddlers) and adequate—con-
siderably more than minimum wage—salaries for those who
take care of children. Caretakers need time to talk with
parents, and time to prepare new activities and clean up
after. Most important of all, day care should *belong to*
parents, children, and paid staff jointly; the funds that must
come from government or commercial foundations to support the paid daycare arrangements needed by our families
must be controlled at the level of the individuals who use
and work at centers.

*Finally, the involvement of the father in a child's care
from the moment of birth provides the child with two trustworthy caretakers at the most intimate level.* Fathers gain
opportunities to learn and exercise all of the caretaking skills
that are often submerged in the course of their worklife.
And mothers increase their ability to nurture their children
by the collaboration of another adult who cares as much and
invests as intensively in the promotion of the child's day-to-
day welfare. Two participating parents more than double the
care a child receives.

It is unlikely, in the present context of nuclear family life,
that mothers will readily or happily "surrender" the pleasures
and responsibilities of child care, unless their own lives are
also substantially changed. Despite the bone-weary fatigue
of unrelieved solo child care, that responsibility represents
for many full-time homemakers the most rewarding and
creative thing they do. It is probably unrealistic to expect
that they can willingly share child care with their husbands
(no matter how beneficial that arrangement will be for their
children and their husbands) unless they also share responsibility for the much less rewarding chores of day-to-day family

maintenance and gain opportunities to do productive work.[20]
The entire puzzle is interlocked and will not "make sense"
if one piece only is moved.

For families with children (our prototype families) the
well-being of youngsters has high priority. For all of us, the
future depends on the people our children become. The
thought is trite only because in this society it has been hon-
ored mostly in the breach. Children—*all* children—have come
last in our social policies, except as objects for others to
control. As we learn to help ourselves, children are our
strongest hope for a better future.

The will to be totally rational
is the will to be made out of glass and steel:
and to use others as if they were glass and steel.
We can see clearly no farther
than our hands can touch.

—Marge Piercy

7 EDUCATION

In striking contrast to our conventional arrangements for
preschool child care, the institution of education—for our
children and for ourselves—is the province of professionals.
The practices, relationships, and organizations of education
for children of school age are only minimally influenced and
regulated by families.

Consider the following paradox:

> When children reach the age of formal schooling (five,
> perhaps, or six), responsibility for their education is
> delegated to professionals. Families, assumed to be in-
> competent to fulfill any major role in educating their
> "school-aged" children, are urged not to interfere with
> the work of professional educators. But the educa-
> tion of older children is in many ways easier than
> that of preschoolers, as their ability to learn and think
> becomes more and more parallel with that of their adult
> teachers.

Before children begin school, responsibility for their education lies entirely with their families. During these years, children learn more rapidly than at any other time in their entire lives. The learning of infants and toddlers is not only rapid and complex but also of signal importance for the child's later life, since the general learning and thinking abilities that children develop during that period (for instance, the construction of language and the labeling and integration of feeling states into the thinking process) are the underpinnings for all later education. There are few workable institutionalized arrangements through which families can gain support, information, and assistance in that responsibility.

If, in fact, only professional educators know how to help children learn, if that near-total delegation (and seizure) of responsibility is meant to be in the best interests of children, then why have professionals been so little involved in safeguarding the education of younger children? And if family members are able to be competent educators of their preschool children, how can we rationalize their exclusion from active participation in the education of their children after they enter school? *It is likely that the interests and preferences of professionals are paramount in this arrangement.* The education of very young infants and toddlers belongs to the homely world of caretaking and intimacy; it is poorly adapted to bureaucratic management and the world of educational technology. I regard this as our enormous good fortune, for child care (that is, preschool education) *benefits* from its own disrepute and inaccessibility to the workings of professionalized bureaucracies.[1] We have, then, an established starting point, a base on which to build a better educational process for our children and even for ourselves.

To educate means to rear, bring up, develop. To take care of children over all the years until adulthood is to educate them in the most organic and essential manner. *Learning* is done by taking in, making some knowledge or skill one's own. *To train*, on the other hand, means to drag or draw, to lay on or hammer into the trainee some knowledge or skills that may or may not become incorporated. Education, as a process similar to nurturant caretaking, focuses on and takes direction from the special characteristics, interests, abilities, and needs of the learner. Training tends to emphasize the characteristics, interests, abilities, and needs of the trainer. In fact, much of what we call education, as carried out by professionals in our schools, is actually training.

Professional educators do not agree about which of the following are the most important goals of schooling:

> 1. To mold "tax-paying citizens": to transmit the knowledge and skills that will enable adults to hold the kinds of jobs that are available in our present society.
>
> 2. To engineer "products" (people) who "fit in" with our present institutions: to transmit the knowledge and skills and beliefs and values and attitudes that will enable adults to accept roles in today's society.
>
> 3. To create experts, managers, and professionals: to transmit the ability to use the knowledge and skills presently seen as useful in the management of our society.
>
> 4. To enable an integration of emotion and intellect (in the broadest sense of energies known and unknown) toward a better society: to encourage and nourish the creative potential for using and *going beyond* the knowledge and skills we presently attend to.

Sometimes this question of goals is dealt with by noting that a designation of priorities depends on, and varies with, the "quality of the material"—that is, the children. Children of different *value* (or "worthiness") are schooled in different ways; they are invested in differentially. This view obscures the fact that we have no valid or reliable means by which any differential value of children can be assessed, except to measure *how well a child is likely to perform in school in the immediate future* by the use of intelligence and achievement tests. The reasoning is circular.

The "worth" of individual children is, in fact, often assumed on the basis of race, ethnically identifiable surnames, sex, the condition of hair, clothing or shoes, or by the reputation of their families. Whole classrooms of children are stereotyped (and labeled) according to assumptions made about "those people": poor, nonwhite, or of a certain religion or ethnic origin. Expectations about capabilities, motivations, interests, and worth of children are also stereotyped by sex.[2] Of course, some children are labeled in a positive way, stereotyped "good," for the same kinds of reasons, and the effect on them can be growth promoting; unfortunately, in our schools their good fortune is often gained at the expense of other children.[3] Families need to have effective means to protect children against schooling practices that demean and cripple them.

Are Schools for Students?

We adults have a self-interest in education over and above our concern for our children and our families. Defined in its most beneficent and growth-promoting potential, education is not just a process of use to children. We all would benefit if formal education were responsive to learning needs as a lifelong process for everyone.

One solution to these concerns is for parents to attempt to "seize control" of bureaucratized schools; often, the power of the bureaucracy to incorporate parents (and to change only cosmetically) is stronger than is the parents' power to alter or to do away with the bureaucracy itself. Another solution is to discover ways to use what help schools can provide, at our own pace and in relation to our own needs. A "neighborhood teacher," a neighborhood resident who works *for* students and their families and those who want to teach, and who is also so knowledgeable (perhaps even professionally trained) in school matters as to be credible to education bureaucrats, could serve as a link between families and schools.

Any efforts by family members to recapture their central

role in the process of education in this society take time and
energy. If we who choose to develop our own informed
human networks are to create necessary opportunities to do
so, these opportunities can come only through a reassess-
ment and rebalancing of our priorities toward family and
work. This is the reason that changes in the institution of
work and jobs must come *simultaneously with* other institutional changes. We can only "get ourselves together" if we
free ourselves (from impossible employment demands) to
do so. We will have that freedom of time and energy only if
we demand it; helping ourselves will not come about by relying on the niggardly concessions of strangers.

It is critical to emphasize again the power of institutions
dominated by experts, managers, and professionals. Many
individual teachers enter their professional training with a
desire to serve their students: they often find, however,
that their training not only fails to instruct them in that
role but actively discourages it.[4] The local school systems
that employ teachers often fail to support creative innovation in and out of the classroom, and positively reward
teachers who don't "rock the boat." Teachers who please
school managers may be offered jobs in administration, which
is seen as a "step up" from the work of classroom teacher.

Entering the administration with the hope of bringing
change from above can also be discouraging, for, like all
bureaucracies, school systems large enough to have full-time
managers are well insulated against real change. Often the
"reformer" becomes discouraged and leaves,[5] or rationalizes
that small cosmetic changes are acceptable substitutes for
real change that alters the system itself. Sometimes potential
reformers are co-opted and identify with the managerial
philosophy that explains why change cannot and *should* not
come about.

The relationship between families and schools is affected
by the power given to educators over children. Schools fulfill
an important role in this society by rank-ordering pupils,
because most of our other institutions also distribute oppor-

tunities and benefits according to a ranking of individuals: "better" people get "better" opportunities and benefits. While we no longer accord automatic privileged status only to persons with established family names or with inherited wealth, we have accepted a similar rationale for valuing some people over others: we reward "achievement within the system," accomplishments of a limited sort (compared to the possible range of human excellence) that reinforce and further the goals of our present institutions. Professional educators have accepted the assignment of nominating children who will be given the opportunity to demonstrate those kinds of achievement. School personnel therefore have not only the opportunity but the responsibility of labeling children as "good" or "bad," "worthy," or "worthless."

We, as parents, know the sinking, sick feeling of being told that our child "didn't do very well on the achievement tests this year" or, worse, brightly, "Jimmy is a very *dear* little boy, and this year he was almost at the top of the lower ten percent in his achievement test scores." Many teachers dislike this function of schools and are uncomfortable giving this sort of information to parents. Perhaps unwittingly, they sometimes compound the situation by allowing rank-ordering information to be recorded and used without telling the children or their parents.[6] The accumulation of these statistics and reports determines not only how well children are regarded by their teachers, but also how well they will be taught. And how well children learn what must be learned to satisfy school requirements is a very important factor in determining how far they are allowed to progress in school.

Despite the power of schools and educators over our children, the convention is that we parents are responsible for our children's performances in school. We guiltily accept the notion that a child's "bad" performance reflects on us as "bad" parents. We are discouraged from participating in their education, but are quickly blamed and accused of *non*-participation when things go wrong. Many parents (myself included) are anguished at a school report that focuses on a child's inadequacies and poor performance. There is a chilling awareness that recorded information has set a course for the child that may be inalterable. I know of few situations in which I personally feel so powerless in relation to another person as when I hear a teacher's report about one of my own children.

Professional educators are buffered from individual consumer demands by the certain knowledge on both sides that parents who cause trouble, who demand changes in schooling that are unacceptable to professionals, can be punished through the child. The children of "trouble-making" parents are not well regarded in schools, and the "data" on which the ranking of pupils is performed are sufficiently arbitrary to put our children into real jeopardy. We cannot forget about our child's fate as it is affected by school ranking. To do battle with schools as an individual may make one's child a pawn; to work constructively to change school policies and procedures may be seen by school personnel as "doing battle."

The consequences of the power relationship between families and professional educators are reflected in (1) school curricula; (2) children's roles in schools; (3) the exclusion of "undesirable" students; (4) the selection and training of teachers; and (5) the nature of the communications between parents, on the one hand, and teachers and administrators, on the other. In each area, a neighborhood teacher would work to reorder the distribution of power and to support families as the *primary* agents for the education of their children.

School curricula are now established almost without exception at the instigation of and according to the interests of professional educators. Despite complaints that schools teach neither in response to concerns of families about their children's education nor even according to the requirements of available jobs,[7] the right to determine what will be taught and how it will be taught is jealously guarded by professionals.

Parents and children could serve, as neighborhood representatives, on school committees that decide what will be taught and how: to discuss the teaching of Spanish in the elementary grades, for instance, or the introduction of a sex education class, a program of competitive sports, or the affiliation between a high school and a neighborhood daycare center. Families could decide on an individual basis whether their child should or should not participate in any given course or class, giving their children an active voice in the decision. The neighborhood teacher would serve as an intermediary in establishing and maintaining these negotiations, urging parents to present their views to school personnel in a manner that will be taken seriously, and urging school personnel to respond directly to those views.

Children's roles in schools are now characterized by an inability to choose what they wish to learn. They are often transformed from eager, active, curious preschoolers into angry or depressed pupils. Preschool children are characteristically exuberant about mastering challenging tasks and becoming competent in knowing and doing; once in school many become passive, disappointed, or even bitter about their education. We *expect* children to dislike school, and they do just that: when one asks school-aged children whether they like school, very few say yes. Is this simply a way of preparing children to grow up to take jobs that they also will not like? Their answer might give us pause: must we really force children to spend so much time doing what they dislike? (Whether children *really* dislike school, or only say so—perhaps as a gesture of peer solidarity in the face of their powerlessness—is not necessarily a helpful distinction; we can bring ourselves to dislike something by saying that we do.) The neighborhood teacher could ask children about their schooling, listen to their replies, and demand that school teachers and administrators acknowledge and attend to "the voice of the consumer."

Children can also be damaged through the "hidden curriculum" that teaches attitudes and behavior toward author-

ity figures in general. Children learn well and early that the
authority of teachers and principals is not easily challenged,
in situations that range from the orderliness of lunch lines to
the "correctness' of a drawing of a house, to the analysis of
current events. A friend of ours, who remembers her thrill of
anticipation and the pride of her family when she first entered
school, can date the exact moment of her first bitter disillu-
sionment: within the first month a new child joined her class,
and as she was helpfully explaining to the newcomer the
essential "rules of conduct" of the classroom, including the
important rule that one *must not* talk after the second bell,
she was shocked and startled to find the teacher furiously
screaming at them that the second bell had already rung!
One of our own children spent a miserable year in the third
grade when he was openly ridiculed and disparaged for wearing a "peace armband" and rather long hair; he vacillated all
year between conforming to the preferences of his teachers
and holding to his own preferences on grounds of principle.
He did not learn very much reading and arithmetic that year,
although he did learn a great deal about prejudice and authoritarianism.

"Socialization" in schools is often believed to require an
effort to *break the child's spirit* (sometimes called "teaching
self-control"). Our institutions generally give broad support
to the violation of children's dignity.[8] Humiliations and
assaults on self-respect during early schooling leave deep
scars—surely as deep as those left by any family difficulties
and dysfunctions.

A pivotal difference between families and schools is that
in our schools there is rarely any opportunity for teachers or
administrators to develop and exercise a commitment to the
well-being of the *individual* child. The situation is all the more
difficult for children because their families are told to "stay
out." Parents, even brothers and sisters, are not supposed to
know what goes on between teacher and child; thus, they
can rarely heal the child's wounds, help the child learn behavior that will be acceptable, or help the child see the school

experience from any safe perspective. Humiliations and belittlements become internalized as "my fault," exacerbated if parents assume that if a teacher is displeased the child *must* have done something "bad." A neighborhood teacher would help families to help their children by serving as a trustworthy conduit of information about school events.

Exclusion of "undesirable" students is as inappropriate as forced schooling between the ages of six and sixteen. Even children who hate school or who have been labeled as hopeless students or who have other pressing learning opportunities in which they would rather participate (such as being apprenticed to a carpenter) are *supposed* to stay in school. Actually, any child who does leave lockstep education has a most difficult time reentering; most do not have a second chance.

The "lockstep or nothing" convention holds true after the years of obligatory schooling as well, so that high school or college dropouts are only rarely able to come back to school and attain credentials that would allow them, for instance, to qualify for professional training. Proposals for "open" educational tracks that allow learners of any age and any kind of experience to reenter school after periods of alternative activity are easy to suggest and difficult to implement;[9] as always, bureaucracies resist schemes for the individualization of services as "inefficient" and economically imprudent.

There has been no serious attention given to estimates of the waste accrued in the loss of children and adults who could benefit from education; such measurements are in the category of imprecise and complex variables, beyond the interest of most efficiency experts. In a system of open education, one role for the neighborhood teacher would be to locate and inform residents of schooling opportunities and to negotiate, when desired, the reentry of children and adults into educational tracks.

The selection and training of teachers is the most obvious point of control of education through professionalization. Every adult knows some information and some skills that he or she could teach to a child; most adults, and many children, are (uncertified) experts in something that they could teach to others. But it has been determined that only *certified* teachers can be dignified by that title, and parents are urged not to try to teach their school-aged children. One consequence of this arrangement is that some essential teaching, some learning that children need, does not get attended to. Many parents feel so scolded and intimidated about the "problems" engendered when they try to act as their children's teachers that they play that role as little as possible.

But most professional educators do not believe that it is their responsibility, or the responsibility of schools in general, to teach children how to balance a checkbook, for instance, how to evaluate insurance advertised for sale, or how to clean and bandage an abrasion. As a consequence, children can grow up *not* learning many skills and much information that they really need for daily living. This engenders the spiral of a sense of incompetence and the need to rely on dependent access to professionals.

Teaching can, on the other hand, be seen as one variant of caretaking. Of course we teach each other all the time, whenever we show, explain, demonstrate, and work together. In this more basic sense parents *are* their children's teachers, not only in the preschool years but on through the years of formal schooling. What is required is a reevaluation of our acceptance of the professional's definition that the only "teachers" are those who have the formal credentials of professional training.

The neighborhood teacher's function here is to facilitate the informal teaching that occurs between families and their neighbors and friends, and to coordinate the transfer of information about the content and process of teaching from professionals to family members. For example, a child wants to learn to play the guitar and an able adolescent down the block is willing to teach. The music teacher at the neighborhood school can serve as a resource and a supervisor for the adolescent, who might later want to teach a group of neigh-

borhood children. The neighborhood teacher, who knows
local families well enough to search out teacher-pupil connections and knows school personnel well enough to suggest
impromptu lay-professional consultations, would serve as
an intermediary.

*The nature of the communications between parents and
teachers and administrators* is affected by the power of the
position of professional educators. It is difficult to form and
maintain easy acquaintances between parents and teachers.
"Objectivity" and distance are trained into teachers. The
scant attention given in their training to the difficult (but
rewarding) aspects of personal caretaking as part of the
teacher role makes teachers apprehensive about "getting
sucked into a family's problems." Our emphasis on failure,
weakness, problems, and lack of perfection makes it hard for
all of us to focus on strengths and health. Teachers find it
difficult to look upon students, and families of students, as
resources of caring, support, and the pleasures of friendship.
The notion that professionals should be "objective" makes
them wary of developing any personal connection, lest they
show favoritism. And yet professionals *always* show favoritism, if they allow any human connection at all to enter into
their relationships with clients. Only by a cold, machinelike
refusal to recognize clients as people can a professional avoid
liking, knowing, and understanding some people better than
others.

The difficulty for the professional is not to avoid empathy
with persons they take care of, but to strive to assure that
those with whom they do not feel that bond of empathy do
not receive poor service. The empathetic bond itself greatly
increases the probability of the best service that the helping
professional can give.[10] One reason that professional services
are generally better in the suburbs than in cities or rural areas
is that most professionals are white and middle class; suburban
families seem to be like themselves and their own families,
and they seem to share comparable histories and expectations
of the future. Professionals' high sense of empathy then

strengthens the quality of the service they give. Not until
significant numbers of "other" kinds of professionals are
selected and trained will the important ingredient of empathy
improve the quality of professional services given to "other"
groups of clients. Blacks have a special potential for giving
good teaching and other services to blacks, Chicanos to
Chicanos, Boricuas to Boricuas, women to women, and so
on. For the same reason, children have a potential for giving
good care (including teaching) to other children.

This alignment of caretaker to recipient will not, of course,
be sufficient in and of itself to improve the quality of professional services for those who are not white and middle
class. At present, for instance, the predominantly white/
middle-class managers of bureaucratic service organizations
also provide impressively better working conditions for professionals who serve white/middle-class consumers. Schools
in poor neighborhoods are much less pleasant places to work
in than schools in middle-class neighborhoods, because of
physical space and especially because of the disproportion
between the needs of neighborhood and family, on one hand,
and the people resources available to respond to those needs.
It is not surprising that professionals who try to bring care
to under-served groups often find their work depressing,
wearying, and difficult.

The emphasis on detachment, objectivity, and denial of
empathy (presented to prospective teachers on the promise
that services provided will be more professional if the personal
responses of the caregiver are not acknowledged) makes it
difficult for them to trust their own tendencies to know students and families as friends. Intuition, organicity, and flow
are sacrificed in the service of proscription, routine, and
efficiency. It is easier to remain cold, distant, and suspicious
when close personal relationships have been portrayed as
"dangerous." Professionals often compound their distrust
by assuming (as they have been taught) that clients or patients are trying to "take advantage" of them, to get services

that they don't "deserve" by presuming on a friendship. In this way a battleground of suspicion is set up.

On the other side, family members are at least equally mistrustful of professionals. Teachers often report that their offers to make home visits to discuss a child's progress in school are refused by parents. On the basis of all of their past experience with professionals, and especially with school personnel, parents correctly perceive that reports from school are potentially dangerous, usually focus more on weaknesses than on strengths, and may catalogue the child as less than perfect or in some degree a failure. The meeting is expected to be unpleasant and uncomfortable—not one that many families want to have take place in their own homes. In addition, parents may wonder whether teachers will judge and rank *them*, and record their observations in administrative records. It can be expected that attempts at communication between any one teacher and any one parent will be wary and subtly hostile.

Personal trust, in this case as in every other, comes about only by repeated face-to-face contacts and demonstrations of trustworthiness. By convention, children have new teachers every year; rapid changes of employment location by teachers (promoted by the dissatisfactions structured into jobs) help to assure that alliances of friendship and trust will not develop between school personnel and students and their families. The parallel between school and employment is striking: students and workers, feeling dissatisfied and helpless, welcome a change to a new classroom or job. But moving on prevents us from knowing and trusting one another, and from "wasting" time and energy in the "inefficiencies" of caring about one another. Nor can we join together—student with teacher, or worker with worker—to improve our circumstances. If we as individuals or as neighborhood groups now overcome this base of mistrust, it is only by rare good luck or by conscious efforts to overcome the barriers to trust that have been created for us. The neighborhood teacher, as a

connection of long-term stability between schools and families, would help us to make that effort.

Education for What?

The kinds of education that we want and need for ourselves and for our children fall into four broad areas: (1)
basic skills—how to read, calculate, paint, carpenter, cook,
sew, find information, write, evaluate the reports of experts,
take care of children and sick people, and so on; (2) basic
knowledge essential for a sound and safe life—how our bodies
work, the maintenance of good nutritional status, the legal
rights of individuals and groups, the beauties and dangers of
the physical environment in which we live, how our behavior
affects others and how others can affect us, the uses and
abuses of the chemical substances we take into our bodies,
how children grow and develop, the responsibilities and priv-
ileges of various kinds of employment, and so on; (3) knowledge and skills that allow a perspective on, and appreciation
of, everyday life—poetry, drama and literature, history, mathematics as a game or a discipline, theoretical and practical
science, the history and theory of music and the visual arts,
sociology, psychology, and so on; and (4) knowledge and
skills directly related to taking and holding paid employment
—how to be a lawyer or electrician or physician or mechanic
or sociologist or priest or administrator or plumber.

Each of us learns some things more readily and with
more enjoyment than we learn other things; some kinds of
learning are more essential, some more enjoyable, some more
relevant in each personal life. Each of us, male and female,
child and adult, from every level of "natural" ability and
income, must have equal access to all varieties of learning
opportunity if we are to evolve a society that fulfills its
promise of equality of rights. Much more of our learning can
(and already does) take place outside of formal "educational"
agencies than within.

Basic skills can be learned both in families and in schools.

Some professional educators wish to broaden the scope of their responsibility and control in this respect, in part because of the disparagement with which professionals regard home-bound lay education; this view is reinforced when family members are instructed to believe that they are less competent to teach than are professional teachers and less wise in selecting what should be taught than are experts.

The basic skills fall into three loose categories: language and number use, personal and interpersonal conduct, and skills of negotiating with the institutions of everyday life. All parents have these skills with some degree of competence; perhaps none of us is as skillful as we would like to be. Family members cannot help but teach their children about the use of these skills, if only by demonstration. On the other hand, to restrict a child's learning of basic skills to family members only would be weakening.

The neighborhood teacher can advise parents and coordinate resources to help children learn basic skills:

> 1. Some children have trouble with talking from the start, some are late or slow, some have such unclear articulation that other people have difficulty understanding them. Some children do not take easily to reading, having more than the usual difficulty with attention or with the discrimination of right–left, up–down, backwards–forwards (called "dyslexia"). Some children with problems of discrimination or motor coordination do not easily learn to print or write. Some falter in learning basic arithmetic. There are parents, also, who themselves have long-unresolved problems in reading or written expression or arithmetic, and who could benefit from special help that would allow them to teach their children.
>
> 2. The skills of personal and interpersonal conduct are obviously taught at home—"Share your toys," "Don't mess in your sister's desk," "Keep your hands off other people if they don't want to be touched,"

"Don't make fun of your brother's sandcastle; he thinks it's beautiful," "You can have your turn minding the baby tomorrow afternoon." Similar skills are also taught in schools, sometimes openly and sometimes in the "hidden curriculum" that reflects the attitudes and beliefs of teachers and school administrators—"Don't doubt my word; what I tell you is correct," "The most important thing in baseball is to win," "The student who does the best work can leave early, and all the rest have to stay and clean up," "Boys who want to cook are strange." Children thus learn skills of dealing with those in authority, those who are younger or less able, those of the opposite sex. They learn about competition and cooperation, working alone and collaborating in a group, and "winning" and "losing." And they learn about the absolutism of rules, the rights of children and other relatively powerless groups, and how one decides what is "right" and "wrong."

Sometimes families have strong feelings about these skills and can convey to their children, and to school personnel, what they approve of and reward, and what they dislike and discourage. Often, however, it is difficult for anyone (school professionals as much as parents) to analyze what children are learning with regard to these skills and what the specific situations and sanctions are that encourage their learning. If parents hope that their children will not become fiercely individualistic and competitive, and yet a child seems to be increasingly concerned about "winning," it is not always easy to determine whether there are situations at home or at school that subtly encourage competitive skills.

This kind of analysis is often easier for an "outside" person—our friends often make important observations about our children that we as parents have overlooked because we are too close to see. A neighborhood teacher, who knows both individual children and the climate of the classroom, can see these connections in a way that is helpful both to parents and to teachers, and especially to children themselves.

3. The basic skills needed to negotiate with the institutions of everyday life are among the least well taught in all areas of education, at home and in schools alike. Although no single adult is likely to be skillful in all areas of negotiation, among a coalition of persons of many ages and varying experience any child might be able to learn how to deal with banks, utility companies, appliance repair services, insurance companies, welfare offices, and government licensing agencies; how to secure and defend their legal rights, how to find a competent physician and safeguard their rights as patients, how to promote their own education and safeguard their rights as students, how to be canny consumers, how to find and use the government agencies whose purpose is to protect the individual citizen; and how to work as individuals or as part of a group, whichever seems most advantageous. Unfortunately, existing teaching in these areas often focuses on producing obedient consumers of services.

These skills must change over time, sometimes quite rapidly, as institutions themselves change; adults as well as children need to be constantly brought up to date. A model for this sort of self-help education has grown in the women's health movement, as women meeting together share their personal experiences and learn from each other what their rights are as patients; how to deal with physicians, clinics, hospitals, health insurance companies, and pharmacists; how to work, both as individuals and as groups, for changes in institutional policies and in legislation affecting health; and how to seek the best health care they can find for themselves and their families.

The professionalized educational system is not particularly expert in knowing, much less teaching, these kinds of skills. The role of the neighborhood school

might be to provide a forum in which experts, such as
attorneys and physicians, who are attuned to the needs
and interests of layfolk would explain how various
institutions work and enable them to learn the skills
of negotiation. The role of the neighborhood teacher
might be central, since school personnel can learn as
much from neighborhood people as *vice versa.*

The *basic knowledge* essential for a sound and safe life is
necessarily taught for the most part by experts. School
teachers are experts in their own fields, of course, but in any
given school only a narrow range of areas of expert knowledge will be represented; thus, schools must bring in the
teaching services of scientists, child-development specialists, attorneys, physicians, nutritionists, experts in environmental health and safety, and so on. We have evidence to
support the proposition that *any* topic can be taught to, and
learned by, any adult or school-aged child in an intellectually
respectable fashion.

In this time of information explosion, parents and teachers
as well as children can benefit from talking with, asking
questions of, and challenging experts. Public schools are a
logical place for experts to exercise their responsibility to
teach what they know to layfolk. Experts themselves can
learn, from experience and from constructive criticism, how
to speak and explain so that others can understand the knowledge that they ordinarily use in their work. When children
and parents learn together, the family household becomes
the place where children's learning is reinforced through
practical use.

The neighborhood teacher may become the person to relay
back to experts the effectiveness of their teaching. As a professionally trained teacher, his or her voice may provide
acceptable reinforcement to the comments of layfolk; as a
resident of the neighborhood, he or she will readily have
access to, and can understand the reactions of, the lay participants in teaching/learning interactions.

The *knowledge and skills of perspective*, which enable us to go beyond the immediacy of our everyday lives, have been a major focus of our institution of education. Unfortunately for our children this teaching, which should surprise and delight them, has been confused with training for employment and generally infused with the forced dreariness of most formal schooling. In that climate, learning can be painful, and teaching ineffective. Although the basic fund of knowledge is the same, instruction in botany is different if one is training a botanist than if one is educating an electrician, for instance, who can gain enjoyment, insight, peace of mind, or the excitement of discovery by "knowing botany." Recognizing, knowing life cycles, and perhaps gathering and eating the plant life that grows in one's home area can extend the fullness of one's life. Compare also a child's visit to a museum or a concert, as an excursion or a "treat," with the art or music instruction in many schools.

Unlike instruction in basic skills and basic knowledge, there are no rules of thumb to determine which kinds of knowledge and skills of perspective will be of special use for any given individual. Personal needs and interests vary widely. We all, adults and children alike, can use opportunities to try learning how to read, understand, and write poetry; how to listen to, understand, and play music; how to learn and do mathematics as a game; how to read, understand, and write history. In our present educational system, if the student doesn't "catch on" to subject the first time around, he or she is labeled as "not very good in" that subject and rarely has a second opportunity to begin fresh.

This philosophy is totally inappropriate for a society in which we are encouraged, even driven, to change our interests and our use of personal time over exceptionally long life-spans. We should be able to reenter the school system at any time (as valid students, not as "exceptional" or "deviant") and begin as beginners to study the violin or ancient history or comparative religion or biochemistry. The school system serves as a logical, central locality for this kind of learning,

since schools employ large numbers of experts and own the
equipment that is necessary for many kinds of instruction.
This kind of teaching can, of course, also become an integral
part of our systems of exchange of unpaid services. I know
enough about harmony to be able to teach you as a beginner;
will you teach me how to find wild foods in return?

The neighborhood teacher, knowing the resources in the
neighborhood and in nearby schools, can make connections
between half-formed interests and learning options both for
children and for adults. The child who loves to sing might
like to know enough about playing the piano to help in learning new songs; the neighbor three blocks away who used to
be the church soloist is having a quiet year with her children
in school and her half-time job, and she might be happy to
teach that kind of piano playing in exchange for lawn mowing.
The old man across the street is a Civil War buff and would
be pleased to talk about the subject he loves with someone
who will do his grocery shopping.

Employment-related knowledge and skills have been the
unacknowledged backbone of our educational system. Much
of this teaching is training, based on the principle that there
is only one right answer, one "right" way to do things. Since
this kind of teaching is directed to taking and holding particular jobs or sets of jobs, it would be well if professional
educators included employers in decisions about what and
how to teach.[11]

If we were to evolve a society in which job opportunities
were really equal, then everyone would have access to training for every job within the constraints of special ability and
the numbers of workers that can be employed. If more students apply for a particular kind of job training than the
employment system can use and pay for, then some lottery
system would prohibit the inequitable use of the advantages
of money, position, and "pull" in selecting among them.

Employment-related knowledge and skills are best taught
shortly before the student seeks employment. Certain jobs
require only brief training, which can be a part of the high

school curriculum. For some kinds of work—auto mechanic
or secretary, for instance—the training is moderately extensive; it can be part of a post-high-school curriculum or taught
in special training schools. For other jobs the knowledge and
skills required are very extensive—nuclear physicist or neuro-
surgeon, for example—and lengthy programs of preparation
are necessary.

Training courses for particular jobs, as we now have them,
are a prime means by which rank-ordered students get perma-
nently channeled into job slots: an auto mechanic will not,
except in the most exceptional circumstances, ever cross
tracks to become a nuclear physicist, nor will a secretary
cross over into the training sequence for neurosurgeons.
Conversely, students who enter training for nuclear physics
or neurosurgery and who are dissatisfied can rarely escape,
and then only with the stigma of the dropout, "failure,"
"quitter."

We now have very few educational programs that teach
anyone how to be a generalist, which usually means the
integration of two or more areas of specialist knowledge and
skills. The recent history of attempts at "interdisciplinary"
teaching and learning at the university level have been discouraging. Specialists have built-in loyalty to their own fields
and are mistrusting of persons in other "disciplines." Many
hopeful programs in interdisciplinary education collapse:
teachers dislike the requirement that they work collaboratively, coordinating what they teach with the teaching of others.
In addition, the bureaucratic organization of the university
is inimical to any program that does not have a clearly identified hierarchy of responsibility.

Although individuals can become generalists by integrating
within themselves the special areas of knowledge and skills
of more than one field, we will probably have few generalists
until the agencies of higher education begin to value and promote generalism. The clear utility of generalists to layfolk
(in their service role) and to the complex and multifaceted
problems of most pressing urgency in our society (in their

creative problem-solver role) may induce more *individuals* to
undertake the generalist position on their own.

The neighborhood teacher is one such generalist. He or
she might be paid a service fee by neighborhood families or
a salary by the neighborhood school system or by some level
of government. Salary payments generate subtle and not-so-
subtle demands for loyalty to one's employer. It is clear that
at present it is families, not professionals, who need special
advocates. It is far preferable, then, that neighborhood teachers be paid by families, perhaps through control of tax monies.
The apparent usefulness of the neighborhood-teacher role is
also a strong argument for an education voucher mechanism,
by which families receive payments in cash from public
revenues to promote the education of family members.[12]

There are, at present, few easy (institutionalized) educational tracks for the neighborhood teacher: preparation for
the role requires that the learner remain closely tied to her
or his neighborhood while simultaneously learning "the ropes"
of professionalized education. The work is essentially free
lance, in the sense that emphases and priorities, working
style, and areas of special focus will be determined by the
neighborhood itself. We who live in families could assist and
encourage individuals who will become our neighborhood
teachers as they progress through professional training. Without our help and support, it is overwhelmingly likely that
students will become professionalized away from us and will
become unable to help us deal with the institution of education.

. . . most of all He envies the bodies,
He who has no body.

The eyes, opening and shutting like keyholes
and never forgetting, recording by thousands,
the skull with its brains like eels—
the tablet of the world—
the bones and their joints
that build and break for any trick,
the genitals,
the ballast of the eternal,
and the heart, of course,
that swallows the tides
and spits them out cleansed.

He does not envy the soul so much.
He is all soul
but He would like to house it in a body
and come down
and give it a bath
now and then.

—Anne Sexton

8 HEALTH CARE

The World Health Organization states that "health is a state of complete physical, mental and social well-being and not merely the absence of disease or infirmity." This point of view is apparently not very relevant to medical education and practice in the United States, for the promotion of health in this sense is believed to be beyond the responsibilities and capabilities of the medical establishment.

Medical Care Is Not Health Care

If health care means the promotion of good health, then there is no profession, no set of experts, no institution whose work is health care. Instead, we have a system for the provision of *medical* services: detecting, diagnosing, and treating illnesses, injuries, and disabilities. The major mission (the focus of the knowledge and skills) of the experts, professional

caregivers, and organizations for research and service that
comprise our medical establishment has little or nothing to
do with the prevention of illness, injuries, and disabilities.
Nor is education provided to layfolk so that they can safeguard their own health and bring knowledgeable and skillful health care to themselves and their families.

We want and need health care. Instead, we are offered only
medical services that patch us up or retrieve us after we
become ill. In this arrangement, the more illness, injury, and
disability that befall us, the more prosperous is the medical
service industry. One need not be cynical to see the rules of
the marketplace at work here.

Several years ago a delegation of healthcare experts from
the People's Republic of China visited the United States.
While in Boston they asked to meet with medical students.
One of the small group of students who met with the Chinese
was asked why she wanted to study medicine; she replied,
"To serve the people." When the interchange was reported in
a national news magazine, the student was described, on the
basis of that statement, as "radical." By contrast, the president of the American Medical Association has outlined the
professional responsibilities of physicians as follows: "to
keep fighting for the preservation of American [sic] medicine
as an individually motivated science and as a creative art . . .
to see that the problems of health-care delivery are solved
within the present system of care rather than at the deadly
sacrifice of that system . . . to retain—and augment—the
people's confidence in medical leadership."[1] These two views
well represent the contrasting purposes of health care and
medical care.

The *health care* that we envision would require of its practitioners devotion to our collective welfare, recognition that
the health and well-being of each citizen is important to all
citizens, and a role of service, a willingness to *respond* to the
needs and demands of clients. The *medical care* that we now
have encourages its practitioners to devote much of their
energy and attention to securing their own personal welfare,

to accept an arrangement by which some citizens have access to more services than other citizens, and to exercise a remarkable degree of authoritarian control in social policies and the personal lives of their clients.[2]

The contrast between these views is poignantly evident in medical schools: the socialization pressures of medical training are so severe that those students who enter training with the intention of "serving the people" find it extraordinarily difficult, painful, and costly to exit from their training with the same purpose and with the knowledge and skills appropriate to that purpose. Some do.

Is Health Care Possible?

Like many of the implicit assumptions of our established institutions, the attitude of medical professionals toward health care appears somewhat irrational. It is argued that the health care that consumers are beginning to demand "is not practically possible." How could this be so? The promotion of good health would not, after all, put healthcare professionals "out of business"; the problems in our society that prevent maintenance of good health are rampant, and their resolution would provide much work for healthcare professionals. New technological developments present new challenges to health maintenance. Newly discovered, health-related knowledge and skills need constantly to be translated into information that layfolk can use in attending to their own health and that of their families. New generations need perpetually to be taught. It is not difficult to propose the changes that would provide us with an institution of health care.[3]

It is also easy to outline some blocks to these changes:

The payment system for workers in health-related fields is such that they are rewarded not for preventing illness, injury, and disability, but for treating these conditions after they occur. Practitioners who work on a fee-for-service basis are rarely paid for time or work that is not "about" a specific (named or diagnosed) symptom or complaint. Neither third-

party payment agencies (Medicaid and Medicare and private
"health" insurers) nor patients themselves are inclined to
think that a visit to a medical professional for informational
or educational purposes is worth a fee. On the side of patients,
at least, this may be in part because medical professionals are
rarely able or willing to answer their questions in an under-
standable and informational way; the professional's manner
conveys that translation into the vernacular would be beneath
professional dignity.

Many practicing physicians believe that health education
and the supervision of preventive health vigilance are not
part of their work, not what they were trained to do, not
what they like to do, and not their responsibility. Physicians
define themselves so clearly as treaters (and not as teachers)
that they are uncomfortable unless they provide every client
with some tangible treatment. Some physicians put more
effort into thinking of a treatment that might be applied
than in trying rigorously to avoid all but needed treatments
and to support instead patients' inner resources for healing.

The great overuse of drugs in our society is due in part to
the habit of physicians of ending patient visits with prescriptions for drugs;[4] even when there is no reasonable treatment
to recommend for the patient's complaint, there are plenty
of nonspecific drugs to choose from. Patients have been
trained to accommodate to this system and to believe that
in order to justify a visit to a physician they must offer a
symptom or complaint; they also know that in order to avoid
the physician's irritation at being "bothered unnecessarily"
—for a fee—they must allow their symptom or complaint to
become a named "illness" with some "remedy" if that is at
all possible. One is made to feel "silly" (soft, infantile) for
having symptoms and for being concerned about them,
unless the doctor can fit the symptoms to a named disease.
In this way patients internalize the physicians' limitation
and often feel guilty for having merely thought themselves
ill. Both patients and physicians alike are comforted by

playing this game because they thereby meet their expectations of themselves and each other.

There is no question that the present organization of medical services is designed to suit the interests and needs of physicians. Medicine is "their" work; they are even paid to design hospital and clinic services to suit themselves. Clinic appointment schedules are designed with doctors' convenience in mind. Access by telephone for follow-up information ("I have developed a rash—could it be from the drug?" "My child still has a fever—should I be worried?" "When should I go back to work?") is rarely planned to suit patients. Arrangements for laboratory testing and X-rays often require extra traveling and delays. Patients are expected to wait for physicians, never the reverse. The physicians' time (and good nature) are obviously presumed to be more important than the patients'.

The training of medical workers, and the conditions and limits of their work, are also regulated by the wishes of physicians. Contrary to what we would like to believe, most nurses are paid to work not for patients but for doctors. The training, certification, and practice prerogatives of nurses, medical social workers, physicians' assistants, and other "allied health workers" are heavily influenced if not determined by physicians' organizations and by individual physicians whom they work "for."[5]

As medical services become more and more bureaucratized into large and complex service organizations requiring management (administration), the manager's concerns for efficiency, economy, and inflexible routine often become even more central than the physician's convenience. But it is not likely that patients' needs will ever become predominant within our present system. A medical care system in which physicians are paid fees for "treating" complaints, with each "sick" patient as a unit-for-pay, can never be a *healthcare* system.

Physicians especially, but also to a lesser extent nurses and

*other medical professionals, are naive and uninformed about
the kinds of knowledge and skills needed to prevent illness
and disability and to promote health.* They simply don't
know how to do it. For instance, defending, promoting, and
protecting the good health of families and neighborhoods
require skills of public education, advocacy, negotiation,
organizing, and confrontation politics. Attending to the
healthcare needs of individuals requires skills of face-to-face
teaching, including the translation of the jargon of science
into the practical information that patients need. Little in
the training or practice arrangements of medical personnel
enables them to learn or use these skills.

Accidents, poor nutrition, and "environmental" poisoning
are now major health hazards in the United States, especially
for children. They are barely acknowledged by physicians as
preventable health problems, since physicians have not been
trained to prevent them, they do not have ready access to
the knowledge and skills needed to prevent them, and they
regard such issues as "beyond the responsibility" of the
physician.

Coping with such problems requires neighborhood-based
doctors who would work collaboratively with other neighborhood residents to achieve the following kinds of health-
promoting solutions, among others:

> Zoning heavy traffic out of the neighborhood (reduc-
> ing automobile accident rates, and lead and other chemi-
> cal poisoning from the inhalation of exhaust fumes);
> Investigating occupational hazards in local places of
> employment, informing both employers and employees
> of potential hazards, calling on governmental investi-
> gatory and regulating agencies, and serving as advocate
> for concerned families (reducing work-related accident
> rates, and chemical poisoning by industrial wastes and
> products);
> Publicizing the nutritional hazards of foods offered
> for sale, insisting that local grocers offer a selection of

little-processed foods in their stocks, educating and assisting neighborhood food cooperatives in the selection and purchase of maximally nutritious foods, and fighting for subsistence incomes (reducing the health hazards of undernutrition and malnutrition).

Although physicians now romanticize their work as "defenders" of good health, only a rare few are willing to take initiative or effective action to rid their neighborhoods of obvious health hazards. All but a few refuse to be of real assistance when asked to cooperate with neighborhood groups in such efforts, especially when these efforts require confrontation with strongholds of money or power. Most physicians do not believe they have, or could or should learn, the skills and knowledge relevant to preventive health care.[6]

The major focus of health-related research today is defined by what doctors already know how to do—to detect and treat existing disease and disability. The body of traditional medical knowledge has expanded in the last several decades to incorporate (and promote) the most profitable areas of technological development. With each year, less attention is given during the training of physicians and medical researchers to taking care of people. Caretaking is given low priority in order to make room for more instruction related to the use of complex machinery (computers, electronic monitoring systems, heart-lung machines, kidney dialysis equipment), drastic surgery, the replacement of body parts, and dangerous drugs. As a corollary, increasingly more human conditions are interpreted as "diseases" to be managed by "heroic" means, both dramatic and expensive. The various addictions (drugs, alcohol) and dangerous behaviors (sexual molestation of children, violent rages) have become "diseases" to be treated by psychosurgery or behavior modification through finely graded electric shock. The development of means to keep "defective" infants alive, to prolong the life of adults with failing hearts or brains, or to replace malfunctioning body parts has made death itself a "disease." We have pushed our-

selves beyond our capacity to decide when or why such
treatments should be applied; they are almost irresistible
simply *because they are available.*

It should be of grave concern that there has been relatively
little attention paid to sophisticated assessment of the effects
of the application of this technology-related research to our
health as individuals, as families, or as a nation. For instance
in one prototypic area, that of childbirth, available data suggest that maternal and infant mortality and morbidity are
not much better, and possibly even worse, than they might
be if we had *not* defined childbirth as a "disease" to be
treated by "heroic" measures: fetal monitoring, heavy anesthesia, and the extravagant use of procedures that interfere
with normal delivery, such as forceps, Caesarian section, the
use of various drugs.[7] What conclusions would we reach with
a *total* assessment in this area?

Most of our major unsolved health problems of high inci-
dence are not, in reality, amenable to resolution by technology alone; they are problems created and perpetuated by the
complexities of *human* behavior interacting with the behavior
of sewage systems, chemical agents, micro-organisms, enzyme
systems, and so on. There are far too many examples of the
nonsolution of health problems by the application of a
medical-technological approach: methadone addiction is
substituted for heroin addiction; social violence is to be
reduced by the personal violence of imposed psychosurgery;
kidney failure that is often a consequence of undetected and
untreated chronic disease beginning in childhood is treated
by elaborate technology (kidney dialysis), while little is
done to detect and treat its causes; surgical removal of wombs
is used to prevent the births of "unwanted" children; depression in middle-aged housewives is treated by long-term prescriptions for drugs that make them "feel better" by feeling
almost nothing at all; and amphetamines are given to little
boys who dislike, and do poorly in, school.

If we are to understand, prevent, and treat most of our
serious health problems, we need the research efforts of

healthcare professionals who are concerned with such questions as the following: (1) how to translate scientific health-related knowledge into information that layfolk can use effectively to monitor and responsibly oversee their own health status; (2) how to recognize and help those who *will* use drugs in ways that are destructive to themselves or to others; and (3) how to help us resist the pressures to buy and use harmful products, foods, and entertainment. We need to study those who presently work in, and control, the medical professions, to determine under what circumstances they would be willing to invest themselves in efforts to promote good health.[8]

The investigators who can do such work are experts whose conceptual and research skills include a tolerance for, and positive acceptance of, the ambiguities of human behavior, a willingness to work with approximating predictions of behavior, an orientation to the solution of pressing immediate problems, and a serious acceptance of the dictum "first of all, do no harm" (*primum non nocere*). Such expert researchers should be drawn from a wider variety of background experience—by ethnic group, class, and sex—than is now the case, so that they can infuse the research-controlling agencies with a broader and clearer understanding of the nature of our most pressing health problems.

Today, medical research is dominated by experts with talent for, and interest in, technological "advance." Medical care, in turn, is directly affected by the products made available by researchers. One major cause for the recent rapid rise in hospital costs, for instance, is the "need" to equip every hospital with the capabilities of the most up-to-date technologies for treatment, including some that have not yet been determined to be acceptably safe and effective. But we are beginning to learn that our technologies may not bring marked improvements in health or even in recovery from illness.[9]

The fee system of our present medical practice, our deficiency of attention to the kinds of knowledge and skills

needed for the provision of health care, and the preoccupation of medical research with narrow and specialized science
and technology all contribute to our present lack of health
care. Each of these is remediable and can be altered by public
policy—each, for instance, can be affected by the expenditure
of government funds.

The Arts of Healing

The philosophy of medical education, since the meteoric
rise in the rate and status of scientific discovery, has drifted
into an assumption that medicine is a science rather than an
art that uses science. Little or no attention is given, in the
course of medical education, to an understanding of the arts
of healing, the effects of "laying-on of hands," the intuitive
processes, the ambiguities of interpreting findings and selecting treatments, the reciprocal power inherent in the healer/
patient relationship, and the balancing of risks—to patient
and to healer—in choosing to interpret symptoms in one way
as opposed to another. The consequences of the assumption
that medicine is only a science and not an art are important
ingredients in the kinds of medical services offered to patients.

Practitioners of the "science of medicine" are members of
an elite and exclusive club because of the lengthy preparation
that has been required of them. The length and expense of
training assure that only the well-to-do will have relatively
easy access to professional status. That training mystifies
"what the doctor knows" by pretending that all health care
makes use of the same level of complex science that is used
by the research technologist. The elitism of medicine has
been reinforced by the expenditure of a great deal of money
for research laboratories, personnel, and salaries.

Scientific orientation is the backbone of medical training
whether the student is to become a laboratory researcher or
a practicing physician. By contrast, little emphasis is placed
on the art of patient care or the service aspect of medicine;
such concerns are disparagingly labeled "soft" and often

looked upon as a waste of precious time that could be spent learning still more science (to what purpose, one might wonder, if *not* to serve patients?).

At one level there is no conflict between science and art for the practitioner: a scientific understanding of disease and healing provides much of the *content* of her or his work, while the art of caretaking constitutes the *process* of that work. There is no reason why a technically competent physician cannot also take pains to understand and respond to each patient as an individual, whole person. At another level, however, there is a severe conflict, for the establishment of new scientific "facts" (and the disproving of much of what was accepted as scientific "fact" only yesterday) can become a time-filling preoccupation and an energy-consuming obsession.

Much of this starts in medical school. Beginning students are rarely certain about what particular kind of medical practice they will do. The range of knowledge and skills that now underlies the entire practice of medicine (in all of its forms, including the most abstruse specialties) is very wide indeed. No single person could know all the "facts" that relate to all of the areas of medical practice: what the cardiologist must know to give patients good care is somewhat different from what the pediatrician, orthopedic surgeon, or general practitioner must know to provide good care. But medical students are told first that they must master "everything" in order to become reputable and competent physicians; then, when they are overwhelmed with the obvious impossibility of retaining and using such a disconnected welter of information, they are gently urged into specialization, away from interest in generalist care that could give patients control of access to services. They thus emulate their teachers who are, for the most part, specialist practitioners who carefully control the patient's access to their time. As they learn to value the depth of their knowledge in a narrow area of science and technology, they tend to adopt a false intellectual humility that excuses their disinterest in that broader goal, the promotion of health.

Workable arrangements that might enable medical students to learn while personally enmeshed in the life of a community, experiencing the health needs of their own families, kin, friends, and neighbors, have not seemed feasible, or even valuable, to most medical educators. Medical students are socialized, in school and in subsequent training, to believe that the most intellectually *respectable* work is not patient care but scientific research. Students know, for instance, that they are firmly rewarded for learning "facts" and are not rewarded, or are sometimes even criticized, for the inefficiency of pausing to consider their patients as human beings. In one typical instance, a student in a group learning about heart disease asked the instructor to talk to the class about the reaction of a patient's family to illness; the instructor scolded the student for ten minutes about learning to focus on the "important" aspects of the work.

This kind of teaching is reinforced by the myth that "handholding" (a disparaging term for offering aid and comfort) and regard for individual patients as people are dispensable, since they have not been demonstrated to cure serious disease. On the other hand, students are often reminded, the failure to remember one critical "fact" might result some day in a patient's death. That most patients recover largely because of their own intrinsic healing power is information paid only lip service, if that, in medical training. What the physician does is taught as the only *important* ingredient in the healing process.[10]

Actually no practitioner can hope to know, remember, and integrate all of the "facts" (and erase all of those learned and then proved not to be "facts") relevant to the treatment of every life-threatening illness. Only some relatively small part of the whole mountain of scientific information that is related to disease can be reliably applied by any one practitioner to the problems of patients in his or her care, and ultimately most physicians-in-training learn and remember only that body of information that they need to be of help to most of the patients they take care of.

In the meantime, concern about the art of medicine has gone out the window: it is not important, it takes too much time, it will not win the student praise from teachers, and it is not much in evidence in the teachers' manner with patients —especially those who are poor or black or otherwise "not important." In the course of everyday illness, injury, and disability, it is likely that physicians do more harm, more to retard healing, by disregard for the art of medicine than by overlooking "facts." What the patient says, for instance, is often brushed aside by a busy physician rushing to fit a complaint into a plausible diagnostic category. Too often one hears of some disorder—heavy menstrual bleeding, for instance, or belly pain or headaches—treated as "nerves" by "tranquilizer" drugs, which was recognized too late as the sign of a malignant growth. Conversely, gall bladders and wombs are sometimes removed to "treat" patients' insistent requests for information, by physicians who misinterpret queries about the normalcy of physiologic irregularities as wishes for surgical intervention. Patients who do not play a properly submissive, dependent role (and who sometimes even overshoot the mark, becoming brusquely aggressive in their frantic efforts to catch their doctor's attention) may—as a consequence of physicians' general dislike for "trouble-makers"—have their sore throats *not* cultured, their pneumonias *not* treated, their constricting casts *not* remodeled.

One difficulty lies in the impossibility of deciding with complete reliability which instances of illness are "ordinary" (susceptible to being helped by a competent and caring generalist) and which fall into that proportionately small handful that *might* be helped by the full panoply of super-scientific specialism and technology. The fact of this impossibility is not generally shared with patients. "Heroic" treatments can harm or kill as well as cure, and they ought ordinarily to be applied only when the risk of death or disability is high. For most ills, patients are better off trusting to their own curative powers, with *assists* from the art of medicine as it is informed by a scientific understanding of disease.

These "ordinary" ills are regarded as relatively uninteresting by physicians who, having been taught to focus on the wonders of the ever-increasing technology of heroic treatments for desperate but rare diseases, feel *themselves* to be deprived when confronted with common complaints.

Many practitioners trained in modern medical schools have reason to be bored or irritated with everyday ills. Medical training teaches heroism, and yet most physicians have only rare opportunities to be heroic. It teaches control of disease, and yet there is no *specific* treatment or cure for most ill health: arthritis, viral infections such as chicken pox or influenza, the memory loss of old age, the infant's colic, most bruises, bumps, and sprains, and so on. Though medical training teaches that the art of medicine is a second-rate concern, most patients ask, directly or indirectly, to be "cared for." No wonder that many physicians, bored and irritated, treat patients as bothersome interruptions to more important work that they could be doing.

No wonder also that relatively few medical graduates have (until very recently) wanted to become "primary-care" practitioners: generalists who attend to all of the symptoms and complaints that patients bring to them, at all hours of the day and night, providing care for some problems, referring others to specialists, without the status of a specialty that uses elaborate technology and a big bag of heroic treatments.[11] And no wonder that many physicians who do try to provide primary care become discouraged and weary; their training has not taught them to discover which knowledge and skills will be most important in their work, and no one has helped them to foresee their own responses to patients' needs and demands for caretaking.

The generalist used to be called a "general practitioner." That term is now rather discredited in medical circles, both because it has been abandoned by the established agencies of medicine (as representing a low-status, low-power non-specialty practice) and because the old-time generalist style of practice had few opportunities for keeping up to date in

modern, scientific medical knowledge and skills. Now, with
consumers demanding access to a·first-line medical practitioner to whom they can go for all of their complaints, problems, and questions (and who will provide care and information for all but "specialist" matters), there is a new kind of
generalist—the "family practitioner."

Family-practice training programs are now attracting some
of the most talented, service-oriented medical graduates. The
programs themselves are still rather unclear in their direction,
however.[12] The field of family practice can easily become a
tug-of-war between factions: old-style generalists, sociologists
promoting behavioral-science technology, and management-
minded bureaucrats. A recently established program for study
and service in the area of "women and primary health care,"
for example, quickly became a program in "women and
primary healthcare *management*," moving away from the
important (but less prestigious) topics related to the actual
provision of care.

Much of the following discussion about neighborhood
doctors might apply to family practitioners. I have avoided
using the term "family practice" because of my apprehension
that this new specialty is already being limited by the accepted and approved models of the bureaucratic agency.

Neighborhood Doctors

Because almost every aspect of medical training, practice,
and management is now infused with scientism, a disparagement of caretaking, and managerial inflexibility, and is af-
flicted with a hunger for control, we need a new breed of
health-care practitioners: call them "neighborhood doctors."
The neighborhood doctor, in parallel with neighborhood
teacher, *belongs* to the neighborhood by virtue of living there
and having some stake in everyone's efforts toward a health-
promoting environment. The major responsibilities of her or
his work are to promote health and prevent disease, injury,
and disability.

The overwhelming majority of the complaints that now
bring patients to physicians' offices are manageable with the
knowledge and skills of a well-trained, up-to-date generalist
physician, working in collaboration with the patient's own
strengths and wit and self-curative powers, and calling upon
a judicious use of modern drugs and procedures. The remain-
der need referral to specialists or to centralized clinical
facilities for more elaborate diagnosis and therapy.[13] The
neighborhood doctor's job will vary from one neighborhood
to the next, since the focus of the work will be determined by
the needs of residents and will depend on their predispositions to disease, the climate, the environmental hazards, the
nature of working conditions, and the kinds of health education that residents want to use.

There are already isolated examples of doctors who work
in this fashion; most often they are solo practitioners, shaping
the manner in which they work in response to just these
neighborhood factors of need. They can be found in urban
neighborhoods and in towns and rural areas; they spend a
large proportion of their time teaching patients; they usually
have modest incomes; they are mavericks. In the world of bureaucratic medicine, the solo practitioner is "what's wrong
with our medical system," a scapegoat to be stifled. While
solo practitioners are less bureaucratically supervised than
other physicians, and are sometimes notably incompetent
and unreprimanded, they are also sometimes remarkably
innovative and responsive to patients. It is not likely that
the managerial functions of unresponsiveness, inflexibility,
and decreasing innovation—and "covering" for employees in
order to maintain the smooth functioning of the organization—will bring a marked improvement to present medical
practice; if we then had fewer very "bad" doctors, we would
probably also have fewer very "good" doctors. The most
innovative, creative, and adaptive solutions to the special
health needs of specific communities that I have heard of
have been developed by solo practitioners or by small multi-
function groups of health workers, responsive not to mana-

gerial demands but to the demands of patients themselves, supervised in that sense by the neighborhood residents to whom care is delivered.[14]

There are many aspiring medical students who believe that they want to practice medicine in just this fashion. What happens to them? In my work in medical education, I see them stumble at the following hurdles:

1. These students are often not admitted to medical school. Aspiring scientific researchers and specialists, students whose families belong to the privileged social classes, and students with very high grades (who are not very oriented to working for people if they have become accustomed to spending inordinate amounts of time studying in laboratories and libraries) are often preferred as applicants, although we know that students of moderate academic ability perform as well in medical school as do those who are "brilliant."[15]

2. The aspirations of these students are belittled as they progress through medical training; the climate of learning in medical school is so anxiety provoking that they are hard-pressed to hold on to their dreams.[16] Concern for the patient as a person, appreciation of the healing power of caretaking, and expressions of empathy for patients' worries, pain, and discomfort are belittled as "acting like a nurse."[17] (This epithet is applied disparagingly to one physician who has developed a training program for nonphysician pediatric caretakers: it is reported that some medical students look longingly at the training given in this program, parallel to their own, for they had hoped that they would learn some of the same caretaking skills in their medical training.)

3. These students are physically and emotionally separated from their communities of origin: most medical schools are isolated ghettos where one sees only other medical students and physicians and, of course, patients, nurses, and other "assistants" to one's training. When medical students are of such low status, it is overwhelm-

ingly tempting to be grateful that those "others" are even lower. The time commitments of physicians-in-training are so heavy that constant fatigue makes them irritable and unable to maintain social contacts. One medical student remarked that the prevailing philosophy of physicians could only be "pounded into students by first ensuring that they would be separated from the families and communities that they care about."

I believe that the students who are most likely to survive this antipatient, individualistic atmosphere and emerge at the other end of their training with an active sense of empathy, concern, and caring are women, blacks, and other members of underrepresented and poorly served ("minority") groups who are brought to a realization that they "don't fit" in the predominantly white, middle-class, male world of medicine. Some of these students deal with the pain of their psychological (and sometimes physical) exclusion by trying to become as much like the majority as they can. But those who have strong communities of identity, from whom they can derive both support and reassurance that their motives for patient care are valid and valued, have a fighting chance of becoming sensitive caretaking physicians.

"Primary care" has become a fad for the funding of research and special training programs. In its management-dominated form it represents the response of the bureaucratic institution of medical care to consumer demands for generalist physicians. If we are to turn this fad in a direction that will be maximally useful for us and for our families, we must insist that the primary caretaker (1) be trained in science to a level of competence to diagnose and treat the majority of our common diseases; (2) know her or his limitations, and know enough about rare disease and the capabilities of specialists to act as patients' advocates in referrals to more technologically and scientifically sophisticated (and perhaps even heroic) medical care; (3) count health education and preventive health activism as major responsibilities; and (4) *allow*

*us, as patients, to determine how, when, and where we shall
consult them.*

It is the latter issue that most distinguishes the neighborhood doctor from the currently proposed models for "family
physicians" and "primary-care specialists." Instead of requiring that patients always come to the physician, or that only
physicians can decide when and where patients will be seen,
the neighborhood doctor can work with the patient to make
that decision, leaving the final vote, in most instances, with
the patient. Instead of restricting telephone access, the neighborhood doctor can give patients opportunities to call whenever advice or information is needed. Instead of telling patients to return "if there is any trouble," the neighborhood
doctor can outline the process of resolution of disease and
can indicate the *kinds* of questions or problems that might
arise and for which help is available—thus instructing the
patient in the knowledge and skills needed to supervise the
healing. When I played this role (albeit somewhat haltingly,
for I had not been very much helped to learn what I needed
to know and value during the years of my own formal medical training), I learned one thing with certainty: my patients
protected me from unreasonable demands and from exhaus-
tion. It was in their own interest that I stay healthy, content,
and connected to my own family, in order that I be most
fully and competently available to them. *By giving over
control of access to patients, caring is returned reciprocally.*

Must this neighborhood health worker always be a physician? Medical bureaucrats are infatuated with the notion
that only science (and not art) is intellectually exciting;
primary care is simultaneously and illogically disparaged as
both "intellectually unstimulating" and "too complex and
ambiguous to be understood." Managers of medical care
often argue that some "paramedical" worker ought to fill
the role of primary caregiver. The question is largely one of
semantics: who is to be called "doctor?" As a doctor, I hope
that the primary-care role will not be preempted; it is a
critically important role for the health of families, and it is
enormously gratifying and complex to carry out.

I believe, however, that entirely new training programs,
free of the inflexible traditionalism and the status-elite hier-
archies of the present agencies of medical care, are needed
to give workers (either doctors or other health personnel)
appropriate preparation for this job. The title itself—doctor,
nurse, health advocate—is less important than the knowledge,
skills, attitudes, and responsibilities to be exercised.

There is real danger, also, that medical bureaucrats will not
allow all of the functions of the "neighborhood doctor" to be
carried out by one person, through the control of training
programs, certification, and licensing. "Emergency medicine"
is becoming a specialty, for instance; it is now very difficult
for anyone who does not work full time in an emergency
room, intensive-care unit, or other "emergency care" job to
be accepted for training—even refresher training—in the techniques of emergency care. It may be that soon no physicians
(not even primary-care physicians)will be allowed to become
proficient in emergency care, unless they do that kind of work
on a full-time basis.

We as consumers of health care have a responsibility to
our families and to our wider communities of identity to
band together as a coalition of clients with any and all health
workers who see the need for appropriately trained primary
caretakers. We have a responsibility to support and encourage
medical students from our own neighborhoods, so that they
do not forget why they wanted to become trained as physicians. We could, for instance, have some voice in the process
of selecting students for medical school admission;[18] could
help finance their education with supplementary public-fund
vouchers, so that poor communities are as able to support
their own interests as are other communities; and could continually inform "our" students of our health needs and ask
students to inform us, in return, during the course of their
training, so that we gain in knowledge and skills along with
our future physicians.

In addition, we have a responsibility to show that we value
good health care when we find it—an especially difficult task

because of natural resentment at the impositions of illness or discomfort and anxiety about the outcome. While a payment structure that rewards the primary caretaker for effort and time expended (not only in diagnosing and treating disease, but also in promoting health and educating families about their own health needs and competencies) would greatly encourage the role of the neighborhood doctor, this need not come through a national health service or insurance prgram; vouchers and prepayments-for-care arrangements can also be worked out with neighborhood control. Finally, some neighborhoods already have competent and caring physicians who might be willing to experiment with innovative practice patterns, given the incentive of working with a mutually responsible and caring community of consumers.

The fact is, much of what we need to know to take good care of our health can be learned and performed within families, with the supervision of the neighborhood doctor. Layfolk can learn, for instance, how to take cultures of sore throats, and can incubate them in their ovens or at a neighborhood health unit with a small and simple laboratory; the cultures can be read by anyone in the neighborhood who has learned this rather easy skill. Many health-maintenance tests are so simple that they can be performed by almost anyone, including children: skin tests for TB, urine screening tests for diabetes and chronic renal disease by dipstick, urine tests for pregnancy, and blood pressure measurements, could all be done on a drop-in basis at a neighborhood health unit—which might, for instance, be in the same building as the local school or daycare center. If a test were positive, or difficult to interpret, one could then check with the neighborhood doctor or another health-team worker. And many techniques of diagnosis and treatment (some easy principles of physical diagnosis, for instance, and some understanding of disease processes, wound healing, and the actions of drugs) *should be known by family members.* [19]

The neighborhood health center can be part of a neighborhood house: a site for teaching, day care, after-school activi-

ties for older children, a crafts center, a toy and equipment
bank, a service and activities center for aged neighbors, and
so on. It can serve as the service site of neighborhood health
care and also as a resource library and an organizational
center for neighborhood action on health needs. It is likely
that health screening, like most health action, could be done
more regularly and carefully if we each were responsible
for ourselves and for members of our families, rather than
relying on the initiative of medical professionals. Tests for
the early stages of those diseases that can be treated before
they develop symptoms, the maintenance of immunizations,
and the monitoring of safety at our job sites and our homes
are matters of immediate and personal concern to *us*.[20]

We do not want, nor should we want, to do without the
competent services of well-trained physicians. When time is
short and the problem urgent ("a matter of life and death"),
we want rapid access to skilled and knowledgeable care,
either to resolve the problem or to facilitate referral to a
technologically sophisticated center. Some of the special
knowledge and skills of the physician are not easy for layfolk
to learn, especially when they need not be used frequently:
reading an X-ray, for instance, or drawing blood from the
vein of a small child. When the diagnosis or the treatment is
ambiguous, or when we are so stressed that we prefer to give
over the responsibility of making a decision, we may want
to "put ourselves in the hands" of competent and caring
skill.

In the latter case, it is important to distinguish between
the better *care* that professionals might give and the assumption of *risk* by professional caregivers. For instance, a child
with a moderately severe head injury with no immediate
signs of residual damage needs to be observed closely for
eighteen to twenty-four hours in case danger signals should
appear and surgery be necessary. In a hospital, nurses do
no more sophisticated observation than parents could do at
home if they were instructed and lent the necessary equipment; a surgical team can usually be mobilized as quickly

when the child comes to the hospital from home, given proper transportation facilities, as when the child is already in the hospital. Parents may, however, prefer to have the child watched overnight in the hospital, knowing that death or permanent and serious disability are possible (though statistically unlikely) outcomes. Professionals are paid to take significant and high-risk responsibility if requested to do so by patients.

On the other hand, the question of hospitalizing an elderly grandparent dying of widespread cancer might be decided differently, taking into account the same questions of responsibility and risk. If cared for at home, the patient might die a day or a week sooner—that is, in the hospital, death might be stayed temporarily. But if the grandparent and other family members do not need additional time to prepare themselves psychologically for the death, then the risk of losing a few days of life might seem insignificant compared to the positive values, both to the dying person and to other family members who care for that person, of dying amidst the familiar comforts of home.

In both cases, while professional knowledge and skills may be more "efficient" than home-based care, that difference is not significant for the ill or injured patient; what is significant is the degree of risk of an unhappy outcome that could bring guilt and double grief for family members. One of the responsibilities of professional caregivers is to assume such risks when asked to do so by informed patients and/or their families.

Providing Our Own Health Care

All of us could learn to be more competent, but only if we wrest the knowledge and skills from experts and professionals; we have a right to be taught and to seek the specific information we need from a variety of sources:

Children in grade school can learn how to take their

own temperatures, to examine their own throats and
decide if a throat culture should be taken, to examine
their lymph nodes for swelling and tenderness. They
can learn the vocabulary of pain well enough to describe
their own symptoms intelligibly: sharp, aching, dull,
steady, off and on, on the skin, just under the skin,
deep, and so on. They can understand why their bodies
need a variety of nutrients for growth, replacement, and
energy, and why their bodies do not benefit from non-
food chemical additives. They can understand how to
wash and bandage abrasions, scratches, and cuts to discourage infection and promote healing. They can learn
how infections spread by the droplets of sneezing and
coughing, by touching an oozing wound, and by fecal
contamination from unwashed hands. They can learn
to foresee the dangers of poisonous substances in the
household, and to run "poison checks" in any space
used by preschool children. And they can learn the
value of testing each other for TB, diabetes, and high
blood pressure. All of these health matters concern
children in their own lives, and they can be taught as
the occasion arises. When children have mild illnesses
or injuries, they can also learn through self-care. This
kind of learning illustrates the use of our own selves as
resources for self-help and for caring for others. None
of this learning is meant to substitute for the privilege
of allowing oneself to be cared for at a time of an illness
or injury, but, if the child wants, the caring can be a
collaboration between caretaker and patient. Health
education in our schools, if it is to have any meaning
and utility for our children, must be related to keeping
ourselves healthy, recognizing when we are ill, and finding help so that we can get better.

   Adolescents can learn more complicated skills: how
to take and read throat and urine cultures, and pregnancy tests, how to take blood samples from a finger prick,
and how to provide simple first aid, such as splinting a

possible fracture and applying a pressure dressing to a
bleeding wound. Adolescents can also learn nursing care
for others: how to keep a home record of fever and
symptoms; a record of fluids taken in and lost, as in
vomiting and diarrhea; how and when to apply dressings
to a skin inflammation like "poison ivy." In addition,
adolescents can learn more abstractly about the helpful
and dangerous effects of drugs and about our bodies'
own mechanisms to ward off and respond to infection,
inflammation, and wounds.

Adults can learn new skills at their neighborhood
health center. Knowledge and skills not used regularly
usually dwindle, of course; those that have been forgotten can usually be relearned quickly as the need
arises. Some of what was learned earlier will have been
superseded by new knowledge and improved skills. But
the most important thing is that we would come to
adult membership in families with an appreciation of
the strengths and fragilities of our bodies, a sense of
competence in dealing with everyday health problems,
and a vocabulary to use in seeking new information. We
would be prepared to be teachers of our children.

While no one who is sick or injured should be denied privacy, the opportunity to use an individual's misfortune as
an occasion for caring and concern can be a comfort to the
patient and a reassurance to onlookers that pain can be
lessened, comforts brought, and, for some diseases, curative
measures applied. Knowledge that a competent resource (a
skilled layperson or a nurse or the neighborhood doctor) can
be found when requested also increases our own abilities to
cope.

But what of severe trauma, cancer, heart attacks, and
strokes? These are massive malfunctions and certainly cannot
be well cared for without heroic methods. Emergency care
and comfort and the assurance that skilled help will be made
available as quickly as possible would go far to allay the

psychic misery of these disasters; their definitive care will
often require hospitalization for access to twenty-four hour
nursing, machinery for monitoring and assisting vital functions, and the closely supervised application of life-saving
treatments that introduce the possibility of harmful effects.
Hospital stays could be shortened, however, if there were
neighborhood resources for competent home-based care, and
supportive supervision for the kin, friends, and neighbors who
take the responsibility for that care.[21] There is evidence that
home nursing is as effective as hospitalization in the period
of recovery from a heart attack.[22] Similarly, midwife-attended
home births are as safe as hospital births for most deliveries,
primarily because the midwife is less likely than the hospital-
based physician to interfere with the normal process of birth
by applying "treatments" with the potential of doing harm.

We have been robbed, by our conventional arrangements
for professionalized medical care, of our competence to
promote the good health of our families and to provide
skilled home-based care. We have even been "relieved" of
our participation in birth and death. We have allowed ourselves to hope that the "science of medicine" will, if we
give it enough rope, keep us all alive forever—for fighting
death has been the physician's major goal. We have almost
forgotten that there is more to health care than the application of chemicals and technology. Physicians have been
taught *not* to take care, and to be not servants but masters
of those they take care of. Medical care has focused on
"being alive," as a product; health care demands attention
to the quality of life, a process. As patients, we have forgotten how to claim what should be ours: the ability to take
good care of ourselves and those we love and trust, in sickness and in health.

even your desertions,
your betrayals,
your failure to understand and love us,
your unwillingness to face the world
as staunchly as we do;
these things
which ravage us,
cannot destroy our lives,
though they often take our bodies.
We are the earth.
We wake up
finding ourselves
glinting in the dark
after thousands of years
of pressing.

—Diane Wakoski

9 GOING BEYOND

There was a time, we like to believe, when we could hope to
choose with confidence between easily defined good and bad
alternatives. Our wish to do "the right thing" is based on our
continuing, if perplexed, adherence to nineteenth-century
philosophy, the historical root of our faith that with the use
of a careful scientific approach and perseverance we will learn
the secrets of a universe that is rationally and morally ordered.

It may once have been functional to assume that there
always *is* one clearly better alternative, more useful, proper,
and moral than all others. When in past experience that
preferable and morally commendable choice was not readily
evident, it was assumed that we did not have enough information to identify the "right" choice. We firmly proposed
that any clear-thinking, fair-minded person could and would
choose the proper path if only enough were known about
the problem; those who did not make the "right" choice
were ignorant or morally reprehensible. Some of us want

still to cling to that model, although it seems to work less and less well for us.

We now live in the midst of a social complex that defies the selection of one clearly "right" alternative. Ambiguities and uncertainties lie on every side. Is it "better," for instance, to be a full-time homemaker, or to spend some of our energies working at paid jobs? Is it "better" for a father to take part-time work, which would permit him to spend time caring for his children, or to work full time or more to gain the money and status that will help his children in other ways? Is it "better" to move to a suburb, safe and clean, or to stay in the city with kin and friends at close reach? How could anyone know, for sure? Increasingly, answers include the qualification, "it depends."

Changes come with dizzying rapidity. Sometimes we create our own changes—we quit our jobs mid-career to return to school or take a different kind of work. Sometimes we passively witness changes washing over us—our children take on work and family styles that we never would have envisioned for them. And sometimes changes are imposed on us without our consent—urban renewal projects destroy our neighborhoods, taxes are raised, fuel rationed, or a war fought. How can we predict the consequences of our choices when the grounds on which they are made, the very grounds on which we stand, seem to shift so unexpectedly and in so many directions? If we focus intently on a desperate, anxiety-ridden holding to *status quo*, it is difficult to see any shifts as part of an organic flow, a connected process; we can then only react, abruptly and reflexively, to single and separate changes as dislocations without meaning. "Who would have thought, five years ago, that we would be . . . ?"

Furthermore, we are connected to a bewilderingly more far-reaching array of events and people than ever before. We are forced to recognize these connections by the notions of a "global village" and a "whole earth"; by our ability to "see it now," all over the world, on television; and by our growing interconnections with other people, both in our

immediate surroundings and in other parts of the world—
often nameless or even faceless people whom we might meet
personally only once, or perhaps never.

These connections make us feel pressed to think of *all*
of the consequences of our decisions, but that "all" can
hardly be comprehended. The consequences and their ramifications appear to be almost endlessly complex, and we
cannot be certain that the information that we find (or that
we are told) is accurate and relevant. We do not know whether we know enough to compose a mental picture of the effects
of hypothetical choices.

For example:

> If one moves from the city to the country and has to
> travel more by automobile than by bicycle, will that
> affect our nation's use of energy resources? Our relations
> with Mideast countries? The resources available to poor
> nations?

> If we fail to intervene to prevent the collapse of
> some of our enormous bureaucratic organizations (for
> example, if some of our major universities fall), will
> the remaining organizations simply be strengthened in
> their present policies, or will they then become more
> responsive to human needs? What will happen to our
> national policies if there are fewer opportunities for
> university education, a populace "less educated" in the
> formal sense? What about those children who look
> forward to being trained for professional jobs?

> If we send food to a starving nation and refuse to
> impose controls on their birthrates, will we help them
> or hurt them? Does it matter what food we send, and
> on what terms? Is it worse to prohibit individual freedom
> (or national self-determination) with regard to concep-
> tion and birth, or to watch while babies starve to death?
> Can we afford to give away our own resources when
> children in this country are starving? Do we, in fact,
> have enough food potential to feed everyone?

Each decision seems connected to so many persons whom
we don't want to hurt, even inadvertently; to so many con-
tingencies that we do not believe we can foresee; and to such
immeasurable ambiguity that we cannot seem to clarify, that
the hope of choosing a clearly "right" path begins to seem
foolish, if not maddening. Much as we would like to believe
that the experts themselves have clear vision and comprehend
as a connected whole "all of the available information," it
seems increasingly apparent that they, too, have only bits
and pieces, which become distorted and garbled by their
own self-interest—for they, like we, are human and not
really made of glass and steel.

One solution to this general dilemma that has been suggested to us is an *extension* of rationalist philosophy: the
hope of selecting the "right" answer with the assistance of
computers—automated processing of information. We are
told that the intuitive ingredient to human thought is now
quite useless, that facts properly nested in facts will cause
the "right" answer to roll from the machine.[1] And indeed
"right" answers do roll out, and then, to our astonishment,
contradict one another in parallel or in sequence. Consider
the "solutions" to our national economic problems; these
solutions are apparently derived rationally, with the assistance
of the most modern aids in the collection and analysis of
data, but one after another they flatly contradict what has
been proposed before. Having been told that our intuition
is no longer to be relied upon, we now discover that neither
we ourselves *nor* our machines can locate, identify, and connect all the information we would need to discover single,
reliable, "right" choices. (Could it be that the imperfect
outputs of our machines reflect the intuitive humanity of
their inputs?)

In point of fact, it is most likely that there never was a
time when making a "right" choice was simply a matter of
having enough information to point the way. "Enough" information was, in other times, an elusive goal at best. It was
believed that by working toward that goal with enthusiasm

and hope, a rational, ordered world and a clarification of our
own rightful places as individuals could be reached; the goal
was hoped for not only as attainable but also as unquestionably desirable.

What has happened is that our technologies have thrust
us into a state of information overload, and we have no
corresponding set of rules by which to arrange, order, and
make use of that information. We know "too much" without
knowing enough to comprehend what is important and what
is not, what is rendered useless by errors inherent in the
collection and dispersal of information, and what important
bits—needed to make the whole—are still missing, whether
by intent or otherwise.

And what of our discredited intuition? It appears to many
to be (still or again) a useful, even valuable, process, a human
capability that has been discouraged and driven underground
by a rationalist, scientistic approach. In actuality, intuitiveness
has always given birth to the real discoveries in science as in
other human endeavors. First a direction, a connection, is
perceived. Only later do we rationally (or even obsessively)
exhaust ourselves with the facts and figures of precise detail.
But because so much of scientific and technological development is relatively mechanistic and uncreative, the role of
intuition appears to have diminished.

One resolution of the gut-wrenching dilemma surrounding
choice is to consider that perhaps one can never find and use
enough information to be certain, and that, in fact, there
may not *be* single "right" choices as universal moral values.
If we trust ourselves to seek the apparent best of all possible
alternatives, by a combination of what we know from a
reasoned connection of facts and what we know through
intuition (being aware that we are always selective on both
sides), then we can learn to weigh risks and benefits in all
possible choices. We can believe that our considered decisions
need to be *best for us*, even if they do not necessarily have
a framework of absolutistic morality. We can also know that

a climate of change means that we will have other chances.
"It all depends."

It is in the realm of personal behavior and family life that
we seem consistently to have the most freedom, and the
most frequent opportunities, to exercise real choice. We can
weigh risks and benefits, and choose courses that seem to
contain the least harm and the most good, only if we know
ourselves and others in our families as well as it is possible
for us to do. We can then try to consider risks and benefits
for each of us as individuals and for all of us as a group.

To be free of the spectre of the single "right" choice
means that we can release ourselves from dependent submission on experts and professionals. If, for example, there
is no absolute "right" way to toilet-train a toddler (if indeed
"it depends" on the nature of the child, the child rearing
propensities of her or his parents, and the history of their
living together and their hopes for the future), then one need
not slavishly follow the faddist dictates of child-development
specialists, nor be worried sick if one's methods differ from
those recommended by the currently popular expert. If
there is no absolute "right" way for parents to distribute
their joint time between work and child care (if indeed "it
depends" on the relative energy levels of mother and father,
the desire of each to become attached to their child, their
need for income and satisfaction in productive work, the
kinds of work available to them, the particular nature and
needs of the child, among other considerations), then one
need not apprehensively wait for some researcher to discover
the solution. We can, knowing our own family constellations,
use "facts" and intuitions to work out our own best solutions. It should not be difficult to recognize intuitiveness as
a critical and essential factor in what we count as important,
essential and true within our families.

To have freedom and range of choice means that many
choices will be discarded. Current talk about broad spec-
trums of possible options is sometimes saddening, if we
mourn all of the options we have *not* chosen. In contrast

with the possibilities that have been foregone, our measly choices seem scant and sparse. And yet I wonder if there is not some misunderstanding of the meaning of "widening options" for substance and style in family living. Surely for any one family there is only a narrow range of possible choices.

Mistakes will be made. Of course, this is severely derogated in our culture: school children—like professional trainees—learn, as a basic lesson, that there are only single "right" answers (which the teacher knows) and that to attempt a flight of imaginative inquiry may bring error and lead to punishment. When we face and accept mistakes as inevitable consequences of making *any* decisions, then we can also discover the options for righting them.

If, in our society, a wide variety of styles of family living were *allowed*, we would have many options to choose among. There would not be an enormous smorgasbord to "pick" from, but the opportunity to select a composite that reflects our own preferences and needs and accommodates the maxim of "first of all, do no harm." For each family group, many possible options will in fact be out of the question; only a few will fall within the range of tolerance or preference of the small, intensely caring group. Among those few, choices can be made according to a best approximation of weighing foreseeable risks and benefits, a process that must be partly intuitive. Changes within a family group will also evolve over time, if personal growth is of any substance. Over the whole life cycle of a family, doing "no harm" sometimes means choosing to repair harm done in the past, unforeseen or unavoidable.

The real change in this incredibly important process by which families make real choices for themselves is to abandon the requirement of looking to authorities for instructions about "right" choices. Authorities rarely know us as more than average statistics. We, ourselves, have the best chance of understanding our own tolerances and preferences.

Experts, managers, and professionals have a great investment in the control, even manipulation, of our choices. Some of our options—in kinds of available jobs, for instance, or in the possibilities of prolonging life—are the direct result of efforts to develop and then use (and sell) new technologies of media, science, education, medicine. Other options— such as new attitudes toward sexuality and sexual behavior, or new interest in food with a minimum of chemicals added— become grist for new efforts to manipulate and control. The development and selling of entertainment (TV programs and magazines, for instance, which serve as vehicles for advertisements) and other products such as "sexy" automobiles, elaborately packaged and partly processed foods, and manufactured vitamins make our interests seem tawdry before we can fairly examine them. As long as we mistrust our own abilities to choose for ourselves and believe that "experts know best" because they hold the key to an assemblage of information pointing to single "right" choices, we allow ourselves to be subject to manipulation and control by people who know us (as people) not at all.

If we cannot look to authorities for *advice* that is reliable and trustworthy, we lose the "magic" contained in the authoritarianism of those transactions. We know that the kind of magic that is based on belief in superpowers can be incredibly comforting and anxiety reducing. Where can we put our hope and our reliance if we are no longer to look to experts and professionals to pronounce the uniquely "right" answers to our perplexities?

Some "healers" from a variety of cultures (our own experts and professionals included) insist that the magic and the power reside in *them*. Others claim that their only magic or power is to energize the potential that always resides in the one who comes to seek help, a potential temporarily blocked but there to be released. Our experts and professionals have been content to believe that the best magic lies in their presumed command of the concepts and technologies of science. By mystifying science, pretending that it could not be understood by ordinary folk, hoping that the cures for all ills could only be found by scientists, and believing that whatever is worth "knowing" is within the realm of scientific techniques, they have diminished their potential for helping and healing. Sharing knowledge and skills is one way of unlocking that potential. The true power of helping and healing resides within everyone.

Magic and trust are curative, more so than many of the drugs in our formularies, many of our technological solutions, and most of the assistance of superbrain computers. If the magic of experts and professionals is demystified and we thus lose the power of *that* magic, must we then flounder, lose our bearings, destroy what good we have attained in our "advanced" civilization?

I propose that a model for transactions of *mutual trust*, the source of a kind of magic we are only beginning to rediscover, is to be found in the assistance provided by a midwife at birth. At a home birth the midwife, fortified with transportable oxygen, suction, intravenous solutions, and a rapid transport system that permits hospitalization in case of unforeseen disaster, comes to attend when labor pains begin to be regular. Assisting in the preparations, instructing family members in their part in the event and their collaborative support of the delivering mother, the midwife encourages and coaxes the birth in its *own due time*. The process builds to the peak of the moment of the crowning head, but the midwife's assistance continues—to clean up after the delivery of the afterbirth, return the house to order, support the exhilarated and exhausted participants and observers, assist in the feeding of the new family member, and share in the rejoicing. The midwife informs, teaches, and allows the magical powers of trust and caring to envelop the family, the mother, and infant. The root of caring is to respect the rhythms, needs, and abilities of another. The family's trust in the midwife, and the midwife's trust in the competence of family members, are the basis of caring that has the power of magic.

There are risks here, as everywhere. Someone must choose

which risks we, as individuals and as families, are willing to
tolerate and find least offensive and frightening. If we are to
choose for ourselves, we must have as much information as
can be fairly laid out without huckstering, without jargon,
and without intimidation.

Caring is not an impossible component in the services of
agency-based experts and professionals but—at least for
now—it a very secondary commodity in bureaucratic settings.[2]
Perhaps our best hope of calling forth the caring potential
of professionals (as people who *can* care) lies in our own
potential for confident self-esteem derived from competence. To become competent to help ourselves, we must
learn to "help ourselves" to the knowledge and skills that
we need. Sometimes we will choose the services available to
us from kin, friends, and others whom we know and trust
rather than professional services. No safe passage, no "perfect" outcome is ever guaranteed to us. Certainly the risks
associated with uncaring and the inability to demonstrate
trustworthiness are important considerations in our choices.

Unless we are to become a nation of isolated, uncommitted, independent individuals who *cannot* care for one another,
we will continue to live in families. Our families are now in
peril, and the most likely source of real help seems to lie in
the magic of caring, to be discovered within ourselves and
all those we learn to trust. As we gain more knowledge and
more skills, we can use and build upon the assistance to be
found from experts and professionals who are not our friends
or neighbors. But helping and healing ourselves is a responsibility that only we can initiate.

This healing potential can expand beyond the family and
the social network. We have so much creativity, intelligence,
and energy locked into guilt, despair at our personal impotence, and self-hate at our presumed incompetence that we
have not begun to contemplate our power and potential
for the active healing of society itself. If we could go beyond
our enforced dependency and presumed incompetence, our
guilt about making mistakes and being "less than perfect,"

our disbelief in and mistrust of trust, our fear of responsibility and our consequent inability to deal successfully with choices, and our constricted denial of the usefulness of intuition, we could release energy, creativity, and the wisdom of our own experience. We could go beyond our immediate families and care about others. Perhaps we can only start and hope to make it possible for our children in their adult lives to live as whole persons.

We cannot guarantee to our children that what they can create within their own families or in their wider society will be "perfect" or unflawed. But what we can hope to achieve, within our own families and on behalf of our children and ourselves, is a valuing and appreciation of the *process* by which we strive; we have, potentially far more control over that process than we have over the end result. The products can be no better than the means through which we work toward them. If "bad lives" make "bad theory,"[3] then we can only hope to heal society with a simultaneous attention to the quality of our personal relations. *First of all, do no harm* can be made to apply in societal affairs, as in professional services, only when it is a governing principle in the process of our intimate relations with our spouses and children, our kin, friends and neighbors, and our communities.

There are characteristics of our family relationships, and characteristics of the behavior of experts, managers, and professionals, that are parallel: lack of trust, individualistic competition for scarce resources, ready use of blame and guilt as explanatory concepts, fear of error, expectation of "right"-ful perfection, and denial of intuition. Experts, managers, and professionals blame families for engendering these characteristics, while family members often feel that their interactions with institutions outside of the family induce these qualities in their own internal relations. Perhaps it is less than useful to seek to fix blame on individuals, either members of families *or* experts, managers, or professionals. Perhaps the institutions that govern us, and for which we are all responsible, drive us not only to hurt each other but also to blame each other for our hurting. Our institutions, which are made up of human networks, are simply our conventional arrangements for getting things done. Like the choices families make with regard to their internal affairs, our institutions are not entirely arbitrary in form; they reflect the ends that they serve. But neither are our institutions fixed and unchangeable; they are not determined either by our biological natures nor by moral absolutes. We use them, and they affect our lives. We could have options in the ways we work, care for our children, find education, and promote our health; we could redirect our institutional human networks to different ends and, in doing so, change their forms.

I do not believe that we can grow out of alienation and mistrust by accepting the ministrations and manipulations of experts, managers, and professionals, who too often simply cover over our wounds and disguise our sickness, treating only symptoms and thereby permitting and promoting new instances in which we must depend on them. Putting our families into their *own* perspective, caring and trusting and respecting their integrity, can release us to let out our intuitive creativeness into broader concerns. Only by helping ourselves to help our families, by attending to the process of caring, can we—with impact and substance—right the institutions of our society.

NOTES

Foreword

1. I have used the terms *patient, client, consumer,* and *layperson* interchangeably, although each has rather different connotations. According to *Webster's Third New International Dictionary, patient* has an archaic meaning of "one who suffers, endures, or is victimized," and a modern meaning of "one who is subjected to action or external force—opposed to *agent." Client* means "a person under the protection of another," as a *vassal. Consumer* means "one who utilizes economic goods," clearly emphasizing the commercial transaction of caregiving. The term that I prefer—in either of my roles as caregiver or as recipient of care— is *layperson,* which means simply "not belonging to some particular profession or not expert in some branch of knowledge or art"; it is good to know that the Greek root is *laikos,* "of the people."

2. A handful of books, autobiographical or fictional, that are said to give authentic portrayals of some kinds of families rarely presented in a positive light, or at all, in our social science literature:

Black families: Ernest J. Gaines, *The Autobiography of Miss Jane Pittman* (New York: Dial Press, 1971); Lorraine Hansberry, *A Raisin in the Sun* (New York: New American Library, 1961); Margaret Walker, *Jubilee* (Boston: Houghton Mifflin, 1966); Anne

Moody, *Coming of Age in Mississippi* (New York: Dial Press, 1968).

Chicano families: Jose L. Navarro, *Blue Day on Main Street* (Berkeley: Quinto Sol Publications, 1973); Tomas Rivera, *Y No Se Lo Trago la Tierra: And the Earth Did Not Part* (Berkeley: Quinto Sol Publications, 1971); Rudolfo Anaya, *Bless Me, Ultima* (Berkeley: Quinto Sol Publications, 1972).

Indian families: N. Scott Momoday, *The Way to Rainy Mountain* (Albuquerque: University of New Mexico Press, 1969), Kiowa; R. A. Lafferty, *Okla Hannali* (New York: Doubleday, 1972), Choctaw; George Clutesi, *Potlach* (Sydney, B.C.: Grey's Publishing, 1969), Salish.

Eskimo families: Charles C. Hughes, *Eskimo Boyhood* (Lexington, University of Kentucky Press, 1974).

Puerto Rican (Boricuan) families: Piri Thomas, *Down These Mean Streets* (New York: Alfred Knopf, 1967); Elena Padilla, *Up From Puerto Rico* (New York: Columbia University Press, 1958); Pablo Figueroa, *Enrique* (New York: Hill and Wang, 1970).

Poor and nonurban white families: Harriette Arnow, *The Dollmaker* (New York: Macmillan, 1972); Kathy Kahn, *Hillbilly Women* (Garden City, N.Y.: Doubleday, 1973); Harper Lee, *To Kill a Mockingbird* (Philadelphia: Lippincott, 1960); Chaim Potok, *My Name Is Asher Lev* (New York: Alfred Knopf, 1972).

With apologies for the books that I did not hear about that should have been on this list, I am grateful to Dorothy Burlage, Manuel Teruel, Carolyn Attneave, Alvin Pouissaint, Lucilla Quinones, Maria Elena de la Garza, and Denice Aguirre Johnston.

1
Breaking Locks

1. R. D. Laing, *The Politics of the Family and Other Essays* (New York: Pantheon, 1971); David Cooper, *The Death of the Family* (New York: Pantheon, 1970); and Shulamith Firestone, *The Dialectic of Sex* (New York: William Morrow, 1970), are examples of recent commentaries on the oppression of family life; they focus primarily on *nuclear* family style.

2. See, for instance, Alvin L. Schorr, *Poor Kids: A Report On Children in Poverty* (New York: Basic Books, 1966); S. M. Miller and Frank Riessman, *Social Class and Social Policy* (New York: Basic Books, 1968); The Children's Defense Fund, *Annual Reports* (Washington, D.C.: Washington Research Project, 1973, 1974); and U. S. Congress, Senate Subcommittee on Children and Youth, *Hearings*

on American Families: Trends and Pressures, Congressional Record
118, no. 142 (1973), for analyses of the effects of U.S. public
policies on the well-being of families.

3. These statistics on changing family composition are from
the following sources: U. S. Department of Commerce, Bureau of
the Census, *Current Population Reports*, series P-20, no. 271, table
4 (Washington, D. C.: Government Printing Office, 1974); A. J.
Norton and Paul C. Glick, "Marital Instability: Past, Present and
Future," *Journal of Social Issues* (forthcoming 1975); Mary Jo
Bane, "Marital Disruption and the Lives of Children," *Journal of
Social Issues* (forthcoming 1975); and personal communication
from Paul C. Glick and Robert Weiss. There is some false security
in "explaining" or "predicting" family events from census data:
what we know as "new data" was usually collected one or more
years before, and often represents events that occurred even earlier.
For instance, divorce occurs, on the average, some seven years after
marriage; if marriage rates for any given year are compared with
divorce rates for that year, we are comparing couples who married
in one year with couples who married, on the average, seven years
before. Those who *remarry* in the index year were married for
the first time, on the average, some nine years before. The three
groups—first married, divorced, and remarried—are different people.

4. See Mary Howell, "Employed Mothers and Their Families,"
Pediatrics 52, no. 2 (1973): 252-63; idem, "Effects of Maternal
Employment on the Child," *Pediatrics* 52, no. 3 (1973): 327-43,
for an analysis of research about employed mothers.

5. The Commission on Population Growth and the American
Future, *Population and the American Future* (New York: Signet,
1972), pp. 127-8; the "potential earnings" of parents who care for
children are so low that it is apparent that the commission assumes
that these parents are always women. The figures are now outdated
by our sharply increased cost of living.

6. See, for instance, Marc J. Roberts, "On the Nature and Condition of Social Science," and Don K. Price, "Money and Influence:
The Links of Science to Public Policy," *Daedalus* 103, no. 3 (1974),
for mild-mannered discussions of the politics and values of "doing
science," by members of the academic establishment.

7. See, for instance, Lenore J. Weitzman, "Legal Regulation of
Marriage: Tradition and Change," *California Law Review* 62, no.
4 (1974): 1169-1288, for a detailed analysis of the legal aspects of
marriage contracts. Rosabeth Kanter, in *Communes: Creating and
Managing the Collective Life* (New York: Harper and Row, 1973),
gives an overview of communal and collective family styles.

8. I am grateful to Dr. Mary Rowe, Special Assistant to the

President and Chancellor of M.I.T. for Women and Work, for this
observation, based on information collected from daycare center
personnel (proportion of fathers who make arrangements for out-
of-family child care), from employers (fathers requesting work releases
for household responsibilities), and from her own extensive counseling
with employed spouses and parents.

9. A recent summary of the options for housewives' wages is
given in David G. Gil, *Unravelling Social Policy* (Cambridge, Mass.:
Schenkman, 1973).

10. Judson T. Landis, "The Trauma of Children When Parents
Divorce," *Marriage and Family Living* 22, no. 1 (1960): 7-13.

11. The nature of "intuitive knowing" is the subject of some
debate; see, for instance, Jerome S. Bruner, *On Knowing: Essays
for the Left Hand* (New York: Atheneum, 1965); Theodore Roszak,
"The Monster and the Titan: Science, Knowledge and Gnosis,"
Daedalus 103, no. 3 (1974): 17-32; and Gunther S. Stent, "Limits
to the Scientific Understanding of Man [*sic*]," *Science* 187, no.
4181 (1975): 1052-7.

12. See Lawrence LeShan, *The Medium, The Mystic, and The
Physicist* (New York: Viking Press, 1974), for a recent discussion
of intuition and scientific discovery.

13. See, for instance, Margaret Mead, *Culture and Commitment*
(New York: Doubleday, 1970); and Women's Research Center of
Boston, *Report of Women's Opinion Survey, October, 1974* (Needham,
Mass.: Women's Department of Issues and Involvement, WCVB-TV,
1974), for discussion and documentation of rapid and radical change
in the way we collectively view our "realities."

14. Robert Massie and Suzanne Massie, in *Journey* (New York:
Alfred Knopf, 1975), offer a poignant illustration of our institutionalized arrangement of excusing the unhelpfulness of bureaucratized human services (medical care, in this instance) by blaming
the helpseeker for her or his "problem." I am grateful also to Ted
Scott for pointing out that to label a child "hyperactive," "minimally
brain damaged," or "having a learning disorder" serves to blame
otherwise "good" children for falling in the lower ranks of schools'
evaluations of their "worth"—a function of schools that sometimes
takes precedence over education.

15. See also "Physical Checkup Rewards Urged," *Boston Sunday
Globe*, 3 March 1975, for a proposed system of "rewards, penalties,
or possibly both" to force everyone to see a physician at least once
a year.

2
The Family Within Us

1. Marge Piercy, *To Be Of Use* (New York: Doubleday, 1973),
p. vi.

2. I am deeply indebted, for both my appreciation of the funny/
awesome diversity of family life and my respect for this essential
sex difference, to these good friends: Louise Kerr, Denice Johnston,
Serena Mailloux, Victoria Roemele, Barbara Rosenkrantz, Mary
Rowe, and Kathy Weingarten.

3. Rosabeth Kanter, "Intimate Oppression," *The Sociological
Quarterly* 15 (1974): 302-14.

4. Recent thinking in the feminist movement has begun to explore
these subtleties of interpersonal control, dwelling not only on "being
in control" but also on the relinquishing of control to another—
either a status equal (often another woman, sometimes a spouse)
or a status subordinate (child, student, client, patient). With status
equals, control can be in finely tuned alternation; with status subor-
dinates, the gradual shift of control, which of course works to decrease
the discrepancy in status, is a goal of appropriate caretaking for a
recipient who is in the process of growth. It is increasingly an effort
of feminist thinking to "go beyond" traditional (male) concerns
toward an understanding of fully mutual, two-sided human relationships.

5. There is another mode of relating through sexual intercourse,
now found primarily outside of families but also sometimes between
people who live together in a household or a marriage. In this mode,
sexual gratification ("relief") is looked upon as a personal need or
drive; one's partner must be controlled to a degree sufficient to
insure compliance and an appearance of enjoyment, but little or no
sharing, intimacy, or caretaking are involved. This mode of sexual
relation is encouraged by the "new" mores of the Sexual Revolution;
it is also the age-old justification for many of the rapes that are
covertly sanctioned by our society's views of individualistic "rights."
It is, however, profoundly in conflict with the kind of relationship
between members of a household that is proposed here as the root
of family life.

3
Stripping the Emperor's Old Clothes

1. For examples of the arrogant concealment of information
by experts who influence policy on the strength of their assertions,
see Daniel S. Greenberg, " 'Progress' in Cancer Research—Don't
Say It Isn't So," *The New England Journal of Medicine* 292, no. 13:

707-8 (on the failure to admit the very small gains for prognosis
in malignant disease in the past few decades); and John T. Edsall,
"Scientific Freedom and Responsibility," *Science* 188, no. 4189
(1975): 687-93 (on the failure to act on the knowledge of the occupational health hazard of exposure to vinyl chloride).

2. For instance, the advertisers in *Science*, no matter how eager
they might be to sell their products, will not send "further information" (promotional material) except to persons who identify
the institution that they work for; research grants (providing money
to purchase scientific equipment and supplies) are usually given
only to applicants under the supervision of "certified" experts working in agencies; and suppliers of scientific and technological equipment
and supplies not only charge the highest prices that "the traffic
[usually foundations or the government] will bear," but also refuse
to fill small, individual orders.

3. I am grateful to Chris Coe for this aphorism: "An expert is
someone who tells you what you already know, in language you
can't understand."

4. "One of the conclusions of the 1959 Woods Hole Conference
of the National Academy of Sciences on curriculum in science was
that any subject can be taught to anybody at any age in some form
that is honest. It is a brave assertion, and the evidence on the whole
is all on its side. At least there is no evidence to contradict it" (Jerome
S. Bruner, *On Knowing: Essays for the Left Hand* [New York:
Atheneum, 1965], p. 108). That *is* an assertion and can never be
definitely settled by evidence; if it were attractive (or "profitable")
for experts and professionals to espouse that attitude, we would deal
with information in a very different way than we now do in this
society.

5. Barbara J. Culliton, "The Sloan-Kettering Affair," *Science*
184 (1974): 644-50, 1154-7; see also "Scientists Find Public
Is Often Misled by Faulty Research Data," *New York Times*, 2
February 1975, for a discussion of inappropriate *application* of
faulty data to policy decisions.

6. These data (presented with caution as "approximations")
were received from the Office of the Assistant Secretary for Health,
the Department of Health, Education, and Welfare, and various
divisions of the National Institutes of Health.

7. For observations on the relationships between professionals
and managers, see R.R. Alford, "The Political Economy of Health
Care: Dynamics Without Change," *Politics and Society* (Winter 1972):
129-64; Matthew Dumont, "Modern Medicine and the Death of
Freedom," *A Statement for the Record of the Government Opera-
tions Ad Hoc Subcommittee on Privacy and the Judiciary Subcommittee*

on *Constitutional Rights* (June 21, 1974); Matthew Dumont, "Down the Bureaucracy!" *Trans-Action* (October 1970): 10-14; and Matthew Dumont, "The Changing Face of Professionalism," *Social Policy* 1 (1970): 26-31.

8. *New York Times*, 15 December 1974.

9. Examples of experts and professionals devoted to sharing information with layfolk (for the most part, *outside* of regular places of work and as volunteer activities) are found in the Medical Committee for Human Rights (P.O. Box 7155, Pittsburgh, Pa. 15213 [health information]); Scientists and Engineers for Social and Political Action (9 Walden Street, Jamaica Plain, Ma. 02130 [general science and technology, ecology and health]); and Community Technology (c/o Institute for Policy Studies, 1520 New Hampshire Avenue, N.W., Washington, D.C. 20036 [use of science and technology at the neighborhood level]). Most of the activity of these groups (and the many others like them) is at the level of relatively impersonal instruction, i.e., through publications; sometimes members will respond to requests for information- or skill-sharing for help with a specific problem or need. None of this activity is "institutionalized"; it is carried on almost entirely by voluntary contributions of time, energy, and money, and is often looked upon with vigorous distaste by other established experts and professionals.

4
Weaving the Network

1. See Mary Howell, "Employed Mothers and Their Families," *Pediatrics* 52, no. 2 (1973): 252-63; idem, "Effects of Maternal Employment on the Child," *Pediatrics* 52, No. 2 (1973): 327-43.

2. Reviews of the assumptions made by professionals and experts in recommending child custody decisions are found in Phoebe C. Ellsworth and Robert J. Levy, "Legislative Reform of Child Custody Adjudication," *Law and Society Review* 4, no. 2 (1969): 167-233; and Andrew S. Watson, "The Children of Armageddon: Problems of Custody Following Divorce," *Syracuse Law Review* 55 (1969): 55-86.

3. Lederle Laboratories' advertisement in *Medical Aspects of Human Sexuality* (June 1974): 28-30. Another ad (same company, same periodical [February 1974]: 82-7) shows a woman reading, in what is apparently a publication for layfolk, the head " 'Pill'-Takers Run the Risk of Stroke" (the statement is essentially correct), with the caption, "Because her 'medical journals' alarm her about 'the pill' . . . ." The professionals who read this periodical are being reinforced in their disparagement of the sharing of information among layfolk, while the book *Our Bodies, Ourselves* (New York: Simon

and Schuster, 1973) has sold over one million copies. The book
was written by a group of laywomen (The Boston Women's Health
Book Collective) who decided that since they knew how to use
libraries and search out references, they *did* have access to the knowledge they wished to learn and disseminate: information about the
anatomy, physiology, psychology, and sociology of women.

4. See, for instance, Carol Stack, *All Our Kin* (New York: Harper
and Row, 1974); John B. McKinlay, "Social Networks, Lay Consultation and Help-Seeking Behavior," *Social Forces* 51, no. 3 (1973):
275-92; William C. Hays and Charles H. Mindel, "Extended Kinship
Relations in Black and White Families," *Journal of Marriage and the
Family* 53, no. 1 (1973): 51-7; and Marvin B. Sussman, "Adaptive,
Directive and Integrative Behavior of Today's Family," *Family
Process* 7, no. 2 (1968): 239-50, for discussions of kin networks
of U.S. families.

5. Mary Daly, in *Beyond God the Father* (Boston: Beacon Press,
1974), analyzes the ways by which our society has systematically
submerged the culture of women.

6. Orlando Patterson, in "Ethnicity and the Pluralist Fallacy,"
Change 7, no. 2 (1975): 10-11, argues that individualistic achiev-
ments outweigh the humanistic values of a collective spirit.

7. See Carolyn L. Attneave and Ross Speck, *Family Networks*
(New York: Pantheon, 1973); and Alfred Jacobs and Wilford Spradlin,
eds., *The Group as Agent of Change* (New York: Science House,
1974), for discussions of network therapy. A lovely description of
the evolution of the rationale of network therapy is found in Carolyn
L. Attneave, "Therapy in Tribal Settings and Urban Network Intervention," *Family Process* 8, no. 2 (1969): 192-210.

8. See, for instance, Julius Roth, "Care of the Sick: Professionalism *vs.* Love," *Science, Medicine and Man* [sic] 1 (1973): 173-80;
Julius Roth, "The Necessity and Control of Hospitalization," *Social
Science and Medicine* 6 (1972): 425-46; Irving Zola, "Medicine as
an Institution of Social Control," *The Sociological Review* 20, no.
4 (1972): 487-504; and "The American Health Care System" and
"Choosing and Using Medical Care" in *Our Bodies, Ourselves*, pp.
236-41 and 242-58.

9. See "Your Family Doctor," *Which* (January 1974): 4-11
(published by Consumers' Association, Caxton Hill, Hertford SG137LZ,
G. B.), for the results of a survey that highlights differences between
what patients expect of their family doctor and what their doctors
would like to do for patients. An analysis of the goals and methods
of "professional helpers" is found in Robert Weiss, "Helping Relationships: Relationships of Clients with Physicians, Social Workers,
Priests and Others," *Social Problems* 20, no. 3 (1973): 319-28.

10. For a discussion of alternatives to a childcare system domi-
nated by professionals, see Alice Collins and Eunice Watson, *The
Day Care Neighbor Service: A Handbook for the Organization and
Operation of a New Kind of Day Care Service* (Portland, Ore.: Tri
County Community Council, 1969); Alice Collins, "Natural Delivery
Systems: Accessible Sources of Power for Mental Health," *American
Journal of Orthopsychiatry* 43, no. 1 (1973): 46-52; Arthur Emlen
and Eunice Watson, *Matchmaking in Neighborhood Day Care: A
Descriptive Study of the Day Care Neighbor Service* (Corvallis, Ore.:
DCE Books, 1971); and Arthur Emlen, B. Donoghue, and R. La
Forge, *Child Care by Kith: A Study of the Family Day Care Relationships of Working Mothers and Neighborhood Caregivers* (Corvallis, Ore.: DCE Books, 1971). My principal reservation about most
daycare programs suggested as alternatives to professionally run
centers is the tendency to accept the propositions that child care is
women's concern only and that solo caretakers (for the whole long
days) are optimally effective.

11. See, for instance, Doris Haire, "The Present Status of Childbirth," *Proceedings of the First International Childbirth Conference*
(Stamford, Conn.: New Moon Communications, 1973); Dorothy
Wertz and Richard Wertz, "Lying In: A Social History of Childbirth
in America" (unpublished manuscript); *Our Bodies, Ourselves*,
2nd edition, (New York: Simon and Schuster, 1975); and Suzanne
Arms, *Immaculate Deception: A New Look at Childbirth in America*
(Boston: Houghton Mifflin, 1975), for reviews of the childbirth
experience as arranged by medical men.

5
Work Versus Jobs

1. See, for instance, Studs Terkel, *Working* (New York: Pantheon,
1972), p. xxxviii.

2. See Chapter I of the Report of a Special Task Force to the
Secretary of Health, Education, and Welfare, *Work in America* (Cambridge, Mass.: M.I.T. Press, 1973).

3. The following salary comparisons document the "worth" of
human caregiving jobs in our present society. (See also M. A. Rutzick,
"A Ranking of U.S. Occupations by Earnings," *Monthly Labor Review*
[Department of Labor, Bureau of Labor Statistics], 88, no. 3 [1965]:
249-55.)

Earnings of Adult (ages 25-64) Fulltime (50-52 weeks/year) Workers in 1969

Caregiver (Human Service) Jobs

Category	Median Earnings
Elementary school teachers	
Males	$9,284
Females	7,608
Registered nurses, dieticians, therapists	
Females only	6,775
Service workers (except private household – includes ushers, recreational attendants)	
Males	6,857
Females	3,666
"All other" service workers (includes health aides, lay midwives, nursing aides, practical nurses, childcare workers)	
Males	6,083
Females	3,825
Health service workers	
Females only	4,181
Personal service workers	
Females only	4,038
Private household workers (includes childcare workers)	
Males	3,549
Females	1,792

Other Low-Pay Jobs

Category	Median Earnings
Plumbers, pipe-fitters	
Males only	$9,693
Postal clerks	
Males only	8,645
Transport equipment operatives (includes bus, taxi, truck drivers, parking attendants)	
Males	7,955
Females	4,898
Laborers (except farming—includes construction laborers, garbage collectors, stock handlers, vehicle washers, carpenters' helpers)	
Males	6,646
Females	4,170
Stenographers	
Females only	6,026
Typists	
Females only	5,251

Source: U.S. Department of Commerce, Bureau of the Census, *1970 Census of the Population, Subject Reports: Earnings by Occupation and Education* (Pub. No. PC[2]-8B), January 1973.

4. See Pauline Bart, "Are You a Housewife or Do You Work? Women in Traditional Roles" in Radcliffe Institute, *Women: Resource for a Changing World* (Cambridge, Mass.: Radcliffe College, 1972).

5. Note the "lapse" into the conventional use of female pronoun only. No amount of determination can support the use of "he or she" to refer to the traditional housekeeper role—it is so unlikely that any significant number of men would accept that role.

6. See David Gil, *Unravelling Social Policy* (Cambridge, Mass.: Schenkman, 1973); Charlotte P. Gilman and Emmeline P. Lawrence, "Does a Man Support His Wife?" *National American Women's Suffrage Association* (New York: Charlton Company, 1911); and Jessie Bernard, *The Future of Motherhood* (New York: Dial Press, 1974).

7. See, for instance, "America's New Jobless: The Frustration of Idleness," *Time*, 17 March 1975, pp. 20-6; "Down and Out in America," *New York Times Magazine*, 9 February 1975, pp. 9-11 and 30-5; and Studs Terkel, *Working* (New York: Pantheon, 1972). Older social science studies of unemployment are flawed in their assumption that only men are affected by unemployment: see, for instance, C. Winick, "Atonie: The Psychology of the Unemployed and the Marginal Worker," in G. Fish, ed., *The Frontiers of Management Psychology* (New York: Harper and Row, 1964).

8. Only in the very recent past has there been any major effort (mostly by women social scientists) to study post-divorced families in a frame that does not pre-label the subjects as "deviant," "damaged," or "problematic." See Ruth A. Brandwein, Carol A. Brown, and Elizabeth M. Fox, "Women and Children Last: The Social Situation of Divorced Mothers and Their Families," *Journal of Marriage and the Family* 36, no. 3 (1974): 498-514; and Mary Jo Bane, "Marital Disruption and the Lives of Children," *The Journal of Social Issues* (forthcoming 1975). According to census figures, only 11 percent of children in single-parent mother-headed families in 1972 lived in families with incomes greater than $10,000 (U.S. Department of Commerce, Bureau of the Census, *Current Population Reports*, Series P-60, No. 90, Table 21 [Washington, D.C.: U.S. Government Printing Office, 1973]). Although divorce is more common in poor families, data also show that, on the average, the family incomes of divorced women fall much more sharply than the family incomes of divorced men; see James N. Morgan et al., *Five Thousand American Families: Patterns of Economic Progress* (Ann Arbor: The University of Michigan Institute for Social Research, 1973).

9. Jane F. Amsler, in "Responses to Stress in Early Motherhood Among Employed and Non-employed Women of Two Social Classes" (dissertation, Harvard University, 1974); Naomi Richman, in "The Effects of Housing on Pre-school Children and Their Mothers,"

Developmental Medicine and Child Neurology 16, no. 1 (1974):
53-8; and W. F. R. Stewart, *Children in Flats: A Family Study*
(London: National Society for the Prevention of Cruelty to Children, 1970), studied mothers of young children who rarely leave
their households.

10. Studies usually show that a majority of workers—generally
about two-thirds to three-quarters—would continue to work even
if they did not need the income. (See, for instance, *New York Times*,
24 April 1971; and Curt Tausky, "Meanings of Work Among Blue
Collar Men," *Pacific Sociological Review* 12, no. 1 [1969]: 49-54.)
It is not clear what these workers believe their true options are: are
they saying that work is better than not-work, that their present
job is better than any other job they could imagine, or that *some*
aspects of their present employment (over and above income) are
valuable to them?

11. Many social scientists continue to write about maternal employment as if it were known to be "harmful" to children, although
there is no clear evidence to support that assertion. See, for instance,
Elva Poznanski, Annette Maxey, and Gerald Marsden, "Clinical
Implications of Maternal Employment," *Journal of the American
Academy of Child Psychiatry* 9, no. 4 (October 1970): 741-61,
for a sample of this entrenched attitude.

12. Mary Howell, "Patients and Family: What Does 'Responsible'
Mean?" (unpublished study, 1973). Graduate training programs for
physicians demand 48 to 168 hours per week; in 30 percent of the
training programs surveyed, the work week is more than 90 hours.
One director of training, asked his views of part-time programs for
parents (which, if half time, would average about 40 hours per week)
replied eloquently and on behalf of many of his colleagues: "If an
individual cannot reconcile the idea of arduous training and sacrifice
of home and family for his [*sic*] profession, he could be an excellent
accountant but only an adequate physician" (p. 10).

13. See, for instance, E. Grønseth, "Work-Sharing Families: Husband
and Wife Both in Part-time Employment," prepared for Conference
of the Gottlieb Duttweiler Institute, Zurich, June 1972; and, idem,
"Work-Sharing Families," prepared for the XIIth International Family
Research Seminar, Moscow, April 1972 (unpublished papers, Institute of Sociology, Oslo University).

14. Agreement between Chrysler Corporation and the UAW,
September 1973. This contract is seen as a landmark: "negotiations
are historic within industry because, for the first time, quality of
workers' lives—rather than how much money they make—is [the]
major issue" (8/26/73, 48:2); "unions, under rank and file pressure,
are compiling long lists of contract demands that are not directly

related to wages and hours . . . are calling instead for improved
working conditions and increased workers' rights" (7/8/73, 6:4);
"demand that overtime be made voluntary has become key and
decisive issue in upcoming negotiations . . . heavy overtime during
last 2 years has enabled auto industry to enjoy record sales and
profits and has swelled paychecks of workers; it has also left many
workers fatigued and angry, wondering if it is worth disruption that
it has caused in their lives" (6/20/73, 1:5). All citations from the
New York Times Index, 1973.

15. See, for instance, U.S. Congress, Senate Subcommittee on
Children and Youth, *Hearings on American Families: Trends and
Pressures, Congressional Record* 188, no. 142 (1973); and the public
hearings held in preparation for the report, *Child Care in Massachu-
setts* (Massachusetts Early Education Project, Richard R. Rowe,
Director [1972]).

16. In a time when our arranged scarcity of jobs is hurting an
especially large proportion of workers, we may be frightened away
from demanding changes in jobs for fear that we, too, might become
unemployed. On the other hand, the painful (and wasteful) consequences of our present conventions about work are brought clearly
to awareness at such a time; we might, in fact, be *better* able to
organize and work for change when so many of us are in economic
difficulty.

17. See discussion about benefits in cash and in kind, in a social
system in which there is a guaranteed income floor for families, in
Alva Myrdal, *Nation and Family* (Cambridge, Mass.: M.I.T. Press,
1968), pp. 134-53. For discussions of various family allowances
or guaranteed minimum incomes, see Lee Rainwater, "Poverty,
Living Standards and Families' Well-Being," *Working Paper No. 10*,
Joint Center for Urban Studies of M.I.T. and Harvard University,
1972; Lee Rainwater, "Public Responses to Low Income Policies,"
Working Paper No. 8, Joint Center for Urban Studies of M.I.T. and
Harvard University, 1972; James Tobin, "Raising the Incomes of the
Poor," in Kermit Gordon, ed., *Agenda For the Nation* (Washington,
D.C.: Brookings Institution, 1968); and Sir Morris Finer, *Report of
the Committee on One-Parent Families* (London: Her Majesty's
Stationery Office, 1974).

18. There is a recent spate of proposals for programs of part-
time and flexible-time work schedules, but little specific information about how these can be implemented in a manner that is maximally beneficial to *families*. See, for instance, Senate Bill S. 792
("to provide increased employment opportunity by executive agencies
of the United States Government for persons unable to work standard
working hours"); Janice N. Hedges, "New Patterns for Working Time,"

Monthly Labor Review (February 1973): 3-8; Alvar O. Elbing, Herman Gadon, and John R. M. Gordon, "Flexible Working Hours: It's About Time," *Harvard Business Review* 52, no. 1 (1974): 18-33; Barbara L. Fiss, *Flextime—a Guide* (Washington, D.C.: Pay and Leave Administration Section, Pay Policy Division, Bureau of Policies and Standards, U.S. Civil Service Commission, 1974); Barbara L. Fiss, "Implications of Alternative Work Schedules for the American Labor Force" (paper prepared for the National Science Foundation conference on Alternative Work Schedules, September, 1974); "Hearings on Flexible Hours Employment Act," *Congressional Record* 119, no. 142 (September 26, 1973); Alvar O. Elbing and John Gordon, "Self-Management in the Flexible Organization," *Futures* (August 1974): 319-28; and 'Employee ('Fringe') Benefits and Your Permanent Part-time Job" and "Flex-Time" (position papers from Catalyst, 6 East 82 Street, New York 10028).

19. See Lawrence R. Berger, "Health in the Work-Place: The Supreme Court in Hammer *v.* Dagenhart (1918)" (paper submitted to the American College of Legal Medicine, 1973).

20. See, for instance, Harry Braverman, "The Structure of the Working Class and Its Reserve Armies," in *Monthly Review: Labor and Monopoly Capital: The Depredation of Work in the Twentieth Century* 26, no. 3 (1974), for a discussion of the recent substitution of women for immigrant groups as "reserve" employees.

21. See Eugene Braunwald, "Presidential Address," Annual Meeting of the American Society for Clinical Investigation (May 1975), for an investigation of the short time-in-office of the chairpersons for departments of medicine.

22. I am collecting reports of instances in which two persons fill one caregiver job (for instance, pediatricians, psychotherapists, and so on) and would be grateful to hear from anyone who has worked in this manner. On the basis of the instances on which I have extensive information, I would guess that it is somewhat easier for parents (and perhaps for some women) to work in this fashion, closely communicative—and collaborative—with another person. See also, Mary Howell, "Sex Stereotyping in Medical Care" (unpublished study, 1973).

6
Child Care

1. See for instance Ann Cook and Herbert Mack, "Business in Education: The Discovery Center Hustle," *Social Policy* 1, no. 3 (1970): 5-9. The authors cite a full-page ad in the *New York Times:*

Evaluating children in the 43 basic skills is part of what the

Discovery Center can do for your child. The 43 skills embrace
all the hundreds of things your child has to learn before he [sic]
reaches school age. Fortunately preschoolers have a special
genius for learning. But it disappears at the age of seven [sic].
During this short-lived period of genius, the Discovery Center
helps your child develop his skills to the advanced level . . . .
You owe it to your child to take him to the Discovery Center
today.

See also Arthur Emlen, "Slogans, Slots, and Slander: The Myth of
Day Care Need," *American Journal of Orthopsychiatry* 43, no. 1
(1973): 23-6, for a discussion of professionals' self-interest in estimates of need for professionally run day care. An alternative proposal for the professionalization of preschool child care is found in
another *New York Times* ad: Albert Shanker, "Early Childhood
Education Is a Job for the Public Schools," in the weekly column
"Where We Stand" of the United Federation of Teachers, 8 September
1974.

2. Elizabeth Prescott and Elizabeth Jones, "Day Care for Chil-
dren: Assets and Liabilities," *Children* 18 (1971): 54-8; and Elizabeth
Prescott, "The Large Day Care Center as a Child-Rearing Environ-
ment," *Voice For Children* 2, no. 4 (1970), discuss the hazards of
large centers (more than sixty children) for staff and children alike.
See also Roger G. Barker and Paul V. Gump, *Big School, Small
School: High School Size* (Stanford, Calif.: Stanford University
Press, 1964), for a discussion of size effects in another setting.

3. It is significant that we do not know where and with whom
U.S. children spend their days. (We know where all our bombs are.)
For *estimates* of the need for daycare services, see Mary D. Keyser-
ling, *Windows on Day Care* (New York: National Council of Jewish
Women, 1972); Women's Bureau, Employment Standards Administration, U.S. Department of Labor, "Day Care Facts," Pamphlet
16 (rev.), 1973; and Seth Low and Pearl G. Spindler, *Child Care
Arrangements of Working Mothers in the United States* (Washington,
D.C.: U.S. Government Printing Office, 1968). Note also the caution
of Dr. Arthur Emlen that inflated estimates of daycare "need" may
serve the purposes of professionals seeking funding, overlooking
the very good daycare services often provided in informal network
arrangements. One must distinguish between the very real need of
U.S. families for arrangements that are findable, affordable, and
mutually satisfactory (for child, caretaker, and family) and the
"need" for professionally controlled services: the two are not necessarily synonymous.

4. The "Introduction" to L. Joseph Stone, Henrietta T. Smith,

and Lois B. Murphy, eds., *The Competent Infant* (New York: Basic
Books, 1973) lists a panoply of false assertions made by experts
between 1930 and 1966, in print, about children's development.
The editors comment that "most mothers knew better," and fault
the experts' tendency to theorize without looking at children directly.
(Many mothers, sadly, would have assumed that their own observations were uninformed and that the experts must be correct. In
any case, false information from experts and professionals is of no
practical help to parents, and may do harm unless layfolk understand
the probable level of inaccuracy in these assertions.) Martha Wolfenstein has reviewed the vagaries of advice given to parents about
the "right" way to rear their children, over the period 1914 to 1951.
For instance, in 1938 the U.S. Children's Bureau, in *Infant Care*,
recommended a stiff cuff bound to babies' arms so that they could
not get their thumbs to their mouths; in 1942 thumbsucking was
said to be a harmless pleasure that should not be interfered with.
She plots the recommended severity in the handling of weaning,
bowel training, bladder training, and so on, showing the extreme
shifts in advice (all given with the utmost assurance) from one decade
to the next. See Martha Wolfenstein, "Trends in Infant Care," *American Journal of Orthopsychiatry* 23, no. 1 (1953): 120-30; and
"Fun Morality: An Analysis of Recent American Child-Training
Literature," in Martha Wolfenstein and Margaret Mead, eds., *Childhood in Contemporary Cultures* (Chicago: University of Chicago
Press, 1955), pp. 168-78.

5. See, for instance, Beatrice B. Whiting and John M. Whiting,
Children of Six Cultures (Cambridge, Mass.: Harvard University
Press, 1975); and Mary Howell, "Nurturance in the Delivery of
Primary Health Care" (unpublished paper, 1973), for data on the
experiential correlates of nurturant behavior.

6. See Eldred Rutherford and Paul Mussen, "Generosity in Nursery School Boys," *Child Development* 39, no. 3 (1968): 755-65;
and Richard S. Crutchfield, "Conformity and Character," *American
Psychologist* 10 (1955): 191-8.

7. Harry Stack Sullivan, "The Juvenile Era," in *The Interpersonal
Theory of Psychiatry*, Helen Perry and Mary L. Gawel, eds. (New
York: Norton, 1953), especially pages 242-3, for a discussion of
the family dynamic of "disparagement."

8. R. D. Laing, in *The Politics of the Family and Other Essays*
(New York: Pantheon, 1971); and R. D. Laing and A. Esterson,
in *Sanity, Madness, and the Family* (New York: Basic Books, 1964),
propose—with illustrative case studies—that conventional (nuclear)
family living often requires a child to enter a grand deception that
prevents valid and direct experience; the structure of the family makes
victims of parent and child alike.

9. See, for instance, Alexander Szalai, "The Multinational Comparative Time Budget Research Project," *American Behavioral Scientist* 10, no. 4 (1966): 1-12, 21-31; and Katherine Walker, "Time-use Patterns for Household Work Related to Homemakers' Employment" (paper presented at the National Agricultural Outlook Conference, Washington, D.C., 1970), cited in Janice Neipert Hedges and Jeanne K. Barnett, "Working Women and the Division of Household Tasks," *Monthly Labor Review* (April 1972).

10. For research on enduring behavioral individuality (including schedule-ability) among infants and children, see Alexander Thomas et al., *Temperament and Behavior Disorders in Children* (New York: New York University Press, 1969); Alexander Thomas et al., "Development in Middle Childhood," *Seminars in Psychiatry* 4, no. 4 (1972); and Alexander Thomas, Stella Chess, and Herbert Birch, *Your Child is a Person* (New York: Viking Press, 1965).

11. Robert B. McCall and Jerome Kagan, "Stimulus-schema discrepancy and attention in the infant," *Journal of Experimental Child Psychology* 5, no. 2 (1967): 381-90.

12. The Commission on Population Growth and the American Future, *Population and the American Future* (New York: Signet, 1972), pp. 127-8; the $60,000 includes the cost of a (relatively inexpensive) college education and the foregone income of a parent who does unpaid work caring for the child.

13. The fall in the rates of unwanted births is, of course, also due to the recent increase in availability of contraceptives and, even more, to the change in women's philosophy that encourages them to make responsible *decisions* about their own fertility. Between 1965 and 1970, however, 15 percent of all births were still classified by U.S. women as unwanted (an under-reporting, since admitting that a birth was unwanted is socially unacceptable): 45 percent of fifth children and 63 percent of sixth and higher children were classified as unwanted during that time. Comparing 1961-1965 and 1966-1970, unwanted fertility among whites fell by 35 percent, among blacks by 56 percent; among women with less than a high school education, unwanted fertility fell by 47 percent during that time, and by 17 percent among college-educated women. In the earlier period, more than 20 percent of all births were classified as unwanted by U.S. women. (See Norman B. Ryder and Charles F. Westoff, "Wanted and Unwanted Fertility in the United States: 1965 and 1970," in Charles F. Westoff and Robert Parke, Jr., eds., *Demographic and Social Aspects of Population Growth* [Washington, D.C.: U.S. Government Printing Office, 1972]; and Frederick S. Jaffe, "Family Planning Services in the United States," in Robert Parke, Jr. and Charles F. Westoff, eds., *Aspects of Population Growth Policy* [Washington, D.C.: U.S. Government Printing Office, 1972].) A

long-term study of children whose mothers' abortion requests were denied early in pregnancy (classified as "children unwanted at conception") documents the subtle and complex difficulties of their early lives: Z. Dytrych, H. P. Matejcek, and H. L. Friedman, "Children Born to Women Denied Abortion: Initial Findings of a Matched Control Study in Prague, Czechoslovakia," (paper presented at the annual meeting of the Population Association of America, New York City, April 1974).

14. Dr. Spock, advisor to so many families during the post-war decade, wrote as if all children lived in "ideal" nuclear families. See Kenneth Kenniston, *The Uncommitted* (New York: Harcourt Brace, 1960), for personal accounts of youth resentful of parental sacrifice on their behalf.

15. I am indebted to Estelle Ramey for the phrase.

16. Cited in "Separated Family Loses Court Plea," *New York Times*, 22 December 1974, p. 40. The suit is a landmark for "families' rights"; it has been brought by the Children's Rights Project of the American Civil Liberties Union.

17. See, for instance, Boyd C. Rollins and Harold Feldman, "Marital Satisfaction Over the Family Life Cycle," *Journal of Marriage and the Family* 32 (1970): 20-8; Wesley R. Burr, "Satisfaction with Various Aspects of Marriage Over the Life Cycle: A Random Middle Class Sample," *Journal of Marriage and the Family* 32 (1970): 28-38; "Marriage Without Children: They're Happy, Study Finds," *New York Times*, 21 November 1974.

18. J. Griffith, "Family, Peers Apply Pressure for Kids," *Family Planning Digest* 2, no. 5 (1973): 7.

19. See, for instance, Arthur Emlen, B. Donoghue, and R. La Forge, *Child Care by Kith: A Study of the Family Day Care Relationships of Working Mothers and Neighborhood Caregivers* (Corvallis, Ore.: DCE Books, 1971).

20. Probably equity between spouses within marriage will not be easily possible until there is equity between the sexes generally in all areas of society: see Mary Howell, " 'But I Always Think of My Wife As My Equal': Between-Sex Exploitation and Gender-Role Change," *University of Michigan Papers in Women's Studies* 1, no. 2 (1974): 89-96. For instance, until women's employment opportunities *and* wage-rates are equal to those of men, it will continue to be difficult to estimate the equivalence of their contributions to their families' well-being: see Howard M. Iams, "The Wages of Women and Men: 1960 to 1970" (paper presented at the annual meeting of the Population Association of America, New York City, April 1974); Herma Kay, *Sex-Based Discrimination in Family Law* (St. Paul: West, 1974); and Alice H. Cook, *The Working Mother:*

A Survey of Problems and Programs in Nine Countries (Ithaca, N.Y.: Publications Division, New York State School of Industrial and Labor Relations, Cornell University, 1975).

7
Education

1. For the wages of childcare workers, see Note 3 to Chapter 5.

2. See, for instance, Carol K. Tittle, Karen McCarthy, and Jane F. Steckles, *Women and Educational Testing: A Selective Review of the Research Literature and Testing Practices* (Princeton: Educational Testing Service, 1974); Scarvia B. Anderson, *Sex Differences and Discrimination in Education*, especially Chapter IV, "Look, Jane, Look! See Dick Run and Jump! Admire Him!" (Princeton: Educational Testing Service, 1972); and Barbara G. Harrison, *Unlearning the Lie* (New York: William Morrow, 1974).

3. Classroom studies of teacher and pupil "expectancy" have often been conducted within the usual framework of rank-ordering of students, with only so much "room at the top" and students ranked against each other. See, for instance, Janet D. Elashoff and Richard E. Snow, *Pygmalion Reconsidered* (Worthington, Ohio: Charles A. Jones Publishing Company, 1971).

4. An illustrative quirk in the jargon of educational administrators: one says, "Teachers *service* [rather than *serve*] students." I have also been invited to look in on a classroom to observe "students in operation," which makes the children sound like windup toys. See also Gerald E. Levy, *Ghetto School*, (New York: Pegasus, 1970).

5. Teachers who want to teach but find the constraints of manager-dominated schools unworkable have formed their own network: see Leonard Solo and Stan Baronides, *A Continuing Directory of Schools* (Amherst, Mass.: The Teacher Drop-Out Center [P.O. Box 521], 1970) ERIC Document No. ED 053 053; also *New Schools: A National Directory of Alternative Schools* (1971), available from Cambridge Institute, 1878 Massachusetts Avenue, Cambridge, Mass. 02140.

6. The so-called "Buckley Amendment" (The Family Educational Rights and Privacy Act of 1974) was a federal legislative effort to prohibit schools from maintaining records evaluating students in secret from the students and their families. In many educational situations (especially post-secondary, graduate, and professional schools) students and their families are now told that the educational system will not "work" without the maintenance of secret records: they are therefore now asked to sign away their legal rights to this information. Since education is competitive and "slots" in schools are

a scarce resource, students or families who refuse to sign away their rights would indeed be at a disadvantage relative to those who do sign.

7. Ivar Berg, *Education and Jobs: The Great Training Robbery* (Boston: Beacon Press, 1971).

8. See David Gil, *Violence Against Children* (Cambridge, Mass.: Harvard University Press, 1970), for a discussion of our society's implicit encouragement of private and public violence against children.

9. For discussions of continuous, lifelong education, see Edward Clarke and John Fyfe, "The Education and Training Investment Program" (position paper prepared for NIE-DHEW, 1973); Council of Europe, Council for Cultural Cooperation, *Permanent Education: A Compendium of Studies*, (A Contribution to the UN International Education Year, (Strasbourg: United Nations, 1970); and Paul Lengrand, *An Introduction to Life-long Education* (Paris: UNESCO, 1970).

10. See, for instance, Louise R. Daniels and Leonard Berkowitz, "Liking and Response to Dependency Relationships," *Human Relations* 16, no. 2 (1963): 141-8; Yakov M. Epstein and Harvey A. Hornstein, "Penalty and Interpersonal Attraction as Factors Influencing the Decision to Help Another Person," *Journal of Experimental Social Psychology* 5, no. 3 (1969): 272-82; Stella Chess, Kenneth B. Clark, and Alexander Thomas, "The Importance of Cultural Evaluation in Psychiatric Diagnosis and Treatment," *Psychiatric Quarterly* 27 (1953): 102-14; and Harvey A. Hornstein, Elisha Fisch, and Michael Holmes, "The Influence of a Model's Feeling About His Behavior and His Relevance as a Comparison Other On Observers' Behavior," *Journal of Personality and Social Psychology* 10, no. 3 (1968): 222-6.

11. Ivar Berg, *Education and Jobs: The Great Training Robbery* (Boston: Beacon Press, 1971).

12. For a general discussion, see *Education Vouchers* (Cambridge, Mass.: Center for the Study of Public Policy, 1970); comprehensive and annotated bibliographies are available from the same source. A detailed proposal for implementation is presented in *An Elementary Demonstration Program*, House Document 5995 (Boston: Legislative Research Council, 1974).

8
Health Care

1. Quoted in *The American Medical News* 18, no. 1 (1975): 4.
2. Attend carefully to the "public service" statements of experts

and professionals, for instance, in magazine or television interviews, as when a physician purports to "explain" to the public about the use of some new drug or treatment. How much real (that is, usable) information is given? How often does the expert "mystify" an answer by implying or stating directly that the matter is too complex for layfolk to understand? How often are direct questions answered evasively or off the point? The final explanation is usually, "Trust your own doctor to provide you with an answer [but not information]."

3. See for instance Juanita Bay and Christian Bay, "Professionalism and the Erosion of Rationality in the Health Care Field," *American Journal of Orthopsychiatry* 43, no. 1 (1973): 55-64; and the Biosocial Curriculum Collective, *Biosocial Medical Education* (Boston: The Biosocial Curriculum Collective, Harvard Medical School, 1973).

4. Charlotte Muller, "The Overmedicated Society: Forces in the Marketplace for Medical Care," *Science* 176 (1972): 488-92.

5. See, for instance, Rose Laub Coser, "What's in an Apostrophe? The Case of Physician's Associates" (paper presented at the annual meeting of the American Association for the Advancement of Science, 1975).

6. For the alarming state of occupational health practices in the United States, see, for instance, Alan Anderson, Jr., "The Hidden Plague," *New York Times Magazine*, 27 October 1974, pp. 20-8, 32; Paul Brodeur, *Expendable Americans* (New York: Viking Press, 1974); and Rachel Scott, *Muscle and Blood* (New York: Dutton, 1974).

7. The notion that childbirth is a disease, and the hospital restrictions that restrain the full use of prepared childbirth techniques (such as moving around into a comfortable position, and screaming), both increase the probability of use of major anesthesia. In many hospitals, epidural ("spinal") anesthesia is routine, and women must go to extraordinary efforts to avoid its use if they wish. Epidural blocks depress the activity of the womb, so that drugs (such as pitocin) must usually be used to balance against the anesthetic. After a time (often only a few hours), these drugs can affect the baby, so that the birth must be brought to its end. Fetal monitoring (an electronic device that registers the baby's "distress") further pins down the woman: she looks and feels, with all of the wires and tubes, like a desperately ill patient. If the birth cannot be hastened to its end, or if the baby begins to show signs of distress, forceps or Caesarian section are resorted to. Doctors are in control of this entire birth process. There is no longer a "normal" birth. What we have not yet seriously tried, to improve our embarrassing (disgraceful) international position as twelfth in deaths of women in childbirth and seventeenth

in deaths of infants, is what is probably a radical idea for U.S. medicine:
to give pregnant women access to nourishing food so that they can
feed themselves. (See *United Nations Demographic Yearbook* [1971];
Sam Shapiro et al., *Infant, Perinatal, Maternal, and Childhood Mortality
in the United States* [Cambridge, Mass.: Harvard University Press,
1968]; Dorothy Wertz and Richard Wertz, "Lying-In: A Social
History of Childbirth in the United States" [unpublished manu-
script]; and Lee Schorr, *Health Care of Children and Expectant
Mothers: A Collection of Some of the Evidence of the Failures of
Existing Arrangements* [Washington, D.C.: The Children's Defense
Fund, 1974]).

8. Elizabeth Herzog, "Who Should Be Studied?" *American Journal
of Orthopsychiatry* 41, no. 1 (1971): 4-12.

9. See, for instance, John B. McKinlay, "Some Approaches and
Problems in the Study of the Use of Services—An Overview," *Journal
of Health and Social Behavior* 13, no. 2 (1972): 115-52; Daniel
Melnick and Vijaya L. Melnick, "Splendid Isolation or Professional
Exclusion: Report of a Pilot Study on Scientists' Attitudes Towards
Health Policy" (paper presented at the annual meeting of the American
Association for the Advancement of Science, 1975); and Women
in Research, "Women in Science: Working Together to Vitalize
Research," *University of Michigan Papers in Women's Studies* 1,
no. 1 (1974): 201-9.

10. In Samuel P. Martin, Magruder C. Donaldson, C. David London,
Osler L. Peterson, and Theodore Colton, "Inputs into Coronary
Care During 30 Years," *Annals of Internal Medicine* 81, no. 3 (1974):
289-293), the authors conclude that in the period between 1939 and
1969, despite "a linear increase" in sophisticated and expensive
technology of care, there were no changes in duration of hospitalization nor in deaths in the hospital for patients with heart attacks.
They suggest that there are "routines that are used because of [phy-
sician's] habit and that overweigh the data available on the natural
history of the illness and the individual patient's progress . . . . One
might suggest the existence of a predetermined treatment and diagnostic pattern for many patients *without reference to their diagnostic
status, severity of illness or clinical course of the episode*. Frequently,
these routines were placed in the patient order sheet on the day
of admission" (emphasis added). Treating the patient "as a whole
person" means individualized, not routinized, care.

11. We might even define "primary care" in health matters as
"unheroic health care," remembering that *heroics* can be "vain-
glorious, unnaturally extravagant, or shamelessly flamboyant conduct, behavior or expression" (*Webster's Third International*, p.
1060). There is a place in health care for "boldness, spirit or daring,"

and there is also a place for quiet, modest, forbearing caregiving.

12. See, for instance, Richard M. Magraw, "Trends in Medical Education and Health Services," *New England Journal of Medicine* 285, no. 25 (1971): 1407-13, for a discussion of some of the dynamics of developing family-practice training programs.

13. Kerr L. White, T. Franklin Williams, and Bernard G. Greenberg, "The Ecology of Medical Care," *The New England Journal of Medicine* 265, no. 18 (1961): 885-92; "Data from medical-care studies in the United States and Great Britain suggest that in a population of 1000 adults (sixteen years of age and over), in an average month 750 will experience an episode of illness, 250 of these will consult a physician, 9 will be hospitalized, 5 will be referred to another physician, and 1 will be referred to a university medical center. The latter sees biased samples of 0.0013 of the "sick" adults and 0.004 of the patients in the community, from which students of the health professions must get an unrealistic concept of medicine's task . . ." (p.891). The obvious conclusion is that if health caregivers are to be trained for the work they will be asked to do, they must leave the university hospital and go "into the community" for at least part of their training; the idea is firmly resisted by many medical educators.

14. Glen E. Garrison, Warren H. Gullen, and Connie M. Connell, "Migration of Urbanites to Small Towns for Medical Care," *Journal of the American Medical Association* 227, no. 7 (1974): 770-3, tells of city dwellers traveling out to small towns for medical care. Descriptions of mental health and general health care in client-responsive clinics are found in Gordon P. Holleb and Walter H. Abrams, *Alternatives in Community Mental Health* (Boston: Beacon Press, 1975); and Susan Reverby, "Alive and Well in Somerville, Mass.: A Political Women's Health Project in a Working-Class Community," *HealthRight* 1, no. 2 (1975): 1.

15. The McMaster University Faculty of Medicine (Hamilton, Ontario, Canada) has instituted an experiment designed to clarify the relationship between undergraduate academic performance and personal qualities in physician performance. Applicants to medical school are admitted from two categories: those selected for their academic performance, and those selected for personal qualities including ability to relate to other people. Preliminary analysis of early data suggests that the two groups of students do not achieve differently during their medical school years.

16. Students are also warned away from "giving" control of decision-making in health matters to consumers by the specter of malpractice suits. It should be of concern to layfolk that professionals and insurance companies are likely to press for an arrangement that will decrease

consumers' ability to regulate the quality of medical services by suing—
a poor mechanism to improve quality, but one of the few now
available. For an alternative arrangement that strengthens consumer
control, see George J. Annas, "Avoiding Malpractice Suits Through
Informed Consent," in *Current Problems in Pediatrics* (Chicago:
Yearbook Medical Publishers, 1975).

17. There is systematic training for cool detachment and disinterest during medical education, and little or no attention to the
possible healing potential of empathy and involvement on the part
of the healer. See, for instance, Morris Daniels, "Affect and Its
Control in the Medical Intern," *The American Journal of Sociology*
66 (1960): 259-67; and Harold I. Lief and Renee C. Fox, "Training
for 'Detached Concern' in Medical Students," in *The Psychological
Bases of Medical Practice*, Harold I. Lief, Victor F. Lief, and Nina
R. Lief, eds. (New York: Harper and Row, 1963).

18. The selection process for admissions to medical school at
McMaster University (See Note 15 above) requires the participation
of "members of the community," although these persons are often
professionals rather than layfolk. See also Victor Sidel and Ruth
Sidel, *Serve the People* (Boston: Beacon Press, 1975), for another
system of selection of candidates for medical training.

19. For hopeful examples of recent experiments in home-based
diagnosis and treatment, see "Home Culturing of Urines Helpful
in Children," *Medical Tribune*, 22 January 1975; and "Hemophilia
Home Care Has Potential Problems," *Pediatric News*, March 1974.

20. It is also clear that no one *needs* possession of medical
records as much as the patient does. Not surprisingly, records are
often mislaid, lost, or even destroyed in hospitals and clinics. We
must each own and be responsible for a complete personal health
history record. See Nicholas Cunningham, "More on Transfer of
Medical Information," *Pediatrics* 43 (1969): 639; and Budd N.
Shenkin and David C. Warner, "Giving the Patient His [*sic*] Medical
Record," *New England Journal of Medicine* 289, no. 13 (1973):
688-91.

21. Caring for our own health needs takes time and energy; again,
the realignment of work *vs.* family priorities is essential for family
health in every sense. See Morris Vogel, "Boston's Hospitals, 1870-
1930: A Social History" (dissertation, University of Chicago, 1974),
for a discussion of the loss by families of home nursing responsibilities as family members found less and less time and energy available
for family needs.

22. H. G. Mather, N. G. Pearson, K. L. O. Read, et al., "Acute
Myocardial Infarction: Home and Hospital Treatment," *British Medical
Journal* 3 (1971): 334-8.

9
Going Beyond

1. See Wade Greene, "Triage: Who Shall Be Fed? Who Shall Starve?" *New York Times Magazine*, 5 January 1975, pp. 9-11, 44-5, and 51.

2. A major restraint on the encouragement of trusting and trustworthy professional caregiving arises from the circumstance that, as in most elite fields of work, the elders (who, in this regard, are frequently bitter and disillusioned by their *own* education and experience in bureaucratic institutions) are firmly in control of the learning of youth who might want to develop new ways of providing care. A distinguished medical educator wrote to me, in response to my concern about a kind of teaching in medical schools that firmly *discourages* an orientation of service: "But can people really be instructed by courses, outlines, textbooks in How to Be Kind and Thoughtful? Or, if they can be, who *wants* their kindness?" Another reminded me of the dictum, "Compassion without competence is crap," as if to be compassionate threatened one's competence, and as if the reverse hyperbole were not also true: competence without compassion is *also* "crap"—with at least as much potential for failing to help, or for harming, the recipient of service.

3. Gloria Steinem in Marc Fasteau, *The Male Machine* (New York: McGraw-Hill, 1974), p. xii.